UNDER
THE BED
OF HEAVEN

UNDER THE BED OF HEAVEN

Christian Eschatology
and Sexual Ethics

Richard W. McCarty

Cover image: *Detail from Eclipse*, 2017. ©Michael Tkach.

Published by State University of New York Press, Albany

©2021 State University of New York Press

All rights reserved

Printed in the United States of America

No part of this book may be used or reproduced in any manner whatsoever without written permission. No part of this book may be stored in a retrieval system or transmitted in any form or by any means including electronic, electrostatic, magnetic tape, mechanical, photocopying, recording, or otherwise without the prior permission in writing of the publisher. For information, contact State University of New York Press, Albany, NY
www.sunypress.edu

Library of Congress Cataloging-in-Publication Data

Names: McCarty, Richard W., 1975– author.
Title: Under the bed of heaven : Christian eschatology and sexual ethics / Richard W. McCarty.
Description: Albany : State University of New York Press, [2021] | Includes bibliographical references and index.
Identifiers: LCCN 2021004746 | ISBN 9781438486253 (hardcover) | ISBN 9781438486260 (paperback) | ISBN 9781438486277 (ebook)
Subjects: LCSH: Sex—Religious aspects—Christianity. | Future life—Christianity.
Classification: LCC BT708 .M4153 2021 | DDC 241/.66—dc23
LC record available at https://lccn.loc.gov/2021004746

10 9 8 7 6 5 4 3 2 1

Dedicated to

The Reverend Doctor John Harper

For your advocacy, friendship, counsel, irreverence, and shared adventures.
Your life and gifts have made room for many to be, to live, and to love.
You have made my life all the better—and all the more interesting.

CONTENTS

Acknowledgments		ix
Introduction: Hiding under the Bed of Heaven		1
1.	Building the Bridge between Christian Ethics and Eschatology	11
2.	Sex in Heaven	31
3.	Christianity's Sexless Heaven	57
4.	New Visions for Sex in Heaven	81
5.	Sexual Metaphors for the Eschatological Life	111
6.	An Eschatological Sexual Ethic, Part 1: The Gifts and Fragilities of Monogamy	135
7.	An Eschatological Ethic, Part 2: The Christian Possibilities of Promiscuity and Celibacy	161
Notes		197
Selected Bibliography		223
Index		231

ACKNOWLEDGMENTS

The author would like to recognize and thank the following:

Taylor & Francis for permitting the use of portions of my previous article, "Eschatological Sex," *Theology & Sexuality* 19, no. 2 (2014), for developing chapter 5 of this book. *Theology & Sexuality* can be found online through Taylor & Francis at: www.tandfonline.com

Mercyhurst University, for granting my sabbatical during the fall 2015 semester, which allowed me to conduct research and begin to draft this book.

The Department of Philosophy and Religious Studies at Iowa State University, and especially Dr. Hector Avalos, for inviting me to present a talk on eschatology and sexual ethics at their 2016 annual Religious Studies Speaker Series. With your passing, I hold you in memory.

The American Academy of Religion (AAR) (2014, 2019), the Eastern International Regional Meeting of the AAR (2014, 2018); Edinboro University (2015), Binghamton University at the invitation of Dr. Douglas Jones (2019), and the Penn West Conference of the United Church of Christ (2018), each for the opportunity to present the constructive arguments of this book as it was being developed and finished.

Michael Tkach—for your enduring friendship, and for the generous contribution of your artwork to this project with the cover photo, "Eclipse."

And, ever so much, to Ryan Graber. You truly are the best among us. I very much appreciate your support and encouragement. Your strength, courage, and largeness of heart should be told in story. You deserve celebration—and all who know you find a reflection of heaven.

INTRODUCTION

Hiding under the Bed of Heaven

There are many ways to learn about sex. Hiding under a bed is one of them. At least that is an approach preserved in one memorable story from rabbinical Judaism. In it, we are told about an apprentice of the Torah who hid himself under his rabbi's bed. He did so to better understand physical intimacy between husbands and wives. The rabbi, on suddenly realizing the presence of his student while in the midst of marital lovemaking, commanded him, "Get up, come out, for this is not the way of the earth [an idiom that means this is not proper conduct]!"[1] Although this was an awkward moment, the apprentice replied in earnest, "It is Torah, and I need to learn."[2]

From the perspective of traditional Judaism, it is indeed a matter of Torah (a commandment) for a man to know how to please his spouse sexually.[3] But such a pleasure-focused directive is not so consistently found in Christianity. In truth, many Christian communities vacillate between recognizing sex as a gift of God and insisting upon the vigilant chastisement of our sexual desires—not just as a matter of prudence, but often with warnings about soul-damning sin. A wide variety of Christians have long warned that a failure to properly chastise sexual desire could result in grave consequences, such as sodomy, lawlessness, shame, disease, and death; perhaps even hell.[4] *Chastity* is the virtue that is designed to temper our wild passions so that we do not get lost in the dark woods of desire. Sex is good, we are told, but only if it is well regulated.

Of course, to regulate something is not necessarily a bad thing. We regulate a lot without assuming that an authoritarian agenda is at play. People regulate their blood pressure, their bank accounts, and even how fast they drive their car. But when the regulation of anything becomes excessive or controlled by peculiar norms, people tend to question the authenticity of the rule. When it comes to the regulation of sex in Christian ethics, it matters a great deal where one puts the theological emphasis. For example, doctrines of *creation* can help people to embrace embodiment and sexuality as good things, generally speaking.[5] But doctrines of *sin* have cast suspicions over what—if any—original goodness remains in human beings, not to mention that sin and sex tend to be closely related subjects in traditional Christianity.[6] That said, Christian theologies of *redemption* tell us that sin does not have the final word in the story of humanity. But in the history of Christian thinking on this matter, theologies of redemption tend to be brief—or regulatory—when it comes to human sexuality.[7] One thing is certain: whatever Christ thought about such things, his interpreters have had more to say.[8]

Human sexuality is complicated, and as a result it can be rather confusing. So, much like that apprentice of the Torah, many people have wanted to "see for themselves" what sex is all about. And why wouldn't we? Sex is everywhere—whether shrouded or unveiled. A lesson about biology can inspire curiosity and experimentation. Engaging with the arts can arouse an interest in aesthetics and eroticism. Even moral warnings about sex can serve as windows to pleasurable possibilities. Like the rabbi's apprentice, people sometimes sit under a bed to get a closer look at sex, which is everywhere around us—and yet something that needs more than a brief peek or a medical illustration to fully understand. We seek out an education about sex in a variety of ways and under a number of beds.

For example, just like voyeurs, some people hide out in domains that provide access to sexually explicit content. From Harlequin romance novels to various media of adult entertainment, these are beds that directly expose people to sexual relations—but not always with the best of examples. Some content categorized as "adult entertainment" not only features sexist, racist, misogynist, and exploitative scenes, but even presents them as desirable. When access to this kind of pornography is the primary bed under which apprentices hide (and learn), there should be real concern that people's sexual and moral education can be profoundly skewed to ignore concepts of justice and mutuality. But not all sexually explicit material is so apathetic toward justice in human relationships.[9] In such cases, what is sexually explicit can be revelatory of both pleasure and goodness.

On the other hand, there are people who are forced to sit under the beds of strict codes found in religious catechisms—the kind that issue rigid laws and result in loud monologues about sexual purity and the damning consequences of sexual sin. The origins of these laws often lie in antiquity.

For example, it was medieval Christian theologians who produced certain sin-lists for sexual ethics from the religious resources of natural law theory, scripture, and church teaching. Consider the theologian Thomas Aquinas, who taught that *sins against nature* (mortal sins all) include those sexual acts that cannot result in reproduction. By definition, such grave sins include masturbation, using contraception, oral sex, anal sex (between any two people), same-sex activity, and bestiality.[10] What is more, the theologian's list of *sins against reason* included having sex in ways that could lead to reproduction but with the wrong person or at the wrong time, including premarital sex, adulterous sex, rape, and seduction.[11]

Today, the Catholic Church still holds to these codes but articulates them in positive terms, namely, that only heterosexual, marital, loving sex that is simultaneously open to procreation is holy and virtuous.[12] For those instructed by these codes, a failure to live up to them is counted as a matter of sin—and often described as sin of the most serious kind. That said, church commentary is not always deployed in accord with the letter of the law. For example, when Pope Francis was asked (in 2013) about how he would serve as a confessor to someone who is gay, the pontiff responded, "Who am I to judge?"[13] When explaining his comments, Pope Francis said, "If a person is gay and seeks out the Lord and is willing, who am I to judge that person? . . . I was paraphrasing by heart the *Catechism of the Catholic Church* where it says that these people should be treated with delicacy and not be marginalized . . . [and] I will say this: mercy is real; it is the first attribute of God."[14] That said, the occasional pastoral response of Pope Francis is not always prioritized among either the Catholic hierarchy or the Catholic laity. Some prefer to emphasize the gravity of mortal sin; and others claim it may confuse the faithful to affirm anything but the marital and procreative norm.[15]

When we turn to examine Christian ethics from Protestant perspectives, the churches of the Reformation do not agree about which sexual ethic should function as the primary instructive bed under which Christians should sit and learn. For example, many evangelical Christians define themselves as traditional, Bible-centered, and family-focused. Yet in truth, many such evangelicals have very permissive attitudes toward the use of contraception (in marriage)—something that contradicts centuries of Christian tradition on marriage, family, and sexual ethics.[16] This shift in evangelical thinking occurred largely in the twentieth century. Due to the advancements and availability of artificial contraception, evangelicals (and Protestants more broadly) revisited sexual ethics, considering whether procreation should really be a controlling norm. This theological inquiry resulted in a revised sexual ethic among Protestants, namely, that the use of contraceptives can be good, both morally and religiously (albeit with various contraceptive methods preferred, according to different denominational standards).

So, too, some evangelicals have created erotic manuals to help people better enjoy sexual activity. For example, Ed Wheat and Gaye Wheat are the coauthors of *Intended for Pleasure: Sex Techniques and Sexual Fulfillment in Christian Marriage*.[17] Chapter 5 of the book is aptly titled, "One Flesh: The Techniques of Lovemaking."[18] Sexual performance is one concern of evangelical books like this, but so too is the discussion of what makes marital sex holy and pure. However, having let go of the procreative norm, evangelicals must now wrestle theologically with questions about nonreproductive activities such as masturbation and oral sex, where to draw the line on types of contraception, and the use of sex toys (to name just a few). These are topics about which the Bible makes no explicit reference—leaving "Bible-centered" evangelicals to innovate new teachings from personal judgment.

Meanwhile, Mainline Protestants are now searching for how best to articulate sexual morality for a wide range of people representing sexual and gender diversities. In truth, there are a number of beds under which these Protestants sit. For some it is the bed of the marital rule, albeit applied to heterosexual and LGBTQ people alike.[19] For others it is the norm of monogamy. For still others it is a principled approach, emphasizing the qualities of mutuality and love over any formal rule or marital demand.[20] These more liberal Protestants are sometimes critiqued by their evangelical siblings for revising sexual morality according to cultural norms instead of drawing on the gospel to change culture. Quite to the contrary, careful studies of the Bible and church teaching, coupled with reason and experience, have resulted in many of these Protestant denominations embracing a sexual ethic that is more inclusive of gender and sexual diversities than those of the past. Among these more progressive churches, an often-spoken refrain is that by taking the Bible seriously new insights into sexual ethics are illuminated (especially in the spirit of being "ever-reforming" according to the word and wisdom of God). Even so, the manner in which each denomination articulates these new norms of sexual ethics is quite unique. As a result, these Protestant churches offer different beds under which to sit and learn about the varieties of sex and how to pursue these varieties well.

But of all the beds under which people might sit and learn about sex and sexual ethics, there is one that is rarely discussed: the bed of heaven. Such a statement may strike some people as odd or offensive. In the Christian tradition (broadly conceived), heaven has rarely been imagined as a place where human sexuality continues. For some Christians, the idea of heaven is so spiritual and otherworldly that any notion of physical sex continuing there is absurd. But for many Christians (of a wide variety of denominational identities), heaven is not merely a spiritual state. For these Christians, belief in the resurrection of the dead means that human spirits will one day receive new and everlasting bodies. According to this view, Christ's own resurrection narratives in the New Testament function as a preview of what's to come. Consider a few examples. Even though he had been crucified and killed, Christ was resurrected into a physical body, and yet one that could pass through locked doors and disappear.[21] What is more, the resurrection narratives infer that Christ's risen body could eat, touch, and be touched, while still being able to transcend the plane of space and time by ascending into heaven.[22] For Christians who believe that heaven will include the mystery of a supernatural body like that of Christ, questions about that body and its functions have been relevant. For example, the fifth-century theologian Augustine offered commentary on resurrected (glorified) bodies within his book *The City of God*. In it Augustine teaches that the redeemed will be resurrected in perfected bodies. These bodies will be demarcated by physical sex, with genitalia fully intact—albeit with no sexual function. For Augustine, the one worthy fruit of sex is procreation, something that will not continue in the resurrection of the dead. Augustine hasn't been the only influential theologian to think about such things. A wide variety of Christian theologians (and artists alike) have speculated about life in the resurrection of the dead, wondering what aspects of this embodied life may continue into the next, as well as what might be radically new.[23]

While traditional Christianity has largely held that there will be no sexual relations in the resurrection of the dead (i.e., the heavenly life), other religious traditions have been open to the idea. Rabbinical Judaism has a few references to sex in the afterlife. Traditional Islamic teaching more explicitly embraces it. What is more, a number of Christian utopian movements in nineteenth-century America revisited the idea of sex in heaven, showing themselves willing to consider that erotic human relations may indeed endure in the life of the world to come. Likewise, twenty-first-century Christian theologians and ethicists have begun to produce a new body of academic literature on sex in heaven and the relationship of heavenly sex to sex and morality in the here and now. The possibility of sex in heaven is important because if Christians are to live on earth as it is in heaven, then understanding the possibilities of sex in heaven could say much about how Christians conceive of sexual ethics on earth.

This book explores the relationship between ethics and eschatology and considers how conceptions of sex in heaven might provide for ways of thinking anew about Christian sexual ethics on earth. By definition, *eschatology* is the study of the end—and in particular, the end of time, with topics concerning the return of Christ, judgment day, resurrection, and cosmic renewal. Within the domain of eschatology, Christian theologians offer different forecasts of what human beings will enjoy. Some argue that the afterlife will be exclusively *theocentric*, defined as a state of being in which the glory, joy, and reward of heaven is the eternal gaze of God; an eternal life of simply enjoying direct communion with God apart from any social reunion with family and friends.[24] Other theologians consider the possibility of a social or *domestic* heaven, in which one not only enjoys direct communion with God forever but also enjoys the company of all the redeemed—who will deepen their bonds of love for all eternity.[25] Eschatology considers all this and more, but it also intersects with ethics.

As a discipline, *ethics* concerns critical reflection on morality: an interrogation of how and why people arrive at the values that they (and we) hold.[26] One assumption might be that eschatology and ethics have little to do with one another. That assumption is mistaken. The vision of the eschatological life (whether one refers to that as heaven or the resurrection of the dead) provides Christians with a vision not just of "the end," but also of a new beginning. The eschatological life is an ideal state of being in which humanity lives in communion with God—and potentially, an eternal life of communion with all beings that have been redeemed by the grace of God. That vision of heaven can function to inform Christians about what is good and worth pursuing on earth. Likewise, Christian concepts of goodness—or morality, as broadly conceived—can inform how Christians describe the ideal state of heaven. In this sense, eschatology and ethics have a mutually informing relationship. That relationship is explored here with respect to sexual ethics.

In chapter 1, the reader is invited to rehearse some basic concepts of Christian ethics in order to build a relationship between ethics and eschatology. There, the argument will be made that *theology is morality*. In particular, chapter 1 will demonstrate that theological views directly shape what many people of faith value, such that any discussion of Christian ethics is really an exploration of how theology shapes the mechanisms of moral analysis. Thus, it is important to review the theological resources that shape Christian concepts of morality: the Bible, church tradition, reason, and experience. But eschatology can also function as a theological resource from which to engage in moral reasoning. As chapter 1 suggests, eschatology can sometimes subvert or overrule particular teachings from the Bible or sacred tradition, despite being derived from both.

With the connection between theology, eschatology, and morality having been secured, chapter 2 turns to consider sex in heaven as an existing promise among certain religious traditions. Rabbinical Judaism, traditional Islamic teachings, and certain nineteenth-century American Christian utopian movements all include ideas about sex in heaven. With respect to Judaism and Islam, chapter 2 provides a brief sketch of their distinct teachings about sex on earth, their general beliefs about eschatology, and their teachings about eschatological sex. Then the chapter turns to consider nineteenth-century Christian utopian movements, examining the Oneida Perfectionist Community as well as the Church of Jesus Christ of Latter-Day Saints (the Mormon Church). All four religious traditions help to establish that the idea of sex in heaven is neither novel nor naughty, but rather a genuine concern that has been expressed within various traditions among the Abrahamic religions (i.e., Judaism, Christianity, and Islam).

Working from the conclusion that sex in heaven is an established promise in certain religions, chapter 3 then turns and explores why the heaven of traditional Christianity is sexless. This chapter considers more directly Christian conceptions of heaven and the resurrection of the dead. It does so by examining New Testament texts and evolving church teaching. It will explore how theological notions of sin, sex, and death directly shaped Christian pronouncements about the eschatological life—and specifically, why so many Christians have not thought that sex will continue in the world to come. That view, however, is not shared by a number of present-day Christian theologians and ethicists who have challenged the traditional view that heaven is sexless. Chapter 4 explores three contemporary Christian arguments that affirm the possibility of eschatological sex. As these arguments unfold, they increasingly encourage us to consider a new sexual ethic borne of eschatological insights.

Building on the premise that there is room to imagine eschatological sex within a broad Christian framework, chapter 5 invites the reader to consider sex in heaven not as a promise but rather as a metaphor. Christians have long used material metaphors to describe the eschatological life—an eternal feast, a wedding between the bride and the Lamb (Christ and the redeemed), streets of gold, and a mansion with room for all. Chapter 5 argues that if Christians draw on sexual relations as emblematic of the goods of heaven, then promiscuity, monogamy, and celibacy would each be (noncompetitive) meaningful sexual metaphors for heaven. Chapters 6 and 7 then change the focus to explore how the eschatological metaphors of promiscuity, monogamy, and celibacy might function to inform a new sexual ethic on earth. In these chapters it is argued that all three sexual metaphors for heaven can be embodied on earth, but none perfectly—and each with complications. Chapter 6 challenges the idea of assuming there is perfection in monogamy while nevertheless naming why some people do well to choose monogamous relationships. Then, turning from reflections on monogamy, chapter 7 affirms the possibility that sexual promiscuity might find praiseworthy expressions in sex with friends, polyamory, and various forms of pornography (as iconography of heaven); albeit with the caveat that the word "pornography" is a problematic one for social, moral, and linguistic reasons. The chapter concludes with a reflection on the choice of celibacy—both its gifts and its limitations.

As a work of constructive religious ethics, this book is written with the intention to contribute to ongoing academic discussions about Christian sexual ethics. It is also written for the theologically minded who wish to wade into the waters of eschatology, ethics, and sexuality. But above all, it has been written as an effort to explore and name real goods that might help humanity to flourish. To say so is to admit that theories of morality (whether from philosophical or religious perspectives) have the potential to shape people's lives, whether for the better or for the worse. Each of us only has a small view of what a better life might look like when defined in such qualitative terms. That certainly means that no moral argument is ever complete or completely right. We can either see this limitation as self-defeating or appreciate it as a summons to engage in ongoing dialogue—offering our ideas as gifts to share and to likewise receive from others (including our critics). Within a Christian context, eschatology provides an unusual yet wonderful resource for identifying what is ultimately worth seeking. Indeed, eschatology can orient people to consider—with both humility and conviction—what it means to live on earth as it is in heaven.

Eschatology deconstructs everything by putting an end to this world and beginning a new one. Thus, there is no institution or systematic way of thinking that is not undone and re-created by the apocalypse of the eschatological imagination. As a result, eschatology can help people of Christian faith (and perhaps others more broadly) to critically interrogate concepts of morality. But it can also provide us with creative reasons to embrace values that promote practical goods in the here and now. Thus, if in this book traditional Christian ideas about sexual ethics are challenged from an eschatological perspective, it is not out of a wanton effort to destroy the faith. Rather, mine is a humble effort to inspire and sustain new conversations about sexual morality. To that end, the reader is now invited to hide under the bed of heaven. There, it is possible to consider anew what can be learned about sex and sexuality within the context of graced relationships and prodigal love—and then, to imagine how the sex of heaven might be incarnated upon the earth.

CHAPTER ONE

BUILDING THE BRIDGE BETWEEN CHRISTIAN ETHICS AND ESCHATOLOGY

I do not know how to find out anything new without being offensive.
— *Charles Fort*

A STRANGE PLACE TO DO ETHICS

By definition, strange things are either unfamiliar or inexplicable. The strange can both allure and repel us—enticing us with new possibilities or putting us off with the ridiculousness of absurdity. So defined, all theology might very well be strange, but eschatology is surely one of its strangest forms. Eschatology is the study of the end. In particular, eschatology steers theological interests toward ideas and theories about the end of the world. It further speculates about what comes after the expiration of everything we know. It entertains mysteries of heaven, resurrection, eternal life, and cosmic renewal. Many Christians believe that this future life will lack human frailties, and therefore, the eschatological life will make moral failings a thing of the past.

Christian eschatology can inspire people to think about what is ultimately worth pursuing; namely, some people think about heaven and wonder if getting there requires right belief, avoiding particular sins, or participating in sacramental rituals. Many Christians (though certainly not all) are deeply concerned that there is some kind of theological, moral, or ritual standard that God will use to sort out who belongs in heaven and who does not. This is what many Christians mean when they talk about salvation, or "being saved." They are expressing their beliefs about what it ultimately takes to be redeemed from sin; to enter into the joy of eternal life and be saved from the torments of hell (or annihilation). However, another approach to eschatology—producing far fewer anxieties—is to bracket any concern about *how* to get to heaven and focus instead on heaven as an ideal. Forget for a moment one's own views about heaven, if it exists, and debates about who goes there. Turn instead and consider that heaven has long been described as a place, or a state of being, into which human life supernaturally extends—and in which people experience the fullness of grace and the pure presence of God. When heaven is also imagined as an eternal gathering of all those who are redeemed (the ultimate communion of saints), this vision can suggest what the fullness of grace looks like in human relationships. That kind of eschatological vision offers a unique portrait of human flourishing. It imagines what human life free of brokenness and sin might achieve in holy community.

Without claiming any kind of special certainty, people of faith might explore how some of the qualities imagined of heaven could help them to reorder what they value now and how they live in relationship with others. Certainly, Christians should admit that no finite, imperfect person will ever embody the fullness of heaven on earth—indeed, they would do well to navigate far away from self-righteousness and the traps of scrupulosity. Nevertheless, Christians might seek to fill this finite existence with at least some measure of heavenly goods, and this has the possibility of improving upon life in the here and now. This is not only a theological matter, but also a moral one—and thus, it belongs to Christian ethics.

The resources that usually shape Christian ethics are important: these include the Bible, church tradition, reason, and experience. But another resource that might shape Christian ethics is the eschatological imagination. If "living on earth as it is in heaven" is taken seriously as a perspective from which to engage in ethics, then contemporary controversies about morality might be argued from descriptions of the eschatological life. For example, consider environmental ethics. One eschatological ethic might see the world heading toward inevitable destruction and judgment day, and thus argue that preserving the planet may be of lower value than other efforts, such as evangelization. Another eschatological ethic, however, might seek to better promote our stewardship of the earth, based on the eschatological vision of a divinely redeemed planet without pollution or destruction. A real question for Christians, then, is what they wish to imitate or incarnate of the eschatological life in the here and now, even if they do so imperfectly. What a person chooses to emulate will directly shape what that person values—and what one values is what one generally pursues, defends, and nurtures. To that end, if Christians sincerely seek to live on earth as it is in heaven, it could change many conceptions of Christian morality. For those who are interested in Christian ethics, the prospect of an eschatologically informed ethic seems like a worthwhile subject to explore.

Imagine, then, a sexual ethic from an eschatological perspective. That may sound like the premise of a joke or the musings of a naughty cleric who hopes for eternal erotic delights. Indeed, it could be both. But if eschatology can inform Christian ethics by shifting the imagination to consider what of heaven can inform life on earth, it would be arbitrary to simply dismiss issues of sexual ethics from our eschatological thinking. There might be reasonable arguments as to why sex does not continue into the eschatological life, and certainly we will consider some of these arguments in the chapters to come. But as a general prospect, since Christianity is a religion that frequently affirms concepts of the resurrection of the dead—in the form of some kind of supernatural body—a robust Christian eschatology needs to account for how human sexuality participates in the redemption of the body. Again, one answer might be: it doesn't, at least not in terms of intimate physical relationships. But that is not the only answer, and it would be a failure of imagination to think so.

But before we get to sex in heaven, a short review of Christian ethics and the relationship between eschatology and ethics is in order. In particular, there is a basic relationship between theology and morality in Christian ethics that needs to be distinguished from nonreligious varieties of philosophical moral reasoning. Christians do draw on a variety of philosophical moral theories to hone their ethical perspectives. Even so, the *theological* frameworks that Christians inhabit distinctively filter the vision of their moral imaginations.[1] Because Christianity has a plurality of theological traditions, there are also significant differences (and debates) within the field of Christian ethics.

This chapter aims to identify what kinds of theological movements tend to be in the minds of Christians when they think about morality. By exploring the various resources and mechanisms by which Christians make moral judgments, it will be possible to see not only why they so often disagree with one another, but also why eschatology (though often strange itself) is not such a strange location from which to think anew about Christian sexual ethics. In particular, upon reviewing the usual theological resources that Christians draw upon in moral rhetoric, it can be seen that eschatology is itself a distinct kind of theological mechanism, and one that can arouse new visions for Christian morality.

THE MORAL IMAGINATION

Morality is a construction.

Relativists take such a statement to mean that morality is a kind of discursive fiction; a world of meaning that each one of us creates by telling ourselves certain stories about what is right, what is wrong, and what is morally ambiguous. Relativists champion the idea, therefore, that there really are no objective moral goods to embrace or absolute evils to avoid. Certain things might seem (or feel) genuinely right or wrong, but such feelings—relativists say—are not grounded in anything other than one's subjective sense of morality. According to this view, the best that we can do is to respect the relativity of our individual moral commitments and then negotiate our differences through a variety of strategies for working out human relationships.

In contrast to the relativists, there are theorists who approach morality from the perspective of critical realism, which suggests that reasonable practical goods *can* be discerned by careful reflection on the many experiences of being human.[2] Without denying that definitions of morality can (and should) be disputed, critical realists affirm that careful and cross-cultural investigations into reports of human flourishing—and suffering—do reveal core concepts of a practical, objective morality. In turn, these core concepts of morality require prudent application when addressing some of humanity's most pressing issues. Examples of such core concepts of morality include statements such as do no harm; women and men are of equal moral worth; Black lives matter; rape is wrong; genocide is evil; and health care is a human right.

These moral statements belong to a wide variety of other moral claims that some critical realists believe are grounded in demonstrable truths. For example, when food, clean water, or medicine are withheld from those who need it, suffering follows. That is a practical reality that cannot be ignored. Withholding care when it is available is not a morally neutral act. Nor is the suffering that real people experience merely discursive fiction. Because we share a common humanity that transcends cultural differences, we can (and do) understand why the causes of so much suffering are wrong.[3] Though human communities disagree with one another on any number of moral issues, these disagreements do not mean that at least some basic, reliable moral goods are impossible to discern.

Moral claims become all the more complicated when religious ideas inform what people take to be good or of the highest moral value. Even the most basic exploration of comparative religious ethics reveals that peoples' value judgments can be reoriented to a remarkable degree through religious belief. One can never predict how those value judgments will turn out. For example, Christianity has produced torturous inquisitions and holy wars, while also inspiring pacifist communities and liberation theologies for marginalized social groups. Each instance has been an interpretation of the faith. Each one has been questioned as to whether it reflects true Christian principles. While the disagreements and divisions are many, when religious people make moral claims, they are often arguing for what they believe to be really and objectively good. Their arguments are either reliant on deference to an established theological authority or made according to their own theological ideas. Thus, for many people of faith, *theology* is the mechanism by which morality is constructed. As traditionally understood, theology is the study of God (or more broadly, the study of divinity, however that is conceived). Theology has also been described as faith seeking understanding. In whatever way one defines it, theology can orient people to understand reality and make value judgments with wholly unique perspectives. In truth, one need not have formal training in theology in order to apply it to morality and daily living.

Consider the following challenging, but poignant, examples. Take, first, Deanna Laney. A twenty-first-century American Christian, Laney's faith in God was fierce. Like many other devoted believers, all Laney ever wanted to do was God's will—even if doing so required much of her. "Not my will, but yours be done," is the Christian statement of both struggle and submission. Deanna Laney keenly felt that struggle, as do many religious practitioners. Choosing between her own will and the will of God proved especially difficult when Deanna Laney heard the voice of God command her to kill her children.

That Laney was hearing the voice of God was nothing new. The Texas mother of three had already been receiving messages from God that the end of time was near, and furthermore, that she was among a select few who had been chosen to witness the coming of judgment day. But as Laney tells it, in order to "prove her complete and unconditional faith," God now wanted her to stab or strangle her sons.[4] This divine command proved difficult for Laney to follow. Indeed, she actively questioned it. "I believed with all my heart it was the Lord telling me that, but I couldn't figure out why," Laney said. "I don't understand. Why? What purpose?"[5]

Experts testified that Laney's struggle was real. It was a battle between her love for her children and her love for obeying the peculiar commands of her God. Ultimately, Laney would defer to the voice in her head. After tripping over a rock outside of her house, Laney decided that she would kill her boys by bludgeoning them to death—a method, she thought, that was preferable to stabbing or strangulation.[6] Two of her sons, Joshua and Luke, were killed. Her youngest son, Aaron, was severely injured and suffered brain damage. Laney's husband never knew of her secret mission from God. Court records quote him as saying that he would have stopped her had he only known.

Laney's criminal trial ultimately centered on the matter of her sanity. The prosecution noted that the very woman who killed and injured her children in an alleged fit of religious delusion also had the clarity to call the police after the murders. This series of events, it was argued, suggested that she knew exactly what she was doing—and did so *the entire time*. Psychiatrists on the case, however, were certain that while Laney was capable of experiencing moments of rational control, she was *not* sane during the attacks on and murder of her children. In the end, the jury acquitted her by reason of insanity.

Deanna Laney's story will likely appall many people. What is more, a wide variety of people who identify as Christian (as Laney did) will repudiate her actions. These Christians will likely claim that she is in no way representative of the Christian faith and, moreover, that the voices in her head are not a valid reflection of the God in whom Christians believe. Such protestations are to be expected. And some of these claims will be reasonable. And yet, Deanna Laney's story—as terrible as it is—echoes a biblical narrative that is often celebrated in Christian churches.

Just as Deanna Laney understood herself to hear the voice of God, so too did the biblical Abraham. In the story, the voice said to Abraham, "Take your son, your only son Isaac, whom you love, and go to the land of Moriah, and offer him there as a burnt offering on one of the mountains that I shall show you."[7] By the end of the story, the same God who had commanded the sacrifice of Isaac interrupted it.

For many Christians, the sparing of Isaac is likely what will distinguish Abraham's story from that of other people—like Laney—who think that God is commanding them to kill their children. Christians do not want God to be the monster depicted by the voices of insanity that Laney heard. However, if the standard by which true divine revelation is distinguished from insanity is God's willingness to spare the human sacrifice after having commanded it, Abraham isn't alone.

Meet Hans Missal, another twenty-first-century American Christian. Missal hailed from Orange County, Florida. It was while living there that

Missal heard God command him to kill his family by burning down the house as they slept. Missal's efforts were interrupted when his wife and children were awakened by the smell of gasoline. Missal had taped the doors shut and doused the house with fuel, but the family succeeded in calling the police and Missal was arrested.[8] Missal compared himself to Abraham. He was merely a faithful man following the command of God to kill his family, only to have the sacrifices interrupted. Missal will sit in a jail cell for the rest of his life. Abraham would have been jailed as well had his story taken place today in any number of nation-states with laws that protect children from parental abuse.

In the cases of Missal and Laney, neither the American judicial system nor a variety of Christian believers accepted that the alleged messages from God were true. Thus, there was no reason to excuse Missal and Laney from incarceration. While many Christians will quickly dismiss the stories of Deanna Laney and Hans Missal as matters of insanity, both Laney and Missal made appeals to the God of Abraham. More generally, they oriented their life around the Bible, in which Abraham and their God are found. This raises the question as to whether the Bible can be trusted as a reliable resource for moral guidance, if for no other reason than its presentation of the abuse of Isaac and his near sacrifice within a collection of writings that are regarded as *sacred* texts.[9]

The story of Abraham should indeed raise some real concerns about which narratives people should grant moral and theological authority. There are, of course, interpretive choices to make with the story of Abraham. Abraham could be insane like Deanna Laney and Hans Missal. But that does not appear to be the intended message of the biblical narrative—nor has sacred tradition preserved the story as a cautionary tale, say, to warn people about trusting every idea that pops into their head. If not a warning against insanity, then perhaps the story could be a parable meant to communicate some larger theological truth about God. Maybe it was intended to distinguish the biblical god from the gods of the ancient Near East. In particular, if some of the gods and religious systems in that time (allegedly) did receive human sacrifices, then the point might be that the biblical god is not about such things.[10] Or, maybe Abraham failed the test by not saying "no" to God when presented with the command to kill his child. After all, in Genesis 18:16–33, Abraham actively debated with God about whether God should really destroy Sodom and Gomorrah—and the narrative reveals God accepting Abraham's terms. What is more, we can find other biblical narratives that depict humans arguing with God when a divine command doesn't seem quite right. For example, in Exodus 32, Moses does not accept God's plan to destroy the Israelites for worshipping the idol of a golden calf. When Moses says "no," God relents. Thus, readers should take seriously the idea that the biblical concept of "passing divine tests" sometimes means challenging divine authority—something Abraham did not do in the narrative about sacrificing his son Isaac. Or the story of Abraham and Isaac could be an example of ancient ignorance to the realities of human brutality and domestic abuse. Or, indeed, the surface reading of Abraham's story could be the meaning itself: God tested Abraham's faith by commanding and interrupting the sacrifice of his son, Isaac.

At issue, is *whether*, *how*, and *in what ways* any theological narrative should function to shape one's moral imagination (especially for people of faith). In the case of Abraham, this biblical character is scripted to believe that the voice in his head was a directive from God. But Deanna Laney and Hans Missal believed that as well. This presents a problem to solve. In particular, people of faith need to be able to account for why some narratives are granted sacred status while others are not—whether that has to do with established scripture or tradition, or instead, with the reason and experience of any given believer. Surely there will be a variety of explanations about what we should honor and what we should not—and some explanations will seem better than others. But to be clear, what is relevant about each of these stories is the way in which the central character's beliefs about God clearly shaped what they valued. Another way of saying it is this: for Abraham, Deanna Laney, and Hans Missal, *theology is morality*. The examples of these three figures are extreme—but sometimes the extreme cases are the ones that help us to better understand how and why people make the decisions that they do. This is to say, the claim that "theology is morality" is not only true for extremists; it is also true for nonradical Christians, as well as for the study of Christian ethics more broadly.

Moral Reasoning

If the study of ethics is the critical examination of how and why people make the value judgments that they (and we) do, then Christian ethics is not only for practicing Christians. It is also a domain of intellectual inquiry for those who are interested in how and why Christians (of any variety) make certain value judgments. As an academic field, it provides space for practitioners and nonpractitioners alike to comment, respond, and offer new insights into concepts of Christian morality. While theology and morality are distinct categories of study, there is a rather strong relationship between the two. To understand this relationship, it is helpful to review the content of each category. Say we start with morality. Morality has to do with definitions of goodness, the pursuit of it, or the lack of it—matters about which people vigorously debate. But in spite of disagreements about moral issues, it might be possible to agree about that which people are doing when they engage with moral concepts. In particular, the effort to assess the character or the value of something is a work of *qualitative reflection*. To think about the quality of a given thing, person, or event, we must rely on some measure, standard, or system by which to make moral judgments.

The study of ethics shows that the standards and systems by which people make moral judgments are quite diverse. For example, from one psychological perspective, basic moral judgments are sometimes made in close approximation to the presence of pain or pleasure.[11] However, the values that people place upon pleasure and pain are significantly complex. For example, the doctor's scalpel or another medical regimen may cause wounds and significant discomfort. However, if the doctor's painful actions ultimately result in healing and an overall better quality of life, then such pains may be worth enduring. At other times, however, when painful sacrifices fail to produce a greater good, we may wonder why we ever choose the path of pain at all. Given the complexities and uncertainties of life, a morality based on the presence of pain or pleasure usually requires a more sophisticated analysis before one can ultimately call an experience good or bad. Thus, as a very basic standard, when needless pain is inflicted upon those who have not consented, we generally judge this as bad. Likewise, anything that brings about wanted pleasure without third-party harm is generally esteemed as good.

Pleasure and pain are important, but they are not the only measures that human beings use when engaging in qualitative reasoning. In the halls of philosophy, a variety of sophisticated moral theories both illuminate and complicate the moral imagination. Virtue ethics, utilitarianism, ethical egoism, rights-based ethics, deontology (i.e., the ethics of law or duty), and moral relativism are but a few of the ethical theories that distinctly shape how people make moral judgments. To that point, whenever human beings characterize something as good or bad, there are internal mechanisms at play. Namely, there is a principle, a feeling, a standard, or a system of thinking behind all moral judgments. Pleasure; pain; greatest goods; rules; laws; careful reflection; virtue; human dignity; retribution; passion; anger;

love—You name it! There is something behind every moral judgment, orienting people to understand morality as they do. And sometimes that *something* is theology.

Theology and Moral Reasoning

Theology is the study of God, or of divinity more broadly conceived. In the Christian traditions, God is often venerated as the beginning and the end of all things. Much of Christianity teaches that it is by knowing God that humans are especially able to live and do well. Thus, for many Christians, morality is not only established in relation to the presence of pleasure or pain or in relation to a philosophical moral theory, nor simply from a gut intuition. More importantly, Christians tend to conceive of morality in relation to their understanding of God, and what (if anything) they believe God values, wills, or requires. God functions as the highest end, or the highest standard, by which many people of faith orient their lives and reorient their sense of religious morality from other philosophical or personal points of view.

For example, Roman Catholic priests practice celibacy as one part of setting themselves apart for priestly duties—for the sake of the church and for service to the wider community. When put within many other relational contexts, celibacy may appear to be a kind of deficiency or insensibility. Within the priesthood, however, it is honored as a good thing that helps to facilitate a lifetime of ministry. Likewise, fasting holds profound religious meaning for many people of faith. However, outside of its religious context (or perhaps for health reasons), fasting can appear to be an unnecessary restriction. Thus, whether it pertains to matters of sex, food, or anything else, faith in God has substantial implications for how human beings live their lives. This includes how religious people engage in their overall moral reasoning within theological contexts.

Consider again Deanna Laney, Hans Missal, and the biblical Abraham. All of them, without exception, ultimately judged the attempted or actual murder of their children as qualitatively better than disobeying the voice they understood to be God. Of these three individuals, only Deanna Laney actively struggled with her decision. That struggle was one not only of sanity, but also of moral judgment. As a reasonable proposition, killing your children is generally a bad thing to do. That was relatively clear to her. In fact, it was a value judgment at play in her moral reasoning that caused her to wrestle with the other voice in her head. She probably assumed the wrongness of killing her children from theological insights, too. Her scriptures contain a commandment prohibiting murder, as expressed in Exodus 20:13. The same scriptures also possess the commandment to actively love human beings, as found, for example, in Mark 12:30–31 and John 15:13. Even so, obeying God was her highest end—a God who was allegedly speaking to her not through interpretations of scripture or church teaching, but by direct communication.

That kind of obedience to Laney's god reset the standard by which she set her moral compass. It also reset the standards by which Abraham and Hans Missal accepted the quality of their choices. And they are not alone. Belief in God—and what one believes God wills for humanity—is the same (general) standard by which a wide variety of religious people live their lives. The Islamic State (ISIS), Christian white nationalists, Jewish Zionists, anti-abortionists, Christian pro-choice activists, the Pope, Protestant pastors, religious civil rights leaders, Christian pacifists, Christian feminists, queer theologians, and Mainline Protestant small-group Bible studies (to name just a few) all draw upon their theological beliefs in order to reflect upon what they value and how they live.

What people of faith understand to be of the highest value in relation to God is the first wheel, which turns the other wheels of thought and action. *Theology is morality* because theology orients the mind to engage in moral reasoning in particular ways. But theology is not a single, monolithic thing. Instead, it exists in many forms and has a variety of expressions. For example, consider the medieval theologian Thomas Aquinas. Aquinas argued that faith, hope, and love should be the forces that shape the mechanisms of right reason.[12] However, the theologian defined faith, hope, and love according to church tradition. Indeed, Aquinas turned people toward the Catholic Church, venerating their doctrines as revelatory of reliable theological and moral truth. In contrast, many sixteenth-century Protestant reformers argued that it is the Bible alone that should have singular authority over one's spiritual beliefs and moral vision. What is more, for mystics, prophets, and those suffering with psychosis, disembodied voices and visions from God have functioned to inform right behavior. For still others, careful reflection on the vast warehouses of global religious teachings functions to shape a moral orientation. Thus, for many different kinds of people of faith, *theology is morality*, not because all religious persons are theologians by training (or even think in a theologically coherent way), but because the practical exercise of theology consists in any person's conceptions of God, which in turn can shape what that person thinks, says, and does. This, for better or worse, has real effects that ripple out from its source.

CHRISTIAN RESOURCES FOR MORAL REASONING

When Christians engage in theological moral reasoning, they do so from a number of standard resources: the Bible, church tradition, reason, and experience. Much has already been written about how these resources have been interpreted and cited. What can be said with certainty is that Christians often disagree with one another about them. They debate about what resources of the faith should be prioritized and how those resources should be interpreted and applied. Too often these disagreements have been remarkably painful. A couple of examples are worth considering. These stories give human faces to what might appear to be purely theoretical issues.

Consider the Reverend Doctor Norm Kansfield. An ordained minister in the Reformed Church in America and the former president of New Brunswick Theological Seminary, Kansfield was ultimately dismissed from his presidency in 2004 as a result of officiating a wedding for his daughter and her female partner.[13] The denomination he had served for decades then put Kansfield on ecclesiastical trial in 2005 and found him guilty of disobedience. Kansfield was ultimately dismissed from the office of professor of theology and suspended as a minister of Word and sacrament.[14] In return for the love of his daughter and his sincere theological beliefs, Kansfield was treated as a heretic.

Consider also the Reverend Anna Blaedel, who was ordained by the United Methodist Church. Blaedel has faced multiple church interrogations and a legion of condemnations for identifying as queer and for having performed a same-sex wedding. With each anti-queer investigation, Blaedel's accusers cited *The Book of Discipline of the United Methodist Church*—a handbook of denominational doctrines and standards (albeit one that is open to revision, and is not regarded as utterly infallible). In response, Blaedel's defenders have turned to the Bible. There they cite gospel values in order to challenge what they believe is outdated and sinful church policy. This crucible in the United Methodist Church went to the highest levels of the denomination.[15] In taking to social media, Reverend Blaedel wrote an open letter to the United Methodist Church, boldly proclaiming:

> I am disappointed, and sad, and angry, and weary, and exhausted by this seemingly endless series of attacks on my being, my loving, and my ministry. Let me be clear: I will not stop seeking justice and liberation through theological reflection, liturgical witness, and collective action. I will not stop committing myself to the spiritual

practices of bearing witness, telling the truth, creating and encouraging creative collectivities, interrogating power, practicing tenderness, and resisting evil, injustice, and oppression in whatever forms they present themselves. These are practices of faith, ways to live with integrity in a wounded and wounding and wonder-full world.[16]

While a number of Mainline Protestant denominations in the United States have moved to embrace queer clergy like Reverend Blaedel, denominations like the United Methodist Church and the Reformed Church in America are breaking apart over the issue of accepting those who identify as LGBTQ—the results of which are not only institutional, but also put the livelihood and well-being of LGBTQ clergy and laity in turmoil.

In the midst of these painful and persisting disagreements among Christians, the Bible, church tradition, reason, and experience are at play. These particular resources distinguish Christian ethics from other forms of religious moral reasoning. One should be careful to pay attention to how different concepts about these resources have the power to shape arguments within Christian ethics. For example, Christians neither agree about what the Bible is nor concur on how it should be interpreted and applied. Consider that fundamentalist Christians tend to deploy literal approaches to the interpretation and application of scripture, which in turn supports their moral values and sense of religious orthodoxy. This approach to scripture is very far removed from the more contextual approach offered by other Christian denominations. These churches tend to approach scripture with the tools of biblical scholarship, including the study of original languages, history, and social context. What is more, Christians do not mean the same thing when they speak of scripture as the word of God. Some mean that the words on the pages of the Bible were dictated by God. Others believe that the texts are divinely inspired but need interpretation to unearth the intended meaning, which is sometimes obfuscated by ancient language and cultural contexts. For still others, the word of God is not a "what" but a "who"—the second person of the Trinity, who became human in the person of Jesus. For such Christians, the word of God is eternal and ongoing; to be heard through the scriptures, but not reduced to them.

Given the diversity of perspectives on scripture, it is important to recognize that a Christian ethic that relies on the Bible is an exercise of interpretation. That does not mean that the Bible is merely a superficial prop that people manipulate to their own predetermined ends. That happens. But people have also been known to change their mind about theological issues and morality through more in-depth studies of the Bible. Even so, those changes of belief still represent interpretations. Recognizing the important role interpretation plays in any appeal to the Bible should cultivate humility over hubris. To that end, Christians, professional theologians, nonconfessional scholars, and self-avowed skeptics alike simply need to admit that there is, in actuality, a panoply of theological and ethical possibilities that can be produced from the Christian scriptures. Of these varieties, some will appear more convincing than others.

Church tradition also plays a formative role in Christian ethics. Here, too, there is no agreement about which church tradition to venerate over others. Church tradition takes different forms according to denomination. For example, Protestant Christians often claim the theological principle of *sola scriptura*, or "scripture alone," to teach and preach the gospel of Christ. With this as their banner, many Protestant Christians give themselves permission to dismiss the traditions and teachings of any other church if it is discerned that those traditions and teachings cannot be found in the scriptures. That said, the principle of *sola scriptura* is very rarely representative of Protestant church teachings in practice. In particular, the Protestant Reformation inspired the formation of many different denominations (or traditions) of the Christian faith, each with a set of catechisms, doctrines, and statements of faith that uniquely represent their particular understanding of scripture and its application. Such Protestants will tell us that their catechisms and statements of faith merely clarify what scripture means, and that scripture retains its primary authority. However, upon closer analysis, the production of these catechisms and statements of faith very often function as authoritative church tradition, by which participant members are seen in good standing and right faith—or not. Although many Protestants often critique the Catholic Church for allowing church traditions to supersede the clear teachings of scripture, the diversity of Protestant church teachings demonstrates that church tradition is very important to Protestants. By nature of the Protestant movement, when a Christian in a Protestant church discerns error in the church's teachings, they move to "protest" and "reform," which sometimes leads to the creation of another institutional church or denomination. The proliferation of such Protestant traditions contributes to the diversity of Christian ethics on any number of moral issues.

In contrast with many of their Protestant siblings, the Catholic Church has a more hierarchical model of church tradition and authoritative teaching. Rather than subordinating church teaching as derivative of the scriptures, the Catholic Church affirms that official church teachings are equal in authority with scripture. This model of church tradition rests upon a particular theological affirmation; namely, the Catholic Church teaches that the authority that Christ granted to his apostles was transferred to their successors. This, the church teaches, has continued on from generation to generation. These living authorities are entrusted with the right interpretation of scripture and the articulation of church doctrine. They carry the titles of bishops, cardinals, and ultimately, Pope (who is believed to inherit the authority of the apostle Peter). Thus, from a Catholic perspective, church tradition should absolutely shape Christian ethics. The *Catechism of the Catholic Church* explicitly affirms, "To the Church belongs the right always and everywhere to announce moral principles, including those pertaining to social order, and to make judgments on any human affairs to the extent that they are required by the fundamental rights of the human person or the salvation of souls."[17] In response to the church's teachings, the faithful are instructed to learn obedience—even as the church also recognizes that the conscience of each person is in a constant state of formation.

In addition to church tradition and the Bible, *reason* and *experience* are two other theological resources that are commonly cited in works of Christian ethics. In truth, reason and experience are the only mediums through which religion is made possible. These are the human faculties that allow for consciousness, imagination, communication, community, and analysis. So, too, there is no scripture or church tradition without the existence of a rational mind that is capable of producing such sacred texts or articulating the doctrines of the church. Indeed, without reason, human beings would function only by appetite or instinct.

Even so, some Christian communities say that they are suspicious of reason. For them, it is as if our potentiality to reason poorly subverts the value of this intellectual power altogether. Indeed, in order to discourage people from trusting their own reason over divine revelation, some Christian communities encourage their followers to sublimate the insights of reason to texts of the Bible (taken literally) or to church doctrines (as orthodoxy). There may be good reasons for being suspicious of particular forms of reasoning, or the reasoning of particular people. But one thing is certain: without reason, the artifacts of religion could not exist. Communities could not be formed, and neither could any sense of meaning be unearthed from the religious texts and traditions that assert themselves as repositories of divine truth.

What is more, without the medium of experience, there could be no meaningful narrative about anything. Experience is the drama of human living: it is shaped by *where* we are, *when* we are, *who* we are, *how* we are—and all of this in relation to other creatures, persons, and the world as a whole.

Without experience, there would be no narrative of the divine manifesting or interacting with humans in different times and places. Moses on the mountain, Jesus in the desert, Muhammad in the cave, Buddha under the lotus tree. Martin Luther and his sixteenth-century spiritual awakening to grace; the Christian abolitionist movement in the face of slavery and racial oppression, twentieth century Catholic base communities striving for liberation in El Salvador—all of these stories and many more are the stuff of experience; and without it, we do not have religion at all.

A mindful Christian ethic should appreciate the power of one's personal and social location. In particular, it is imperative to consider how our location on the map of humanity shapes our assumptions and values. This includes physical sex, gender identity, sexual orientation, economic status, geographical location, social status, racial or ethnic identity, political identification, religious heritage, physical or mental abilities, and so forth. Together they produce our experience, placing us in particular locations that others do not inhabit—sometimes to our privilege and sometimes to our marginalization. These experiences, in turn, shape the processes of our moral and theological reasoning. For example, before a person ever approaches the Bible, the location of their personal and social experience will have already colored how they will first receive the text. Consider, for a moment, that a white slave owner likely heard the statement "slaves obey your masters" as a clear scriptural justification of slavery—while the enslaved likely heard the story of the exodus from Egypt as a biblical indication that God is actually on the side of slaves. So, too, a person's experience postures them to resonate or disagree with church tradition (think back to the stories of Reverend Kansfield and Reverend Blaedel). This is true not only for marginalized people, but also for those with power and privilege. Thus, it should go without saying that people who are in positions of power and privilege have a profound responsibility to interrogate their own views. A failure to do so can too easily result in self-righteousness and tyranny. Indeed, it is difficult to understand how any Christian community can look back on the social and moral atrocities committed by Christians in the past (e.g., the Inquisition, the crusades, slavery, domestic abuse, and other injustices) and *not* think that they might have some reason to pause at their own claims to rightness or orthodoxy today. That said, it is also worth noting that it is out of people's experience and reason that great liberation efforts have been grounded in biblical interpretation and engagement with church tradition, including movements for LGBTQ equality, women's rights, and civil rights for racial and ethnic minorities, to name just a few.

ESCHATOLOGY AS A THEOLOGICAL MECHANISM FOR MORAL REASONING

Scripture and church tradition as mediated by reason and experience are indeed the resources from which concepts of Christian morality are produced. These are also the resources that shape particular Christian *theologies*. Eschatology is one such example. Eschatology is constructed by weaving together biblical interpretations and church teachings—and sometimes, eschatology is shaped by claims of direct revelation from God (remember Deanna Laney). Such eschatological views do not merely repeat texts and traditions, but rather expand upon them. For example, nowhere in the Bible does one text explicitly say that the end of time will be marked by a rapture of true believers followed by a seven-year tribulation, the rise of an anti-Christ, and a final battle between good and evil. And yet, that is an eschatology that has become popular in certain segments of Protestant Christianity and Hollywood films.[18] It is an eschatological theory that draws on a variety of biblical texts but does so by imposing interpretations on them and stringing them together in a particular order. There is an important point to grasp here; namely, a stated eschatology can create a new way of understanding the world—one that draws on the resources of the Christian faith, but that expands upon them so much that the eschatological perspective is itself a unique statement. Thus, eschatology can produce a new set of values and priorities for human living. When it does so, it creates an *eschatologically informed ethic.*

To be clear, at issue here is the authoritative weight that eschatology can possess in shaping the moral imagination. In particular, eschatology can supersede the authority of particular biblical texts and church teachings—even if it had been constructed from these resources. We can see instances of this within the Bible itself. For example, in Paul's first letter to the church in Corinth, matters of everyday living, including issues of sexual ethics, were upended by his eschatological concerns. The text reads this way:

> Now concerning virgins, I have no command of the Lord, but I give my opinion as one who by the Lord's mercy is trustworthy. I think that, in view of the impending crisis, it is well for you to remain as you are. Are you bound to a wife? Do not seek to be free. Are you free from a wife? Do not seek a wife. But if you marry, you do not sin, and if a virgin marries, she does not sin. Yet those who marry will experience distress in this life, and I would spare you that. I mean, brothers and sisters, the appointed time has grown short;

> from now on, let even those who have wives be as though they had none, and those who mourn as though they were not mourning, and those who rejoice as though they were not rejoicing, and those who buy as though they had no possessions, and those who deal with the world as though they had no dealings with it. For the present form of this world is passing away.[19]

Without question, these verses of scripture are perplexing. They challenge a wide variety of conventional norms about sex, marriage, family, work, wealth, and property. In truth, Paul's advice here is probably not something we would hear even the most conservative (or traditional) Catholic or Protestant pastor recommend for couples about to be married. Just imagine the premarital counseling session in which the pastor begins with Paul's words, "Those who marry will experience distress in this life, and I would spare you that." Which is to say, Paul's writings here transgress a number of conventional religious norms about marriage (then and now). The apostle does so from the perspective of eschatology.

Consider the passage again. Paul appears to be answering a question about the moral and theological status of marriage. For reasons either theological, philosophical, or both, the church in Corinth wanted to know if marriage was permitted for followers of Christ. Paul's answer is complex. First, Paul admits that he is not giving an answer from God, but rather is articulating his own opinion. Second, Paul does not forbid marriage, and thus he affirms that something of the existing models of marriage and family were permissible for the Christians in Corinth to pursue. However, Paul then turns to say that those who are married should live as if they are not; that those who have possessions should live as if they don't; and that those who deal with the world "as it is" should stop doing so. The theological perspective by which Paul suggests these radical life changes is nothing other than his eschatological vision. In particular, Paul writes, "For the present form of this world is passing away."[20]

Scholars and theologians have various theories about Paul's eschatological imagination.[21] Some suggest that Paul believed the end of time was imminent. Other scholars read Paul as simply asserting his belief that judgment day will come one day—and that Christians should live in light of that hope.[22] In truth, Paul's timeline for judgment day doesn't matter. Whether he had a heightened eschatological timeline in mind, or not, what Paul did do was to invite the Christian community in Corinth to live by an eschatological ethic. That eschatological ethic had the power to supplant other temporal teachings about marriage, sex, and social order. While Paul did not absolutely insist that the Corinthians should live by a radically ascetic eschatological ethic, the apostle did offer an eschatological vision as a theological orientation from which to live life in the here and now.

Paul wasn't the only early Christian to advocate for an eschatological ethic. For example, consider the second-century New Prophecy movement. Its adherents believed that the Holy Spirit gave the gift of divine revelation to true believers. Possessed by such a religious belief, the members of the New Prophecy movement dared to proclaim eschatological visions and lived ascetically so as to prepare themselves for judgment day. They did so in ways that included rather negative attitudes toward sexual relations. As scholars note, the eschatological asceticism of the New Prophecy movement was distinctive in a number of ways.[23] They refused to set up ecclesiastical structures.[24] They denied any good reason to believe that this world would be around much longer. Indeed, for those who were committed to the New Prophecy movement, a real Christian's attitude and ethic was supposed to reflect the seriousness of the coming apocalypse. The world was ending, and in their view, true Christians should respond accordingly.[25]

That type of eschatologically informed ethic is not far off from more recent examples of eschatological living. Consider Harold Camping, a twenty-first-century radio evangelist. He predicted that Christ would return to earth on May 21, 2011. At that time, Christ would supernaturally rapture his true believers into heaven, after which he would return, on October 21, 2011, in order to destroy the world.[26] Neither the rapture nor the destruction of the earth came to fruition. But in the time leading up to the prophesized dates, followers of Camping quit their jobs, leveraged their material possessions and finances, and abandoned family members in order to warn others about the imminent judgment to come.[27] For Camping's followers, the present form of this world was indeed passing away, and they had little time to live in the world as it is in the rush to prepare for what was to come. They had, in short, adopted not only an eschatological theology, but also an eschatological ethic.

The fact that eschatology can shape Christian ethics appears certain. However, the suggestion here is not that eschatology will always lead to a radical transformation of how one lives, but only that it can. Namely, not all Christians with eschatological beliefs (or expectations) are going to sell their homes and divest themselves of all their wealth in preparation for the coming of Christ. For many Christians, their eschatological views function to give them a sense of hope that this life is not the end—and that whenever the end does come (by death or by judgment day), there is a path forward into eternal life. Such a view can also shape Christian ethics; namely, if a Christian believes that "the end" will one day come and that there is a right way to walk toward the end in relationship with God, then that path forward will not only function to confirm what this person takes to be required spirituality, but it will also have the power to shape what that person values morally. For example, if one agrees with a church's teachings about which things are sins and which are not, then one's vision of heaven will likely assume that what is righteous on earth may have a chance of continuing on—and likewise, what is sinful will be purged or left behind. In this sense, a Christian eschatology might function to confirm traditional codes of morality rather than reform them.

Ultimately, eschatological views demonstrate two things. First, a stated eschatology can create a new narrative by which people sincerely interpret their lives on a timeline toward judgment day. And second, an eschatologically informed ethic may take any number of directions. Not all eschatological visions are oriented toward the reform of conventional moral codes. But some certainly are. What is more certain is that eschatological perspectives (however they are constructed) can powerfully inform the moral imagination. For the apostle Paul this meant thinking of new ways to live in Christian community. For the New Prophecy movement it meant adopting an ascetic orientation. For Harold Camping and his followers it meant radically reorienting how they treated finances and family members in the face of a certain date of Christ's return. For many others, eschatology either reifies, revolutionizes, or gently informs their ethic. In all of these examples, and many more to be examined in these pages, eschatology proves itself to be a unique theological place from which many Christians do engage in ethics.

CONCLUSION

Eschatology may very well be strange theology, but it also demonstrably empowers ways for thinking about Christian ethics. Eschatological visions can motivate people to live on earth as it is (or will be) in heaven. To that end, sexual ethics is one of the moral issues that a Christian eschatology might address. If the eschatological life is described as the continuation of human life in some supernatural form, then questions about the continuation of gender, sex, and sexual activity are authentic ones. In the next few chapters, we will investigate how such questions have already been answered by a variety of religious communities, before going on to imagine new possibilities.

CHAPTER TWO

SEX IN HEAVEN

Men and women will retain their sex in heaven.
—*Pope John Paul II*

AN ANCIENT PROMISE

In 2008, Dr. Eben Alexander, an American neurosurgeon, discovered life after death. While suffering from a severe meningitis infection, Eben Alexander went on an incredible journey into a life beyond this one. There he experienced a realm of unspeakable beauty, palpable love, and spirits both angelic and human. His critics claim that the neurosurgeon was simply hallucinating. But Dr. Alexander doesn't think that this critique is valid. He notes that his meningitis infection was demonstrably decimating the portions of the brain associated with consciousness. His body was comatose, and yet something of Eben Alexander was still conscious and experiencing a spiritual odyssey. His unexpected recovery provided him with the opportunity to share with the world his beliefs about life after death. By his own admission, Dr. Alexander says that of all the wonders and mysteries he encountered, the truths of heaven can be distilled to these phrases: "You are loved and cherished. You have nothing to fear. There is nothing you can do wrong. You are loved . . . unconditionally."[1]

Eben Alexander's narrative of a mystical realm of spiritual bliss is hardly a new one. The details of his spiritual journey are unique. But they fit within a larger history of religious beliefs about life beyond death. For example, the Persian prophet Zarathustra promised rewards of pleasure in a heavenly paradise for the righteous. The Hebrew prophet Isaiah saw a vision of a heavenly mountain, upon which the people of the earth will one day be gathered and where they will then turn from the ways of war to the practice of peace. The Christian prophet John, while imprisoned on the Greek island of Patmos, saw visions of a mystical city, an eternal feast, a celestial marriage, and the formation of a new heaven and a new earth. Likewise, the Arabian prophet Muhammad envisioned a heaven that includes sensual beauty and eternal rest. And the American prophet Joseph Smith offered an eschatological vision in which righteous families that stay together on earth are also able to stay together in heaven. Among these visions of heaven, some of them include the pleasures of sex.

This chapter considers descriptions of sex in heaven as they appear in a number of religious traditions. As it turns out, eschatological sex is not such a new idea. References to sex in heaven can be found within Judaism, Islam, and a variety of nineteenth-century Christian utopian movements in America. Notably absent from this list are Catholic and Protestant varieties of Christianity. To be sure, Catholic and Protestant Christians do not lack discussions about sex in heaven. However, these discussions are either new ones by scholars and theologians who seek to find room for sex in heaven (see chapter 4) or older discussions controlled by those theologians—especially from antiquity—who have negated the possibility of sex in the resurrection of the dead (see chapter 3). Unfortunately, Christianity's global influence has led to a wide variety of people who never even think about the possibility of sex in heaven or who assume that a sexless heaven is the norm. This chapter serves to disrupt their assumption. To do so will require investigating cases where heavenly sex has been affirmed among existing religious traditions. By taking these religious traditions seriously, we will find that eschatological sex is neither a modern novelty nor unimportant to the study of theology and ethics. What is more, by investigating where eschatological sex has been embraced, we can later turn and consider why much of Christianity has *not* included the pleasures of sex as emblematic of the goods of heaven.

JEWISH DELIGHTS

"Without question the best thing about being Jewish is the free sex vacation to Israel." So writes Rose Surnow about her weeklong trip to Israel through the Birthright program. She explains, "The goal of Birthright, which is partially sponsored by the Israeli government, is that young Semites will meet, marry, and procreate, yielding little mini Jews. I am not religious but I do love hummus and making out, so obviously I had to go."[2] Rose may not be religious, but the religion of her family possesses plentiful discourses on sex and bodily relations. Some of that discourse reads as restrictive. But other portions may open up quite a few erotic possibilities.

Jewish Views on Sexual Relations

Jewish views on sexual relations can be found in a number of biblical and theological texts. Among the oldest teachings of Judaism are those found in the Hebrew Bible (what some Christians call the Old Testament). Within the pages of the Jewish scriptures it is possible to find a wide variety of statements on sexual relationships. These references include descriptions of marriage, procreation, suave seduction, and erotic passion. The same texts also describe patriarchal privilege, ritual purity codes, slave wives, war booty, rape, and social codes that assign women to be the property of men.

The Hebrew Bible consists of three parts: the Torah (the Law), the Nevi'im (the Prophets), and the Kethuvi'im (the Writings). Each section of the Hebrew Bible presents different approaches to Jewish sexual relationships. The complexity of the Jewish scriptures suggests that no simplistic reading of these texts is possible. Nevertheless, it is illuminating to sample each section of the Jewish Bible for statements on sexual relations in order to have a better understanding of the landscape of Jewish sexual ethics. For example, in the Torah, the texts only explicitly sanction sexual activity between men and women.[3] And yet, there is no anticipation of marital or sexual monogamy for Jewish men. In fact, the Torah gives instructions for how men can take more than one wife. It even allows men to take concubines.[4] Furthermore, the Torah accepts that female slaves are men's property as sexual objects and outlets.[5] And in another unsettling set of laws, it is permitted that a woman can be killed for not being a virgin before marriage; and if she is raped before she is engaged, she is to be wed to her rapist.[6]

These patriarchal and polygamous Torah arrangements are further complicated by layers of other biblical laws. Consider, for example, that the Torah allows men to take certain relatives such as cousins and sisters-in-law as legitimate spouses.[7] In the case of the sister-in-law, the Torah commands men to take their sisters-in-law as wives, but only if they are widowed and childless—a matter seemingly focused on procreation. In fact, the command to marry a widowed sister-in-law is featured in a cautionary tale found in the book of Genesis. It is the story of a man named Onan, who was struck dead for ejaculating outside the body of his sister-in-law, whose first husband had died and left her childless.[8]

While reproduction is an important concern for taking childless sisters-in-law as wives, procreation is also a biblical command more generally. In fact, one of the first commandments described in the Torah is for humans "to be fruitful and multiply." Even so, the law of reproduction is often upstaged by other, more pressing Torah concerns involving sex and bodily relations. These concerns are informed by codes about ritual purity and cultural distinction. These codes are meant to distinguish the Jewish people from all the other nations of the earth, in terms of both ritual worship and cultural purity. With respect to cultural distinction and sex, the Torah forbids Jewish men from taking women as wives if they come from certain foreign tribes.[9] The specific concern in this commandment has to do with intercultural mingling. In particular, intercultural mingling was regulated in order to avoid the dilution of Jewish heritage and to minimize the corruption of their religious practices and devotion to Yahweh (the biblical god).

What is more, when turning to consider Torah concerns about ritual purity, the texts forbid people to have sex when the activity itself—or the sexual partner—is *ritually impure*. To be sure, there are a number of ritual impurities that Torah-observant Jewish people must attend to in sexual relations, including matters related to bodily fluids, parts, and functions. For example, concerns about ritual purity may be one part of the Torah's prohibition against anal sex between men. Because the anus facilitates defecation, it is a part of the body that is in a regular state of *ritual* impurity. So, too, semen is a bodily fluid that is ritually unclean.[10] The reader should distinguish, however, between ritual impurity and issues of sexual morality more generally. These ritual codes function to determine if a Jewish person can enter into sacred space and how they can relate (bodily) to other Jewish people. They are not codes about philosophical or religious morality written for a panhuman audience.

Another notable Torah concern with ritual impurity includes the prohibition of sex during a woman's menstruation. Very explicitly, the Torah categorizes women as ritually unclean during their monthly menstruation—so much so that a woman not only has to abstain from sex during this time but also has to abstain from sleeping in the same bed with her husband until she has been made ritually clean.[11] Lynne Meredith Schreiber, a twenty-first-century Orthodox Jewish woman, explains the observance of this ritual code in personal terms:

> I can't touch, kiss, or have sex with my husband for twelve days after my period starts. Two little drops of reddish brown on my underwear. *Here we go again.* Since I had kids my cycle is irregular, which wouldn't be a big deal except that I'm an Orthodox Jew and I can't even pass the salt to my husband—let alone touch, kiss, or have sex with him—for twelve days after my period starts.
>
> We never know when we'll have to sleep in separate beds or place a vase with a single rose between us on the dinner table as evidence of our separation.[12]

While Schreiber goes on to say that these codes of ritual purity do not ultimately extinguish the passion in her marriage, she does note the kind of sincere conscientiousness that it takes to practice these Torah commandments.

Admittedly, these are only a few examples of the laws concerning sexual and bodily relations in the Torah. They are not the only perspectives about sex in the Hebrew Bible. For example, when one turns to the Kethuvi'im (the Writings), these Jewish scriptures provide portraits of sexual relations that sometimes privilege the experience of erotic passion without rehearsing the Torah concerns about procreation, ritual purity, or cultural distinctiveness. The Song of Solomon is one biblical book that is rich with such textual evidence. Without question, the book depicts explicit sexual escapades that are easily imaginable through the poetic metaphors that are employed. In one instance, the male lover describes the female lover's body with great care— including her dove-like eyes; her fawn-like breasts; her large, rounded stomach; her ample thighs; and her "channel of fruits and spices."[13] The woman is described, here, as a veritable paradise—and she in turn describes her lover's body in fine detail. His is the appearance of ivory-work, with a kind face, yet with a body of pronounced features like the wood of a massive cedar tree.[14] The woman shows her awareness of her own capacity for sexual pleasure, as she calls her partner to "come to his garden and eat its choicest fruits."[15] In this description it is very likely that we are reading a scene that is intimating cunnilingus.

As the text goes on to describe their sexual exploits, the reader is clearly a third participant, a voyeur—watching as the lovers kiss, caress, and stimulate each other; his head is "wet with dew" while her inmost being "yearns for him."[16] A person may as well be reading contemporary erotica. If this text were simulated on film, it would likely be categorized as adult entertainment. However, noting the eroticism of both the man and the woman in the Song of Solomon is not to suggest that the text is free of sexist, violent, or patriarchal problems.[17] But even if the text has its "thorns," as Danna Fewell says, it can be argued that the Song of Solomon often achieves an explicit celebration of sex in ways that some religious folk might condemn as too vulgar to reveal anything divine.[18] Phyllis Trible offers a positive reading of the text. Trible says, "Born to mutuality and harmony, a man and a woman live in a garden where nature and history unite to celebrate the one flesh of sexuality.... Neither escaping nor exploiting sex, they embrace it and enjoy it.... Testifying to the goodness of creation, then, eroticism becomes worship in the context of grace."[19]

Thus, while sexual relations are sometimes restrained in the Hebrew Bible for reasons concerning ritual purity, and the letter of the law often assumes the patriarchy of the ancient social context out of which it is written, the Jewish scriptures nevertheless accept that sex is a natural part of being human—and that its pleasures are worth savoring. What is more, the living traditions of Judaism have also embraced a view of sexual relationships as natural and good. For example, traditional Jewish celebrations of the Sabbath include the expectation that one should have "sexual relations with [one's] spouse" as part of embodying the joy of Sabbath rest.[20] This insight will reappear in Jewish eschatological conceptions of sex, too.

Consider, also, the thirteenth-century Jewish philosopher Nachmanides, who said, "We believe that God created all things in accordance with his wisdom.... If our sexual organs are a disgrace, how could it happen that God created something shameful or ugly?"[21] Furthermore, George Robinson notes that rabbinical rulings in the Talmud "specifically state that 'a person will be held accountable to God for refusing to enjoy those pleasures that are permitted.'"[22] What is more, when turning to the tradition of Reform Judaism, it is possible to find teachings about human sexual relations that are inclusive of sexual and gender diversities. In fact, Reform Judaism largely accepts that any sexual relationship can be holy so long as it is just and kind. As the Jewish rabbi Yoel Kahn has argued, the practice of justice in human relationships was the primary concern of the biblical prophets (as found in the Nevi'im). Thus, when applied to sexual relationships, emphasizing the prophetic concerns of justice and kindness can reorient Jewish thinking away from Torah concerns about ritual purity and cultural distinction and toward an ethical concern for the quality of human relationships more broadly conceived.[23]

Jewish Views on Eschatology

While Judaism has always advanced statements about sex and bodily relations, it has not consistently held eschatological views. Depending on the time, place, and theological leanings of the Jewish people, comments about the afterlife have greatly varied. For example, certain texts of the Hebrew Bible make references to *sheol*—roughly translated as the "place of the dead."[24] In one instance in the Hebrew Bible, the spirit of the prophet Samuel was brought back from sheol by a witch at the behest of a desperate king.[25] This particular narrative suggests that sheol might be conceived as some kind of continuation for the life of a human spirit. Jewish theological reflections on sheol suggest a variety of possibilities. For example, David Novak notes that "whereas in biblical teaching *she'ol* means a kind of amorphous oblivion, having no specific opprobrium attached to it, rabbinic teaching, with its more intensive concept of hell (*gehinnom*), sees *she'ol* as the place where the otherworldly punishment of the wicked will take place."[26] The reader should be careful to note, therefore, differences between references to sheol in the Hebrew Bible and how the concept has been developed by a variety of Jewish theologians. That said, the same Hebrew Bible also contains the Book of Ecclesiastes, in which the author is positively agnostic about the fate of any kind of spiritual life after death.[27] There we read, "For the fate of humans and the fate of animals is the same; as one dies, so dies the other. They all have the same breath, and humans have no advantage over the animals; for all is vanity. All go to one place; all are from dust, and all turn to dust again. Who knows whether the human spirit goes upward and the spirit of animals goes downward to the earth? So I saw that there is nothing better than that all should enjoy their work, for that is their lot; who can bring them to see what will be after them?"[28]

Beyond notions of where spirits go after bodily death, ideas about an eschatological resurrection from the dead did eventually develop among the ancient Jewish people. George Robinson notes:

> Belief in the resurrection of the dead, a key element in traditionally observant Judaism's vision of the Messianic age, dates from the period of the Pharisees, and may be an outgrowth of Greek or Persian influence. While the Pharisees accepted the idea of resurrection, the Sadducees rejected it emphatically. According to at least one Jewish historian, Louis Jacobs, the idea of the resurrection of the dead gained its first currency at the time of the Maccabees,

around the second century BCE, a period of great suffering for the Jews. In the face of such trauma, the old ideas of reward of good and punishment of evil seemed untenable [while living on earth], but the notion of another life after death promised a final, cosmic justice.[29]

Robinson further explains that in the Mishnah (a written compilation of the sacred oral law tradition), it is stated that "corporeal resurrection will be a part of the world to come, except for one 'who says there is no resurrection of the dead.'"[30] And as David Novak notes, "There is no doubt that 'resurrection' here means the resurrection of the physical body, not the immortality of the soul."[31] Which means, historically and theologically, that concepts of the resurrection of the dead (among the Abrahamic religions) began with Judaism and were not introduced by either Christianity or Islam (even if both have also included concepts of resurrection within their eschatological theories).

Judaism and Eschatological Sex

Although Judaism as a whole includes a variety of conceptions about the eschatological life, not all Jewish people emphasize it or even believe in it. But when the rabbis have described the eschatological life, sex has sometimes been included. As Rifat Sonsino explains, "There are only a few references in the early Rabbinic literature describing the features of paradise. For some of the Rabbis of this period, the present world is a foretaste of paradise in the world-to-come, which is a place of reward for the righteous, with its celebration of Shabbat, sunshine, and sex (BT *B'rachot* 57b)."[32] In other words, the pleasures of the life to come are to mirror the pleasures of earthly Sabbath—which includes the enjoyment of sex.

The extent to which such eternal pleasures are to be taken literally or metaphorically is a matter of disagreement among Jewish theologians. For those whose eschatological imagination includes the coming of a messiah and the bodily resurrection of the dead, the possibility of sex in the life to come can be a real one.[33] But for those who deemphasize bodily survival and assert a spiritual postmortem, any references to the pleasures of sex (if they are made at all) are probably meant to be mere approximations of the joy one will experience in the near presence of God.[34]

To that end, there is no single doctrine of eschatological sex in Judaism. Even so, the faith does refer to it with literal connotations and metaphorical possibilities. The receptivity of Judaism to eschatological sex, however, presents no direct challenge to the practice of traditional Jewish sexual ethics on earth. Namely, some Jewish people have drawn on the positive qualities of sex to approximate the life to come. But nothing of the traditional Jewish descriptions of eschatological sex exceeds what is already permitted on earth. In other words, Jewish eschatology has been informed by the pleasures of sex, but the enjoyment of sex on earth is not (yet) reconceived by any eschatological example of it.

THE BEAUTIFUL COMPANIONS OF ISLAMIC HEAVEN

In 2015, a would-be Pakistani suicide bomber understood himself to be a righteous warrior engaged in a holy struggle (jihad) against sin. Death was his preferred weapon, even if it meant the elimination of his own life. On being arrested and interrogated, the jihadist was asked if his Muslim family supported him. They did not. When asked if he was married and if not, whether he wished to take a wife, he allegedly responded, "72 virgins are waiting for me in heaven—so why should I prefer only one here?"[35]

In this era of global religious terrorism, terrorists like this man have not only obscured traditional Islamic teaching, they have also perpetuated caricatured doctrines of Muslim eschatology. The promise of seventy-two virgins is one such caricature. That the Qur'an promises beautiful heavenly companions is true. But the nature of their companionship, the number of companions assigned to each heavenly citizen, and the effect this eschatological promise has on Islamic ethics is far more complex than the way in which this Western report of an incarcerated Islamic terrorist describes it.

Islamic Sexual Ethics

Before it is possible to describe the eroticism of Islamic heaven, it is first necessary to consider Islamic sexual ethics more generally. As with all things in Islam, the teachings of the prophet Muhammad are central to Islamic sexual ethics as a whole. Much like his Jewish contemporaries, the prophet Muhammad was opposed to the idea that a religious life is best practiced in celibacy. To the contrary, Muhammad's religious framework included sex as part of the good life for the righteous. For example, in the Qur'an we find a number of references to the natural goodness of sex between husbands and wives, including allowances for polygamy.[36] Like the Torah, the Qur'an forbids sexual activity between spouses during menstruation, just as it forbids forms of sexual activity that are deemed unnatural.[37] While Qur'anic references to "unnatural sex" are likely references to same-sex activities, these have also been cited by Islamic religious scholars to condemn oral and anal sex between husbands and wives.[38] To that end, the prescribed form of sexual activity in traditional Islam is marital vaginal intercourse. But such prescriptions are not made from a belief that sex itself is especially corrupted by sin—something that many Christian theologians of Muhammad's time supposed.[39] Rather, traditional Islam prescribed marital vaginal intercourse from a deeply held belief that God created sex for men and women to enjoy, in that particular way and at particular times.

Although a surface reading of the Qur'an explicitly presents a heterosexual marital norm for sexual ethics, contemporary Islamic scholarship has begun to offer affirmations of sex and sexuality that are more inclusive of gender and sexual diversities. For example, Ghazala Anwar argues:

> If vaginal heterosexual intercourse were permissible only because it led to impregnation, then it would eliminate the need for vaginal intercourse ninety-nine out of a hundred times that it is engaged in. Vaginal intercourse may lead to conception, but the intention must always be mutual pleasure as insemination can be achieved without penetration. It is not vaginal or anal intercourse but mutual consent, desire, gentleness, and permitting one's body to express one's love, to please and be pleased, that fulfill what the Quran ordains between lovers. It is entirely unnatural and counter-intuitive to reduce sexual expression between lovers to vaginal heterosexual intercourse.[40]

Anwar recognizes that much of Islamic jurisprudence does not support this point of view. Even so, she argues that traditional Islamic sexual ethics can be incompetently deployed. In particular, she believes the traditional view can ignore the emotional and relational dynamics of a sexual relationship "to the great defeat of love and mercy in heterosexual marriages and the oppression of sexual minorities."[41]

Muslim scholars and communities will debate such specific issues of sexual ethics for some time. However, what traditional and progressive Muslims seem to agree upon is an underlying positive attitude about sex, generally speaking; namely, that sex is a natural good in God's creation and that the enjoyment of sex can reflect one part of God's will for the life of human beings on earth. What is more, when we look for references to sexual activity across the whole scope of Muslim theology, it appears that sex might also have a place in the life of the world to come.

Islamic Eschatology and Eschatological Sex

In agreement with traditional Judaism, Islam affirms a belief in life after death and in a final resurrection of the dead. The Qur'an teaches that the day and the hour of the resurrection is something God only knows.[42] Until that time, some Muslims believe that the spirits of deceased humans exist in an in-between state—a spiritual plane of existence between this mortal life and the resurrection of the dead. Once in this spiritual state, traditional Islam teaches that there is no coming back.[43] The Qur'an states, "When death comes to one of them he will say: 'O Lord, send me back again that I may do some good I did not do [in the world].' Not so. These are only words he utters. Behind them lies the intervening barrier [stretching] to the day of their resurrection."[44] The Qur'an does not go into any profound detail about this interim spiritual state of being. What it emphasizes instead is belief in the resurrection of the dead.

When we consider Islamic conceptions of resurrection, it is there that heavenly companions show up as interesting characters. In particular, the Qur'an promises righteous men eternal companionship with the *houri*, a term that seems to reference beautiful female companions.[45] In surah 44, the Qur'an declares: "Surely those who fear and follow the straight path will be in a place of peace and security. In the midst of gardens and of springs, dressed in brocade and shot silk, facing one another. Just like that. We shall pair them with companions with large black eyes. They will call for every kind of fruit with satisfaction. There they will not know any death apart from the first death they had died, and will be kept safe from the torment of Hell."[46] In surah 52 a similar eschatological promise is offered: "Those who fear God and follow the straight path will surely be in gardens and in bliss, rejoicing at what their Lord has given them; and their Lord will preserve them from the torment of Hell. 'Eat and drink with relish,' [they will be told, as recompense] 'for what you had done.' They would recline on couches set in rows, paired with fair companions [who are clean of thought and] bright of eye."[47]

While the promise of men being paired with such fair companions does present itself in the pages of the Qur'an, it is further promised that righteous women will also enjoy paradise. The Qur'an states, "But he who performs good deeds, whether man or a woman, and is a believer, will surely enter Paradise, and none shall be deprived even of an iota of his reward."[48] But whether such righteous women are to enjoy any similar delights of heavenly companionship (as the men allegedly will), the Qur'an is silent or opaque apart from the intervention of interpreters.[49]

However, what can be said with more certainty about Islamic eschatology is that it is sensual. The scriptural references to food, drink, and comfortable furniture are all heavenly promises that draw on the experiences of earthly sensual delights. What is more, the Qur'an's references to beautiful heavenly companions tilts the imagination toward the idea that righteous men might enjoy erotic rewards in Muslim heaven. However, what is absent from the Qur'an is any specific reference to "seventy-two virgins" for sexual delight. That eschatological promise is only found in the writings of Islamic religious scholarship. In other words, the more explicit promise of the famed promiscuous sex in Muslim heaven is found in the interpretive work of imaginative theologians. Religion scholar John Portmann captures one striking example:

> According to Koranic commentator Al-Ash'ari (d. 935), 'Each time we sleep with a *houri* [a heavenly female companion] we find her a virgin. Besides the penis of the Elected never softens. The erection is eternal; the sensation that you feel each time you make love is utterly delicious and out of this world and were you to experience it in this world you would faint. Each chosen one will marry seventy *houris*, besides the women he married on earth, and all will have appetizing vaginas.'[50]

Even as Al-Asha'ri made such explicit eschatological comments about appetizing vaginas and eternal erections of delicious pleasures, regrettably, he did so in culturally circumscribed ways that objectify female sexuality through patriarchal and heterosexist views.

And yet, women are not the only objects of beauty featured in the eschatology of the Qur'an or that of Islamic scholars. As Stephen Murray and Will Roscoe note, "In the Qur'an, Paradise is furnished not only with female attendants (the houri) but also with immortal [male] youths who serve as cupbearers to the faithful."[51] The Qur'an specifically says, "Youths of neverending bloom will pass around to them cups and decanters, beakers full of sparkling wine."[52] Here the idea appears to draw upon an understanding that young men could be found just as aesthetically beautiful as women—and yet, neither the Qur'an nor other traditional Islamic religious texts ever explicitly permit, let alone praise, a man who indulges in this attraction through sexual activity.[53] At best, such a teaching disrupts any number of narrow understandings about aesthetic attractions between men. At worst, this view of young men might be read as the objectification or exploitation of young people, who, along with women, have often been treated or abused as the property of older men.

While sexism and patriarchy can be identified in some articulations of traditional Muslim eschatology, one should not lose sight of the fact that traditional Islam embraces human sexuality (generally speaking) as a gift from God. More specifically, Islam is a religious tradition in the Abrahamic family that does not regard sex as an impurity that must be purged before entering the eschatological life. With traditional Judaism, Islam affirms that the pleasures of sex are God-given and that the experience of sexual pleasure—properly pursued—is good. Indeed, according to traditional Islam, sexual pleasures may well continue into the next life.

However, just as traditional Jewish thinking about eschatological sex did not reform Jewish codes of sexual ethics, so too, traditional Islamic views on eschatological delights have not reformed Islamic sexual ethics on earth. Even if Al-Ash'ari turns out to be correct that citizens of paradise will receive more than seventy beautiful companions for the enjoyment of sex, that view has not increased the number of sexual consorts that Muslims are able to take on earth. At most, a Muslim man is only allowed to take four wives, and then, only if he is capable of caring for all of them equally.[54] Thus, like Judaism, Islamic eschatology is informed by what is considered valuable, attractive, and good upon the earth. Or, one could say it another way: that traditional Islamic eschatology is significantly informed by Muslim ethics and aesthetics.

POYLAMORY AND PROMISCUITY IN CHRISTIAN HEAVEN

Cristy and Dave Parave are bodybuilders who love Jesus. They love one another, and they love their swinging sexual lifestyle—an approach to sex that involves trading mates with other couples for excitement and pleasure. "'I don't think God would be mad at what we are doing,'" Cristy reported in 2014. "At first I was conflicted, but the more we looked at it, the more it makes sense to us. . . . God put people on the Earth to breed and enjoy each other. . . . I feel God is always with me and he has put us here for a reason.'"[55]

Dave and Cristy are so committed to their Christian swinging that they created an online network for those who want to join them at FitnessSwingers.com (a website that is still active as of this writing). There, the website seeks "[opposite-sex] couples and single *females* who desire intense sex, to explore new experiences and who are able to separate lust from love."[56] The website's emphasis on opposite-sex couples and single females seems to differentiate itself from groups that are more inclusive of bisexuality. Most notably, the swingers of this online community generally shy away from bisexual men.

Cristy and Dave Parave are not alone in their Christian commitments to swinging. Another Christian wife defended the swinging lifestyle this way:

> I can provide insight to how a couple can be both a faithful Christian and an active swinger. Both communities have things in common. They place a high value on marriage, and family life. Sixty-seven percent of swingers say that it is possible to love both swinging and Jesus, almost half regularly attend religious services, and more than half say they are very religious.
>
> ... Additional attractions include its relationship to the biblical practice of polygamy, its admonishments to remain "Safe, Sane, and Sober," and "Don't cheat. Swing." A careful study of scripture may cause a Christian to discover the difference between adultery [which is forbidden] and swinging [which is not].[57]

The belief that sex with multiple partners is *not* contrary to Christian teaching is a unique one. Most keepers of tradition would find such a statement incompatible with Christian teaching. However, such a nonmonogamous view does show up in some sectors of Christian history, and especially in the formation of new religious communities.

Consider, for example, the Oneida Perfectionists. Grounded in the teachings of John Humphrey Noyes, the Oneida Perfectionists (c. 1848–1878) were a nineteenth-century Christian community in Upstate New York who were primarily oriented by their eschatology. They embraced an eschatology that they called *full-preterism*.[58] This view accepted that all end times prophecies were fulfilled in the first century. This included a belief that the Second Coming of Christ happened (spiritually and invisibly) as a form of judgment against Temple Judaism, which was exacted when Jerusalem was destroyed by the Roman Empire in 70 CE.[59] With the belief that the Second Coming had already occurred, Noyes affirmed that human beings could live perfectly, without sin, now, in a new age of the reign of God. To that end, the Oneida

Community embraced a perfectionist identity. This was not a claim that everyone had already achieved perfection, but rather an assertion that they could achieve it as part of living out the new age of the reign of God on earth.

As William Kephart has noted, "Noyes preached that Christ had already returned to earth and that redemption or liberation from sin was an accomplished fact. It followed, therefore, that the spiritual world was autonomous, free, and quite independent of the temporal order."[60] In this sense, the Oneida Perfectionists understood that they were free to pursue the utopian vision of the eschatological reign of God—which for them included a sense of freedom from the conventional order of sexual ethics. In their time and place, sexual morality was largely controlled by the norms of heterosexual marriage, sexual monogamy, and procreation. However, the eschatological teachings of John Humphrey Noyes would change much of that for their community.

Noyes taught that romance and monogamy were nothing else but manifestations of possessiveness, exclusivity, and selfishness, sins to be eradicated from the perfect community. As a result, the Oneida Community embraced *complex marriage*. According to this form of social ordering, all people belonged to one another (in the same way that all land, property, and funds belonged to each member). Within this model, sexual relations were negotiated through a mediated form of mutual consent. That said, the sexual pairings could only take place between men and women. Kephart reports that Noyes

> taught that all men should love all women and that all women should love all men.... Sex relations within the group were reportedly easy to arrange.... If a man desired sexual intercourse with a particular woman, he was supposed to make his wish known to a Central Committee, who would convey his desire to the woman in question. If the latter consented, the man would go to her room at bedtime and spend an hour or so with her before returning to his own room. No woman was forced to submit to a sexual relationship which was distasteful to her, and the committee system presumably afforded her a tactful method for turning down unwelcome suitors.[61]

What it also provided was a framework to pursue sexual activities for pleasure rather than reproduction. The Oneidas did not reject reproduction, but they did practice it according to a very selective process (a kind of eugenics program). They believed that reproduction that occurred in the perfect age of the reign of God needed to be carefully planned.[62]

Noyes defended the practice of complex marriage as an eschatological ideal by looking to Christian scripture. David White notes that he primarily cited the Gospel of Matthew 22:23–30.[63] The passage reads this way:

> The same day some Sadducees came to [Jesus], saying there is no resurrection; and they asked him a question, saying, "Teacher, Moses said, 'If a man dies childless, his brother shall marry the widow, and raise up children for his brother.' Now there were seven brothers among us; the first married, and died childless, leaving the widow to his brother. The second did the same, so also the third, down to the seventh. Last of all, the woman herself died. In the resurrection, then, whose wife of the seven will she be? For all of them had married her." Jesus answered them, "You are wrong, because you know neither the scriptures nor the power of God. For in the resurrection they neither marry nor are given in marriage, but are like angels in heaven."[64]

What Noyes discovered in this passage was not the end of sex, but the end of marriage as it is traditionally practiced among Christians. In particular, Noyes interpreted Jesus to mean that exclusive, monogamous marriage ends in the eschatological life. But where marriage ends, the pleasure of sex continues, albeit within a new formulation of marriage and sexual relationships.

Noyes settled on complex marriage as the vehicle by which Christians should engage in sexual activity—whereby all members of the community were married to one another (i.e., all men to all women). Noyes believed that it was a clear command of scripture that followers of Christ should live in community with one another and share all things.[65] An example of such communal Christian life can be found in the New Testament book of Acts, in which one early Christian community was described this way: "All who believed were together and had all things in common; they would sell their possessions and goods and distribute the proceeds to all, as any had need."[66] For Noyes, the sharing of all things included sharing one another's bodies through sexual relations, without claims or requirements of exclusivity.

Contemporaries of Noyes would often castigate him for advocating "free love"—with insinuations that the Oneida Community simply followed every passion to fulfillment within the free rein of promiscuity. That critique is not quite true. The promiscuity that Noyes championed was actually controlled by the practice of *coitus reservatus*; which Noyes called "male continence." As Lawrence Foster has explained it, "Under male continence, a couple would engage in sexual congress without the man ever ejaculating, either during intercourse or after withdrawal.... In [Noyes's] view, regular intercourse [was] wasteful, sowing the seed where one does not want or expect it to grow."[67]

To that end, the polyamorous Oneida Community did practice a form of sexual restraint according to their special concern for "wasted seed" and eugenics. However, apart from that concern, the sexual ethic of the Oneida Community is unique for Christianity because it prioritized the enjoyment of sexual pleasure. But because of the rule of male continence, men's enjoyment of sexual pleasure was restricted. Allegedly this restriction on men benefited women's sexual experiences. Foster explains:

> However men may have reacted, women at Oneida evidently found the practice an improvement. In describing his early experimentation with male continence, Noyes observed: "my wife's experience was very satisfactory, as it had been never before." The medical historian Norman Himes opined "that the Oneida Community stands out historically as perhaps the only group experiment, at least in the Western World, placing great emphasis on the full satisfaction of the woman, and this in a culture dominated by male attitudes." The sex researcher Havelock Ellis concluded that some women did reach orgasm when male continence was practiced.[68]

Of course, reports from men about female sexual satisfaction should always be received with a healthy dose of skepticism. But one might at least hope that many of the Oneida men were able to hone their practice of continence to the benefit of the Oneida women who desired sexual satisfaction.

As for the ease or difficulty of such a contraceptive practice for the Oneida men, Noyes only asserted that it was "easy for *spiritual* men."[69] Beyond what can be conjectured about the enjoyment of such sexual practices, one thing is certain; namely, the eschatological imagination of Noyes and the Oneida Community resulted in a rather radical reorientation of social order and sexual ethics (at least for their time and place). They faced intense scrutiny from their fellow Americans, and therefore their decision to be part of such a countercultural community was intentional and meaningful. Such eschatological views of social order and sexual ethics came with a price. For example, Noyes himself had been driven out of other localities because of his teachings. Only New York State offered a stable home for his eschatological experiment of communal utopia.[70] To that end, the Oneida Perfectionists provide one very poignant example of how eschatology can directly reshape Christian sexual ethics. Indeed, this is a distinction the reader should make very clearly. The Oneida Community did not project an ethic of complex marriage onto their eschatology. Rather, it was their eschatological beliefs that caused them to revise their sexual ethics. They would not be the only nineteenth-century Christian community to draw on eschatology to shape their theological and moral claims about sex and marriage. The Church of Jesus Christ of Latter Day Saints also came to advocate for a kind of eschatological sex that offered a new vision of Christian heaven.

GOD HAS SEX

Originating in New York State, the Church of Jesus Christ of Latter Day Saints (LDS) operated under the prophetic authority of Joseph Smith. This American prophet claimed that he was receiving a new revelation from God, which provided for both a new collection of scriptures as well as a living and direct line to God through the prophet. Smith's visionary leadership has proven to be very successful. While the eschatological utopia of the Oneida Perfectionists eventually disbanded, the LDS church has flourished into the twenty-first century. One part of this new religious movement includes an interesting vision of the eschatological life, and the (potential) place of sex in it. However, before turning to discuss the views of the Latter Day Saints on eschatology and sexual ethics, it is important to address the often-cited controversy concerning their practice of polygamy.

When accessing the archives of the Latter Day Saints (or Mormons), it is very clear that the practice of polygamy was at one point indeed sanctioned. However, the practice of polygamy only took place around a prolonged episode of exile. Because of the nonconforming nature of LDS theology, as well as the church's tenuous relationship with local, state, and national governments, the early Mormons quickly found themselves on the run and often under attack. With a concern that the dwindling numbers of the faithful would result in the end of the new religious movement, Joseph Smith believed that polygamy was both a biblical and a practical means by which the LDS could faithfully repopulate their community.[71] Citing the patriarchs of the Hebrew Bible, Smith argued that polygamy itself was not sinful—even if Christianity had moved toward a monogamous norm. Monogamy, Smith argued, wasn't wrong—but it wasn't the only norm for sexual ethics either. Thus, Smith proclaimed that polygamy was a provisional good. However, when finally settling into their more stable life in Utah, the marital practice that Mormons returned to was the monogamous norm of nineteenth-century America. In fact, those Mormons who refused to abandon polygamy would go on to form their own sectarian religious communities apart from the LDS church—some of which still endure today. By comparison, while the Oneida Community practiced nonmonogamy from their eschatological ideals, the Mormon embrace of polygamy was not so similarly motivated.

That is not to say that Mormon polygamy was completely divorced from the eschatology that Joseph Smith articulated. In fact, Smith found some extra justification for polygamy in the same New Testament passages that the Oneida Community had used to support their practice of complex marriage. In particular, Smith cited the Gospels of Matthew and Luke, which contain Christ's teaching that marriage will not persist in the resurrection of the dead.[72] Joseph Smith understood such passages in light of his new revelations about marriage, which affirmed that marriage does continue in heaven (whether monogamous or polygamous), just not in the same way it is lived on earth.

To understand Smith's perspective more clearly, consider the Gospel passages again. In each one, the Sadducees had come to expose what they took to be the folly of believing in the resurrection of the dead. They did so by questioning whom a woman would belong to in the resurrection if she had married seven different brothers on earth. A plain reading of the Gospel narratives show that Christ's answer is twofold. First, that the Sadducees were wrong about eschatology. Namely, Jesus affirmed that resurrection from the dead will happen. Second, Jesus taught that in the resurrection of the dead there will be no marriage. But Joseph Smith understood Christ's teaching only to mean that marriage will not continue as it is practiced now. Whether polygamous or monogamous, Smith taught that earthly marriages would eventually transform into *celestial marriage*.[73] In heaven, as Joseph Smith explained it, spouses are in for a big upgrade—not the eradication of marriage altogether. From the perspective of LDS theology, heaven offers the opportunity for spiritual evolution into godhood, which husbands and wives enter together (but which prioritizes the apotheosis and authority of the man).

For Smith, the problem with both the Sadducees of scripture and traditional Christian teachings is generally the same; namely, both are in error about the eschatological life—either in terms of it existing at all, or what it will be like. Joseph Smith believed that the vision of celestial marriage offered far more interesting possibilities for eternal life than what traditional Christianity had been teaching. This included the possibility that those who are married on earth can endure in powerful new ways in the life to come. Ultimately, the LDS church teaches that this is a matter of achieving divinity and setting out to be God of a new world. This is a theological claim in need of more explanation.

The Latter Day Saints did not believe that they were living in the eschatological age in the same way that the Oneida Community did. Rather, the nineteenth-century LDS accepted that the world to come was still on the horizon of human time. But they did believe that they were living in the "latter days" (hence the name). Thus, for the LDS, life on earth was preparation for life after death. Indeed, according to LDS theology, the earth was created in order to test the spirit children of God the Heavenly Father. This test was to see whether God's children would still love him if their love and obedience came through faith, and not by sight. This particular theology asserts that all human beings once lived in a spiritual preexistence with God.[74] According to Mormon theology, each person has to eventually leave this spirit-existence, passing through a mystical veil when born. Purportedly, this veil robs each human being of any memory of their preexistence. Once upon the earth, humans are tested in matters of faith and morality. But according to LDS theology, life here is not the end. Life on earth is only one stop on a larger journey. It is a spiritual journey that is primarily ordered toward both heaven and deification.

In particular, the eschatological narrative that Joseph Smith articulated was one that included a domestic heaven and provided for a kind of supernatural evolution—allowing humans to achieve apotheosis (i.e., ascension into godhood). With respect to a domestic heaven, Joseph Smith imagined an afterlife that challenged theocentric models of it. The differences between domestic and theocentric models of heaven are important to note (both now and for later chapters). According to Mormon researcher Samuel Morris Brown, "The theocentric model of the afterlife emphasized the majesty of God at the expense of human relationships. Worthy believers would in the afterlife pay no attention to other humans, as all creatures and their creaturely associations paled in comparison with God's divine glory."[75] Contrary to the theocentric view, Joseph Smith taught that the world to come would be one lived in community. Brown reports, "In public pronouncements that irritated estranged followers and Protestant neighbors, Smith announced publicly that he preferred hell with his friends to heaven alone" and that "preservation of human ties represented the core of his preaching, what he defended with a revelation announcing that the 'sociality which exists among us here will exist among us [in the afterlife].'"[76]

But for Joseph Smith, the domesticity of the afterlife was not pictured as merely a heavenly reunion of friends and family playing in an eternal paradise. This domestic heaven also provided for the continuity of marriage. Smith taught that husbands and wives would be joined together (again) in heaven. However, this marriage would not exist for the sake of romantic love and companionship alone. Rather, Smith taught that marriage was all part of the process of apotheosis; the very progression into godhood. Upon attaining godhood, celestial marriage provided the possibility of giving birth to new worlds and new children, who themselves (like humans now) might one day come to share in the power and glory of divinity.

Smith grounded his visions of apotheosis and celestial marriage in his doctrine of God. In a break with traditional Christian views, Joseph Smith "announced to the [church] the 'secret' that 'God himself who sits in yonder Heavens is a man like unto one of yourselves.'"[77] Smith's doctrine of God reimagined the God of this world as a being who was once mortal, but who had spiritually ascended to godhood through a supernatural evolution that all mortal males can hope to achieve. This teaching would be summarized by the church president Lorenzo Snow (1891–1901) in the short statement, "As man is now, God once was; as God is now, man may be."[78] While the authority of godhood is something that only males are able to achieve, LDS theology does not leave women out from the progression to divinity. Brown explains:

> The [God] of early Mormonism stood as the "head" God of the heavenly-family. He was the Father of the Sons of [God], the figure they would imitate in the eternal progress of the Chain of Belonging. The familialized Chain pushed Mormonism into one more radical doctrine. The God of early Mormonism was not a holy bachelor, existing in the cosmos outside of family entanglements. He participated in a recognizable family structure, bound not only to offspring but to a spouse. Distinct from the dyadic divine feminine of other esoteric traditions, the Heavenly Mother of Mormonism, preached perhaps as early as 1835, was God's wife.[79]
>
> What seemed to have mattered most to Smith and his early followers is that God the Mother placed God the Father into the family context. Both were fully integrated into the heaven family tree, a married spousal unit. Together they were the parents of Jesus and the Sons of [God].[80]

Thus, the eschatology of the nineteenth-century LDS church was not only domestic, it also implied a sexual or erotic dimension; namely, deified men and their wives will continue in celestial marriage. They will engage in a form of heavenly intercourse that will allow such higher beings to create new spiritual offspring. All of this is to say that Mormon eschatology (the end of our time) is actually the beginning from which whole new worlds of mortal beings will emerge.

Whether celestial intercourse is the same as earthly intercourse is not certain. On the one hand, the affirmation that "God is a man like humankind," albeit of an elevated sort, suggests that the intercourse of deified men and their wives could closely approximate sexual performances on earth. There is nothing in LDS theology suggesting that celestial sex is antithetical to celestial marriage in the life of the world to come. On the other hand, Mormon doctrines of God suggest that the capacities and characteristics of godhood far exceed the current finitudes of humanity. Thus, a man who has gone through apotheosis (with his wife) may not retain (or need) every function of human life as it is now known. It is feasible that the creation of new worlds and spiritual children could result from the intermingling of their love and willful desire for a new creation. Admittedly, this Mormon theology is a matter of deep mystery. But insofar as the LDS doctrine of God sustains that "God is like a man in yonder heaven," the eschatological promise of celestial marriage intimates that sex—or something very much like it—continues in the life to come.

LIVING FOR HEAVEN

Swinging bodybuilding Christians; Orthodox Jewish couples who keep to the rules of Torah; Muslims who hunger for righteousness in this life and the next; nineteenth-century exiled utopians with new visions for Christian living: these disparate people of faith reveal that concepts of sexual morality can take wildly different forms when drawing on the resources of faith. Traditional Christianity shares little in common with their sexual ethics. Thus, the examples of this chapter show us unique insights into sexual ethics among religious varieties. Some of them also reveal that the idea of sex in heaven is not new or novel. With respect to the concept of eschatological sex, there are two orientations to consider here: an *ethically informed eschatology* and an *eschatologically informed ethic*.

A paradise of love, pleasure, and ecstasy are common descriptions of the life to come. But look more closely at the terminology that is often used for heaven. It is value-laden. As such, descriptions of the afterlife tend to draw on the lexicons of both ethics and aesthetics. Love, pleasure, ecstasy, goodness, grace, peace, beauty, vitality, fulfillment: these are all *qualitative* terms. Near-death-experiencers, prophets, and theologians alike draw on this kind of language. Such a linguistic strategy suggests that the relationship between ethics and eschatology can be mutually informing; namely, insofar as eschatology can function as a theological mechanism for making moral judgments (as noted in chapter 1), it also appears that concepts of value and morality can (and do) shape descriptions of the eschatological life.

The way people of faith describe heaven indicates to us what they take to be good and inclusive of what is ultimately worth seeking. For example, some religious traditions describe heaven as a final resting place that promises eternal feasts. We can read that cynically, perhaps, as a way to simply assuage or anesthetize the suffering of starving people on the earth. But alternately, the vision of eternal feasts can be read as a meaningful moral statement on the good of fulfillment. That is to say, the vision of heaven as a place of feasting can function as a critique (morally and theologically) of the reign of starvation upon the earth. Likewise, some Christian descriptions of the eschatological life speak of a heavenly mansion, in which there is room for all. If we read that as a moral statement (projected onto an eschatological screen), then it is clearly a statement about the good of shelter. To that end, those who study religion and ethics need to attend not only to how the eschatological imagination might inform ethics (in the here and now), but also how concepts of morality (now) can shape visions of the life to come. Certainly, some of these eschatological descriptions are deployed as metaphors. In other cases, descriptions of heaven appear to function as actual promises of what should be expected in the life to come. Either way, these descriptions of heaven are statements about what is qualitatively good and worth seeking, whether in heaven, on earth, or both. As we have seen, this sometimes includes the affirmation of eschatological sex.

Arguably, Judaism and Islam offer examples of an ethically informed eschatology. In each religious tradition, the pleasures and goods of earthly life appear to forecast the joys of heaven—including sexual pleasures. Even so, none of the erotic rewards of Jewish or Muslim eschatology have functioned to radically challenge conventional codes of religious ethics. But for other religious traditions, an eschatologically informed ethic has reformed both social order and moral codes. The Oneida Community and the Latter Day Saints demonstrate this very well. For the Oneida Community, complex marriage was believed to be a reality of heaven, and thus a reality to embody on earth—even if transgressive of conventional values. For the Latter Day Saints, the promise of celestial marriage has informed the way Mormon spouses practice their marriage on earth.

Sex in heaven is certainly not the only concern for these religious groups. However, the presence of eschatological sex in the religious traditions described in this chapter can illuminate a number of discussions about religion and sexual ethics. First, when religious traditions include the pleasures of sex in heaven, this challenges religious attitudes that would denigrate sex and the enjoyment of sexual pleasure as lower sorts of goods on earth. In truth, it is not difficult to find an array of philosophers and theologians who have demeaned sexual activity as animalistic or as valuable only in terms of the reproduction of the species. A wide variety of theologians and church leaders in Western Christianity have especially been suspicious of the pleasures of sex.[81] By contrast, to assign sex as one of the pleasures of heaven is to affirm that human bodies in the throes of erotic delights reflect one of the eternal, holy goods of paradise. When religious traditions affirm eschatological sex, it invites us to believe that sex is not antithetical to heaven, but rather it is worthy—or reflective—of it.

Second, descriptions of heavenly sex reveal both complexities and possibilities about sex on earth. Consider the complexities. There is a reason why traditional Judaism, Islam, and utopian Christian communities placed boundaries on sexual activity; namely, on earth, it is possible to get sex wrong. For example, traditional Judaism affirms that sex might be included in the resurrection of the dead. But this eschatological promise does not eradicate the need for codes of ritual purity on earth, which keep traditional Jewish people distinct from all the other nations. Likewise, traditional Muslims believe in the resurrection of the dead and hope for a paradise of sensual bliss. But earth is not yet heaven. On earth, the struggle to submit to God for the sake of righteousness still requires some effort. Sex has a place in that effort toward righteousness, but it is well regulated. Even the Oneida Community placed limitations on sexual activity. They believed that they were living in the promised reign of God, but their earthly location required the practice of perfection according to certain codes of conduct. The restrictions that each of these religious traditions placed on sexual activity admit to the need for caution. In other words, living and doing well in sexual relationships still requires guidance and discipline. Sometimes—as these religions suggest—this requires withholding from inclinations that one might otherwise want to indulge.

But even as visions of eschatological sex sometimes fail to change conventional codes of morality, the promise of sex in heaven can also open up new possibilities for rearticulating sexual ethics on earth. For example, when visions of heaven include the enjoyment of sexual pleasure without restriction to one person (as in the Oneida Community), then religious codes of sexual ethics might consider promiscuous possibilities of living on earth as it is (or will be) in heaven. What is more, where visions of eschatological sex celebrate sensual pleasures as goods unto themselves, we might explore the value of pursuing sexual pleasures apart from conventional norms of marriage and reproduction.

However, to pursue this line of thinking within the context of Christian ethics requires us to investigate the absence of eschatological sex within traditional Christian theology. The story of how and why traditional Christianity failed to develop sex in heaven is an unfolding one. In truth, the denial of eschatological sex is not a definite New Testament teaching. Rather, it is a theological conclusion. In the next chapter, the traditional Christian case *against* eschatological sex will be explored.

CHAPTER THREE

CHRISTIANITY'S SEXLESS HEAVEN

If the apocalypse comes... beep me.
—*Buffy ("the Vampire Slayer") Summers*

The end of the world has been a topic of profound fascination at various points in Christian history. The dawn of the twenty-first century is no exception. Then, as the calendar turned from 1999 to 2000 (Y2K), technologically advanced societies heard rumors that some computer systems were not designed to roll over from one millennium to the next. Fear gripped segments of the population, with speculations that society would fall into ruin. Utility grids would go down; aviation systems would fail; banks would collapse; and the world would succumb to chaos. "Are you ready for Y2K?" doomsday-preppers would ask. Such questions sometimes came in the form of commercial advertisements, selling emergency supplies of food and bunkers to face the uncertain future.[1] Accompanying those concerns and commercial ventures were eschatological fears stoked by particular religious communities. These saw the potential chaos of Y2K as a signifier of the end of the world and the return of Christ.[2] In March 1999, the *Los Angeles Times* reported that "a full quarter of Americans surveyed ... believe the onset of a new millennium heralds the second coming of Jesus Christ."[3] The *Los Angeles Times* also reported that "among those who take the [Bible] literally, 40% believed that the new millennium is tied to Christ's return. Among those who are not biblical literalists only 18% said so."[4]

As the world survived the unrealized apocalypse of Y2K, other portents would fuel the flames of early twenty-first century eschatological fervor. Some Christians claimed that the terrorist attacks on September 11, 2001, were a sign of the end times.[5] The subsequent invasion of Iraq by the United States had some end-times communities rethinking how the final battle of Armageddon might play out, given the wars in Iraq and Afghanistan.[6] Barack Obama's stunning rise to the presidency of the United States made some people quite certain that he was the Antichrist, who signaled that the end of the world was nigh.[7] The Mayan calendar—though not a Christian artifact—spooked more than just a few people into thinking that 2012 was the end of the world. Still other Christian churches have seen the ongoing violence and controversies within and around the nation-state of Israel as the fulfillment of end-times prophecies.[8] To be sure, Christians have said a lot when it comes to talking about the end of the world.

Admittedly, the expressions of Christian eschatology that often make headlines are the predictive ones. Church leaders who have revealed timelines and "super signs" about the end of the world can (and do) garner the attention of the general public and national media. Indeed, they sometimes land their eschatological publications on the best-seller lists.[9] The less predictive studies of eschatology—especially the ones that do not stoke the flames of fear—are often relegated to the more stoic or contemplative work of scholars, theologians, and pastors. But even among this cohort there is much debate about eschatology. Arguments about when Christ will return, how, and to what end (e.g., whether to bring retributive judgment or cosmic restoration) flavor much of the debate among Christians. However, if there is any agreement among Christians, it is in their generic descriptions of heaven, which are broadly pleasant. That realm will be one in which sickness and death are eradicated. The near presence of God will be known. Hunger and thirst will be fulfilled. Rest and release from toil will replace exhaustion and anxiety. Some Christians take these material descriptions of heaven to be literal, while others read them as metaphorical. For both groups, however, sexual pleasures are often missing from the lists of heavenly delights.

Indeed, a sexless afterlife has been a hallmark of traditional Christian theology. At first glance, this may not seem like an important matter for Christian theology or ethics. However, upon more careful reflection, the theological status quo of a sexless afterlife reveals a particular agenda according to those who have controlled Christian doctrine. This agenda is not only theological, it is also moral in scope. By eradicating sex from the afterlife, privileged Christian theologians have subsequently categorized sex as something temporal at best, or at worst, something to be devalued. Thus, if eschatology represents the highest end of the Christian life (presumably eternal life with God), then what life looks like in the eschatological age can illuminate what should be counted as important in the here and now. If sex is absent in heaven, then its meaningfulness here is (some will argue) fleeting and only useful in a limited and prescribed sense.

In order to understand how and why Christianity developed in this direction, it will require thinking about wider issues of Christian eschatology. This will include New Testament texts on eschatology, the codification of eschatological doctrines, and the relationship between eschatology and sexual morality. This may seem like a detour from the quest to explore sex in heaven. Indeed, it is easy to get lost in these texts and theological discourses. Entire books have been written on particular Christian scriptures, theologians, and the development of doctrine. Therefore, an attempt to offer a comprehensive review of such sources and their relevance to eschatology and sexual ethics is beyond the scope of this chapter.[10] What will be offered in the next several pages is an exploration of particular Christian scriptures and theological attitudes that were eventually leveraged to give rise to Christianity's eschatological doctrines and its vision of a sexless heaven.[11] This will require pausing to visit some issues of interpretation with respect to eschatological passages in the Bible. In particular, we will take a look at some of the eschatological references in the New Testament and try to elucidate why Christians have such different views on final judgment and salvation. Next, this chapter will note the rise of church doctrines about sin, death, and sex and how they relate to visions of eschatology. By looking at these constellations of issues, one can better understand why traditional Christianity came to deny the continuation of sexual relationships in the eschatological life.

NEW TESTAMENT ESCHATOLOGY:
FIRES OF CONDEMNATION AND REDEMPTION

Christian eschatological warnings about judgment day can be traced back to the New Testament scriptures. That is not to say, however, that New Testament authors invented the category of eschatology or the genre of apocalypse. As other scholars have argued, eschatological and apocalyptic themes in the New Testament probably borrowed from a variety of Jewish and extrabiblical traditions.[12] Given that the New Testament is more like a whole shelf of books than a single volume, it lacks any single or systematic eschatology. But the New Testament, on the whole, does have a number of references to the end of life as humans now know it, with scenes of final judgment. For example, Matthew's Gospel offers a warning from Jesus about a day of reckoning. In Matthew 25:31–46, the reader is warned that there will be a final separating: those who will inherit the kingdom of God and those who will "go away into eternal punishment."[13] The criterion of judgment that Jesus names is a relational one. Those who have served and offered hospitality to the least of all humanity will be welcomed into eternal life. Those who do not will instead go into eternal punishment. Or, to paraphrase Jesus from the Gospel of Matthew, "Whatever you did [or did not do] to the least of my brothers and sisters, you did [or did not do] unto me."

There are at least two ways to read this eschatological narrative. The first employs a predictive surface reading of the text; namely, that Matthew's gospel affirms a coming judgment day and says that a person's eternal destiny will depend upon the exercise of basic human kindness and compassion. However, a second way to read this text understands a persuasive rhetoric to Christ's narrative. In particular, this eschatological narrative may not be a statement on what will be, but rather a story meant to transform those who hear it—a prophetic exaggeration with a purpose. To the point, the story can provoke a change of character and behavior (in the here and now). Any such moral transformation would therefore alter any definitive statement on who (precisely) will experience eternal punishment or reward. Such a reading of this text emphasizes the value of the interim period between the present and a future judgment day. In this interim, repentance and transformation are possible, which increases the number of people who will be "saved" at judgment. Such repentance and transformation of the individual person, when multiplied throughout the world, would seemingly also lead to social reformation.[14] Thus, if caring for the least among us is the criterion for eschatological salvation, then the liberation of marginalized and oppressed people would be a key indicator of those who are destined for heaven.[15]

Whereas the Gospel of Matthew's eschatological narrative can be interpreted as either predictive or persuasive rhetoric, other New Testament texts on matters of divine judgment suggest a possible hope for universal salvation. Romans 5:18 reads this way, "Therefore just as one man's trespass led to condemnation for all, so one man's act of righteousness leads to justification for all."[16] 1 Corinthians 15:22 also draws upon inclusive language, promising that "for as all die in Adam, so all will be made alive in Christ."[17] What is more, earlier in 1 Corinthians the apostle Paul (the attributed author) seemingly describes judgment as a purification process. If so, it would have implications for embracing the idea of universal salvation. The text reads:

> For no one can lay any foundation other than the one that has been laid; that foundation is Jesus Christ. Now if anyone builds on the foundation with gold, silver, precious stones, wood, hay, or straw—the works of each builder will become visible, for the Day will disclose it, because it will be revealed with fire, and the fire will test what sort of work each has done. If what has been built on the foundation survives, the builder will receive a reward. If the work is burned up, the builder will suffer loss; the builder will be saved, but only as through fire.[18]

Christian theologians and biblical scholars debate about how best to interpret this text, especially in terms of who will be saved upon the "foundation of Christ." Some see the passage as possibly referring to all human beings.[19] Others see it as an assurance of salvation for Christians alone.[20] The theologian Jan Bonda sees a possibility of universal salvation in this passage. Bonda writes, "Strange words: suffer loss and yet be saved."[21] It reads as if the judgment is purifying, not retributive. It is a judgment to be faced—and yes, with the difficulty of facing fire—but perhaps, as a refining judgment through which people are renewed for entrance into eternal life (not unlike when gold is melted to take away any impurities before being fashioned as a permanent piece of beautiful jewelry).

Not all New Testament references to judgment day read so hopeful. For example, in 2 Peter the reader will find the following statements: "For if God did not spare the angels when they sinned, but cast them into hell and committed them to chains of deepest darkness to be kept until judgment, and if [God] did not spare the ancient world, even though [God] saved Noah.... Then the Lord knows how to rescue the godly from trial, and to keep the unrighteous under punishment until the day of judgment—especially those who indulge their flesh in depraved lust, and who despise authority."[22] The author of 2 Peter is not alone in declaring that unrighteous people will be duly punished by God. The author of Jude (1:12–13) and the prophet of the Book of Revelation also offer visions of the unrighteous being in torment forever (e.g., Revelation 14:11 and 20:10).

Fear of eternal punishment—as sometimes narrated in the New Testament—has captivated the minds of nervous Christians throughout the centuries. They fear they may be going to hell for getting their beliefs wrong, missing rituals, or as some say, "backsliding" into sin. Other Christians have deployed the same visions of eternal punishment with the agenda to evangelize (or condemn) those who do not believe as they do. Still other Christians have seen utterances of eschatological condemnation as prophetic exaggerations and believed that the redemption of all of creation is the hopeful omega point of history.

What can be said of the New Testament is this: within the same canon of texts, there are scriptures that seem to anticipate universal salvation and there are passages that seem to confirm the possibility of eternal condemnation (or annihilation). For individual theologians and Christian communities alike, decisions have to be made about which biblical texts to prioritize. There is no *one* message about eschatology in the New Testament—except, perhaps, for a general belief in some kind of life beyond death. But even that general belief is articulated in different ways. Some New Testament texts seem to suggest that humans continue on as spirits upon death of the physical body.[23] Other texts emphasize a future resurrection of the dead.[24] The language of *resurrection* suggests that if human spirits endure after death, they will be rejoined with (re-created) supernatural bodies. Christian conceptions of heaven, therefore, can mean anything from living in the near presence of God as a spirit to the resurrection of the dead in which supernatural bodily existence endures—even if not in the same way as bodily existence occurs now.

Those who expect the New Testament to function like the systematic theology of a singular author set themselves up for frustration with the texts or even an utter rejection of them as incoherent. In truth, one cannot simply read the Bible; it must be carefully studied. As scholars of religion and many Christian theologians have noted about the New Testament, the texts are embedded in historical, theological, and sociological contexts, not all of which are immediately clear to the contemporary reader. In addition, the New Testament texts are written in different genres, including (but not limited to) liturgical, pastoral, prophetic, symbolic, theological, apologetic, apocalyptic, and poetic expressions. These genres are then applied to various topics of concern—whether to God, Christ, sin, salvation, ethics, social order, church organization, or eschatology (to name only a few). To that end, no one should expect any sort of simple theological consistency in the New Testament—except that the texts will reveal a variety of reflections and instructions from early Christian leaders (disparate though they were), who were seeking to make sense of and apply their understandings of Christ and the gospel to human life. They did so in their particular historical and contextual experiences of it. Or, as one biblical scholar put it, the New Testament "rather resembles the creative processes through which the early faith communities wrestled to understand the will of God for their particular time."[25]

The complexities and varieties of religious teachings in the New Testament require the reader to return to the complicated work of interpretation. As noted in chapter 1, the reader of the New Testament must make certain interpretive choices. Those interpretations reveal, to some extent, the agendas and ethos of the interpreter. This includes whether one chooses to use eschatological texts as tools of condemnation or to see in these texts more hopeful possibilities. Admittedly, there are long histories of preaching hell and damnation from New Testament eschatological passages. But there are also other (more generous) interpretive options, some of which have given rise to the hope of universal salvation. For example, Origen of Alexandria, an influential third-century Christian theologian, supported an idea of universal redemption. The scholar Ilaria Ramelli suggests that Origen's universalism actually had antecedents in the second century and was shared by some of Origen's third-century contemporaries.[26] Which is to say, hopeful readings of Christian eschatology are not inventions of twenty-first-century liberals seeking to make Christianity "nice."[27]

Admittedly, any claim about what the New Testament texts mean (individually and collectively) is a creative work of interpretation. Scripture doesn't speak for itself. It is read and understood through the reason and experience that one brings to the texts (recall chapter 1). That said, *how* New Testament eschatological references were drawn upon to establish church doctrines is something that can be traced more definitively. So, too, it is possible to see how these emerging Christian doctrines about eschatology were eventually drawn upon to negate the possibility of sex in Christian heaven.

HEAVEN, HELL, EUNUCHS FOR CHRIST, AND OTHER SEXUAL ASCETIC PRACTICES

With the rise of institutional Christianity, authoritative teachings about eschatology eventually took shape with the weight of doctrine. By the end of the fourth century, Christianity was no longer just a loose confederation of competing house churches with diverse theological teachers. As historians note, for the first few centuries of Christianity there was a competition between various faith leaders and religious communities for the right to define true Christianity. As in any competition, there are winners and losers. Ultimately, the version of Christianity supported by the Roman Empire edged out the competition in terms of theological rhetoric, influence, and resources. This is not to say that a variety of heterodox Christian churches failed to endure—they did; but they were often persecuted as heretics. The emergent institutional Catholic Church began codifying what counted as *authentic* Christian doctrine and what beliefs were identified as *heresy*. The church's creeds reveal such a doctrinal program at work.

One matter that was important to the formative leaders of the organized church was eschatology. Consider, for example, the Nicene Creed of 325 CE, which articulates a belief that Christ "suffered, and the third day he rose again, ascended into heaven; [and] from thence he shall come to judge the quick and the dead." But after the First Council of Constantinople of 381 CE, the creed was revised with an addition to the ending, which now reads: "we look for the resurrection of the dead, and the life of the world to come. Amen."[28] As the revised Nicene Creed promised final resurrection from the dead, Christians were encouraged to hope for a better world than the one in which they lived. And yet, these Christians still needed to live in *this* world until death or judgment day. To that end, church leaders had to answer a difficult question; namely, what does daily living look like for a Christian if Christ might return any day? Is there time for conventional things like jobs, marriage, and a family? Or, should the Christian vision of Christ's return motivate a more contemplative life of prayer, repentance, and daily preparations to face eternal judgment?

Among the New Testament texts, church leaders found that some of the biblical authors advocated for a rather eschatological reorientation for daily living. For example, when Paul wrote to the Corinthians, his advice was to live not as the world is, but in light of the world to come, "for the present form of this world is passing away."[29] Contrasting with Paul, less imminent expectations of judgment day can also be found within the New Testament. For example, words of patience are found in the text of 2 Peter, when the author writes:

> But do not ignore this one fact, beloved, that with the Lord one day is like a thousand years, and a thousand years are like one day. The Lord is not slow about his promise, as something of slowness, but is patient with you, not wanting any to perish, but all to come to repentance. But the day of the Lord will come like a thief, and then the heavens will pass away with a loud noise, and the elements will be dissolved with fire, and the earth and everything that is done on it will be disclosed.[30]

Alternately, one might also consider the eschatological perspective of the Gospel of Matthew, which does seem to anticipate the return of Christ in some apocalyptic event; but which also cautions the reader that "about that day and hour no one knows, neither the angels of heaven, nor the Son, but only the Father."[31]

The idea that judgment day is coming, but potentially far off, was a significant theological matter for the institutional church to address. But it was hardly a theological scandal or an embarrassment. The fact that the church was organizing as a religious institution centuries after the time of Jesus obviously meant that the delay of Christ's return did not diminish the vitality of the Christian faith. The leaders of the institutional church of the third and fourth centuries seemed to have accepted that there was both an *already* and a *not yet* nature to the reign of God.[32] That is to say, the reign of God was already present with the coming of Christ and the Holy Spirit, but it would not be fully present until the day of judgment and beyond. To that end, even if the delay of Christ's return had to be explained, it appears Christian leaders were not too troubled by it. Church historian Jaroslav Pelikan agrees and adds, "One looks in vain for proof of bitter disappointment over the postponement of the Parousia [i.e., the second coming of Christ] or of a shattering of the early Christian communities by the delay in the Lord's return. What the texts [of the church] do suggest is a shift within the polarity of already/not yet and a great variety of solutions to the exegetical and theological difficulties caused by that shift."[33] Thus, with the rise of institutional Christianity, belief in the return of Christ and judgment day endured. However, the church did not insist that its members live with the kind of acute apocalyptic expectations that would interrupt the pursuit of employment, government, marriage, family, and so forth. In other words, it was acceptable to live with a hope for Christ's return but without a sense of when that would be. From the perspective of traditional Christianity, God alone knows the day and hour of judgment—and *no one else* (even if many Christians have tried their hand at eschatological predictions).

But what the church did teach is that each human being would face divine judgment immediately after death—and thus, even if Christ's return turned out to be far off, death was very much still immanent, putting all people on high alert. As the architects of Christian orthodoxy further considered the state of the human spirit after death (but before the final resurrection), a three-tiered spiritual afterlife ultimately emerged. Following Saint Augustine's suggestion that some sins are punished by eternal condemnation and others only receive temporary punishment after death (*City *of God*, 21.13), the church formalized a belief that three options await the spirits of the departed. The first is *heaven*, the domain of the righteous. The second is *purgatory*, the domain of those who are destined for paradise but need to purge the last vestiges of venial sin. The third is *hell*, the domain of the damned.[34] For the most part, the architects of Christian orthodoxy accepted that stratification as a reliable description of the spiritual afterlife. That is not to say that all agreed. Some influential theologians (like Origen) held out hope for universal salvation.[35] However, it was the doctrines of both heaven and hell that eventually became normative in Christianity. These doctrines had profound implications for Christian ethics—including Christian sexual ethics. Namely, whatever counted as a righteous act leading toward heaven would often count as a moral good, too. Likewise, whatever could lead a person to hell, in terms of sinful activity, was also denounced as immorality in Christian ethics. The relationship here is a rather tight one.

In fact, the relationship was so tight that it led to things like self-made eunuchs for Christ. Within the early centuries of Christianity, castration for Jesus was a real thing. In particular, some Christian men maimed their genitalia as a grand gesture of devotion. For them, to become a eunuch for Christ was to eradicate sexual desire (and all conventional possibilities of marriage and procreation). They did so in order to devote their entire life, love, and service to Jesus. These men were spiritually yoked to Christ in this life, and they looked forward to being in full communion with him in the resurrection of the dead. They wanted nothing to come between them and their love for Jesus—and so they castrated themselves to remove any temptations "below the waist" that might dislocate their passion and service for Christ.

Even so, the institutional church frowned upon such self-castration. Mathew Keufler notes that

> The first decree of the Council of Nicaea condemned self-castration in Christian clerics, so it was obviously a more general practice than most scholars have acknowledged. Ambrose of Milan decried it still in the late fourth century, arguing that Christian men should restrain their sexual impulses with the force of their wills rather than resorting to self-castration (*De viduis* 13.75–77). John Chrysostom went further, stating that eunuchs gained no merit from their virginity because they could not do otherwise (*De virginitate* 8.5). And John Cassian praised the Egyptian monk Serenus for waiting for God to send an angel to castrate him in a dream rather than doing it himself.[36]

While church leaders condemned self-castration, the men who practiced it cited Christian scripture in their defense.

In particular, eunuchs for Christ could look to Matthew 19:12, which reads, "For there are eunuchs who have been so from birth, and there are eunuchs who have been made eunuchs by others, and there are eunuchs who have made themselves eunuchs for the sake of the kingdom of heaven. Let anyone accept this who can."[37] A closer examination of those who became eunuchs for Christ—as well as other Christians who were highly concerned about matters of sexuality—shows that both ethical and eschatological concerns were at play.

With respect to *ethics*, castration for Jesus likely reflected the negative moral judgments that many Christians then held about sexual desire and genital relationships, especially from the second century forward.[38] Many of these Christians believed that sexual desire was motivated by sin itself, and that the pursuit of sexual activity for pleasure alone was also a sin (even when engaged in with a sanctioned spouse).[39] Furthermore, many such Christians believed that the only benefit of sexual activity between spouses was reproduction.[40] Virginity and celibacy were often held preferentially as the models of moral perfection regarding matters of sexual ethics. For Christians living in this period, the keepers of orthodoxy tolerated sexual activity only in heterosexual marriage—and even then, sex had to be specifically for reproduction or otherwise had to be given up.[41]

The developing sexual asceticism in early Christianity may seem grossly sex negative or even phobic to some contemporary readers. Some of it surely was. But behind the appearance of pure erotophobia, there were other moral agendas at work. In particular, there was a social and moral effort among Christians to prove the validity of the new Christian movement in relation to competing philosophical and religious traditions. Uta Ranke-Heinemann explains, "Christians did not yet view themselves as the teachers of the world, which would be living in darkness without them. They were not thought of as having to furnish the pagans and atheists with models of good behavior. It was the other way around: the pagans labeled the Christians as 'atheists,' and the Christians wanted to show that they could match the high ideals of the pagans."[42] Thus, for the Christians who came after the time of Jesus and Paul, the teachings of Christ and the apostles were read and applied competitively as part of a strategy to show that this new religion (Christianity) promoted real good.

Ranke-Heinemann explains this in more detail. In particular, during the time and places in which certain forms of Christianity matured, "public opinion at that time was swayed by the idea—stressed by first- and second-century Stoics—that marriage had to serve exclusively for procreation, as well as by the pessimistic, Gnostic, body-hating idealization of virginity."[43] Consider those statements again. As Christianity was taking institutional shape, it was interacting with (if not influenced by) moral perspectives that either promoted marital procreation as the highest good of sexual activity; or, by the view that virginity and celibacy are the best states from which spiritual illumination can be achieved.

Does any of this sound familiar? It should. The marital procreative norm and the praise of virginity and celibacy have endured in many sectors of Christianity. Admittedly, they are now articulated in new ways, with emphases on family and spiritual purity. But without question, the rise of these norms can be traced back to attitudes among early church leaders—many of whom adopted ascetic attitudes about sex. It is important to note that what these sexual ascetics taught (and what proliferated in Christianity) are not necessarily the teachings of Jesus or the apostles (as those are reported in New Testament texts). In other words, sexual asceticism is only one interpretation for Christian sexual ethics—so it need not be sustained.

Arguably, such Stoic and Gnostic narratives influenced the emerging moral theology of Christian sexual ethics (at that time). In particular, the early Christian adaptation of *both* views seems, in part, to have been an attempt to show that Christians could be the best of the best—as that was then defined in relation to the norms of the Stoics (with marriage and procreation) and of particular Gnostics (with virginity). Of course, this was not the only reason that Christians moved in this direction. Early Christians were not merely cultural chameleons. Certain readings of particular New Testament texts might have convinced some ancient Christians to adopt a form of sexual asceticism apart from Stoic or Gnostic influences. Nevertheless, Ranke-Heinemann's insight about the philosophical and cultural context in which Christianity emerged should not be ignored. In response to the Stoics and the Gnostics, early Christianity could affirm procreation as a good of God's creation while simultaneously affirming virginity as the best state of being from which one could devote oneself to Christ and service to the church. And so even if the historical Jesus or Paul might not recognize how their teachings were applied within particular worldviews that assumed sexual asceticism as a moral good, Christianity as an organized religion grew in this direction.

But such early Christians were not only concerned with moral excellence, they were also concerned with living on earth in preparation for the world to come. In other words, they also had an *eschatological* orientation. Indeed,

Christian ethics—as it was defined then, in part, by sexual asceticism—was all part of living on earth in preparation for heaven. Thus, when certain men castrated themselves for the sake of Christian perfectionism, when certain people embraced celibacy over sexual-genital fulfillment, or when Christians promoted reproduction as the only worthy goal of sexual relations, they all did so believing that this would not only help them achieve moral excellence on earth but also allow them to actively cooperate with God's grace in order to live with Christ forever. There is (seemingly) no part of the imagination of these Christians that separated personal and social ethics from their eschatological concerns about eternal salvation. Thus, those who became "eunuchs for the kingdom of heaven" did so, in part, with eschatological hopes for salvation. Likewise, those who avoided sex for the sake of virginity, were likely also seeking to avoid sin—and thus, without exaggeration, to avoid hell. And those who dared to marry and reproduce (that is, those who dared to have sex) always had to be on guard lest they slip and fall into the sins of sex, which according to the architects of Christian orthodoxy might also mean slipping into the path of the wrath of God.

Sex, of course, was just one of many ethical and theological concerns among the Christians of antiquity. However, because sexual desire stirs so often, and because humans so often seek out sexual pleasures through non-reproductive (or nonmarital) sex, *sin* and *sex* became closely associated in the rise of the new Christian religion. And if closely associated, then there was something about sex (whether in terms of desires or activities) that bore heavily on the status of one's righteousness—and thus, one's salvation. To that end, sex became a pressing matter in Christian moral theology. In other words, how sex was navigated could bear directly on one's eternal destiny.

SIN, SEX, AND DEATH

Of the many issues that pertain to eschatology, the subjects of sin and death are important ones. Without death there would be no conversation about an afterlife. Without the concept of sin, there would be no anxiety about humankind's relationship with God. What is more, it has been the view of many churches (including the Catholic Church and many Protestant denominations) that death is the result of human sinfulness. The *Catechism of the Catholic Church* explains it this way: "Death entered the world on account of man's sin. Even though man's nature is mortal, God had destined him not to die. Death was therefore contrary to the plans of God the Creator and entered the world as a consequence of sin. 'Bodily death, from which man would have been immune had he not sinned' is thus 'the last enemy' of man left to be conquered."[44]

Traditional Protestant views differ little with the Catholic conclusion that death is the result of sin. For example, in John Calvin's *Institutes of the Christian Religion* the reformer writes:

> For in every little transgression of the divinely commanded law, God's authority is set aside. Do they deem it a small matter to violate his majesty in anything? Then, if God has revealed his will in the law, whatever is contrary to the law displeases him. Do they fancy God's wrath so feeble that the death penalty will not immediately follow? ... [God] says: "The soul that sins shall surely die" (Ezekiel 19:4, 20). Likewise ... "The wages of sin is death" (Romans 6:23). ... Let the children of God hold that all sin is mortal.[45]

Those Christians who think along these lines see all human beings as born into a world of sin and inheriting a *fallen* nature. As a result, they believe that all people (now) die because of sin. For those Christians who radicalize this view, it is believed that certain people suffer given tragedies and illnesses because their particular sins evoke the wrath and selective punishments of God.[46]

Even so, other Christians suggest that the relationship between sin and death isn't so causal. Indeed, one of the problems of stating that sin caused death is the reality that death was present on this planet long before the rise of human beings.[47] From single- and multiple-cell organisms to plant life, reptiles, and mammals, death has been a part of life in its natural unfolding. For example, the fruition and death of a plant leads to the spreading of its seeds. The volcanic eruptions that destroy plant and animal life establish formations upon which new life can emerge. Animals too must mature, reproduce, and die to continue the species without overpopulating the biosphere.

As the theologian Hans Schwarz has put it, "It would be shortsighted to conclude that biological death can be inferred from sin and the fall, as if there had been a time when death did not prevail."[48] But that is not what many Christians have taught. Many hold that sin caused biological death. However, that theological view (if read literally) contradicts the way that life emerged on this planet. Schwartz correctly notes that the theological idea of ancient *deathlessness* would bring "us into deep conflict with science, since paleontology shows that biological death already prevailed for millions of years before humanity emerged."[49]

Admittedly, some Christians will be just fine setting their theological beliefs about sin and death in opposition to scientific insights. But this is not the only Christian view. Consider another possibility; namely, that instead of reading church teachings or texts of scripture about sin and death biologically, Christians can read these texts *theologically* so as not to impose such a simple cause-and-effect relationship. The issue is a hermeneutical one. For example, it is true that one can find statements in the New Testament like Romans 5:12, which reads, "Sin came into the world through one man, and death came through sin, and so death spread to all because all have sinned." Likewise, Romans 6:23 reads, "for the wages of sin is death." But the interpretive question remains: what do those texts really mean? Are they to be taken literally as a statement on the origins of biological death, or should they be read in another way? Some Christians do take a literal approach to such things. But Schwarz has argued something else about these passages:

> Paul does not intend to speak biologically of a person who lived long ago and whose sinful activity had cosmic consequences.... The natural biological aspect of death is at most somewhere in the back of his mind, since he wanted to talk in an existential and theological way about the emergence of the age of death.
>
> [However] unlike animals, we no longer experience death as a merely biological death. Knowing about our sinfulness, our alienation from God, and our shortcomings, we encounter death as the final irreversible termination in which these distortions of life can no longer be patched up or concealed. Fear of death becomes fear of judgment, the fear of this final inescapable confrontation with the God who is not only our creator but also our judge.[50]

Schwarz's insight provides a theological option for interpreting these texts in ways that do not deny the place of death in the long chain of natural life. Namely, Christians might suggest that biological death is *not* something that sin caused, but something that sin affects. From such a view, one might affirm that human sinfulness facilitates a kind of anxious attachment to life, which in turn makes the experience of death bitter and difficult to accept.

This more qualitative understanding of the relationship between sin and death is a persuasive one when drawing upon critical and contextual readings of scripture. Admittedly, we cannot be certain what these (or any) authors of scripture absolutely intended. But to treat the scriptures overly literally (for religious reasons or to dismiss them) refuses to acknowledge that many layers of meaning can be discerned in scripture. If the scriptures were not this complex, biblical scholarship would not be so prolific. Furthermore, since contemporary concepts of science and history (as disciplines) were not existing frameworks from which authors of ancient scripture were writing, it would be odd to insist that they meant something scientific or historic about the relationship between sin and death. The authors of scripture were advocating theological arguments—many of which rely on interpreting other scriptures and sacred traditions, which include many different genres of texts and theology (e.g., myth, law, liturgy, devotion, etc.). Thus, to adopt Schwarz's insight about the relationship between sin and death allows the Christian theologian and scholar of religion to investigate any deeper theological meanings in scripture about these things.

That said, what can be said more surely is that institutional Christianity eventually infused suspicion about the relationship between *sin, death,* and *sex*. It did so to such a degree that it became normative to think of sin and death as transmitted through sex. In particular, traditional Christianity has long taught that it was the first human community who introduced sin into the world. When that happened, both they and human nature (itself) fell from a state of grace—not erasing the image of God within the human creature, but injuring the human condition permanently (apart from the intervention of God's grace). Therefore, traditional Christianity has perpetuated the idea that it is through sex and reproduction that new human beings inherit a sinful nature due to the fallen state of humanity. For traditional Christians this view does not render reproduction evil, but it does mean that every human being is in need of salvation from sin and condemnation. In categorical terms, many Christians call this the legacy of original sin, which (they say) is inherited by each and every person.

What is more, given that traditional Christianity apprehends all people as fallen, the very appetites and desires of sinful flesh have long been treated as prone to disorder—including the desires for sex. For example, by the thirteenth century Thomas Aquinas was teaching that "the desire for sexual pleasure was of a most difficult sort to order, and had 'greater need of chastisement and restraint' than any of the other desires for the pleasures of touch [such as for food, or drink]."[51] At issue for Aquinas was not that sexual desire or activity were innately evil, but that sin had so disordered human nature that humanity became prone to "seek sexual pleasure for its own sake."[52]

Indeed, traditional Christianity has long categorized sexual desire for anything other than marital reproduction as the sin of *lust*. Activities that could not achieve reproduction were condemned (and categorized) as sins of *sodomy*.[53] Those sex acts that could achieve reproduction but did so in the wrong relational contexts were considered sins against reason.[54] Punishments for acts of sodomy (e.g., masturbation, mutual masturbation, contraceptive use, oral sex, frottage, anal sex, and bestiality) were considered proper, and sometimes included the threat of the death penalty. Given that acts of sodomy (so defined) were all designated as mortal sins, punishment on earth was just the beginning. These sexual sins had the power to hold humanity captive to sin and eternal death in the fires of hell. It is not an exaggeration to say that such a vision of eternal punishment for sexual sin was often threatened to keep the faithful in line. To that end, it is no wonder that those figures in Christianity who are often regarded as the most holy tend also to be those people who are celibates and virgins—not only in this life, but in the life to come.

CHRISTIANITY'S SEXLESS HEAVEN

Among the influential Christians who argued that there is no sex in heaven, Augustine is significant. In order to understand his conclusions on eschatological sex, one must understand his sexual ethic. In particular, Augustine held that there was only one worthy fruit of sexual activity: biological reproduction, as produced by a married man and woman.[55] Augustine believed that all sexual desire had become corrupt by the fall of humankind into sin. In fact, he went so far as to say that the desire for sexual pleasure—even with one's spouse—was lust itself. Thus even spouses were sinning in marriages if they longed for one another for the sake of enjoying mutual pleasure.[56] But even if the motivations for sex were sinful, the outcome could prove holy through procreation (even if that act of reproduction created a sinful human being in need of salvation).

We have to be careful to see that Augustine's comments here deploy a variety of theological claims at the same time. On the one hand, Augustine valued the vocation of parenthood. On the other hand, he was suspicious of the close relationship between sin, desire, and sex. Such a view of sin and sex, in part, inspired Augustine to affirm virginity and celibacy as "first place" in the kingdom of God.[57] At the same time, Augustine affirmed the original goodness of humanity (and of the human body) in terms of what God had intended for creation.[58] In fact, the theologian even entertained the possibility that before the introduction of sin, sex could have existed without all of its lustful trappings, for the purpose of procreation.[59] Thus, the good of reproduction is the one good thing of sexuality that has endured after the fall. Such complex views about sex would go on to inform the details of Augustine's eschatology.

With respect to eschatology, Augustine believed in the resurrection of the body. At the resurrection, the theologian believed, humans will return to a state of grace in perfected bodies.[60] If Augustine is correct, it raises the question of whether eschatological bodies will have sexual capacities. The question is an important one. After all, it is the position of many Christian theologians that all human inclinations are—in the here and now—tainted by sin: whether in terms of our desires for food, drink, or sex, or even in our intellectual desires to pursue what we do in life. But the promise of the resurrection is that human beings will be *wholly* sanctified, such that our desires and inclinations will only be for the good. Sexual desire and intimate relations have long been left out of that eschatological picture. That should make any Christian theologian pause and seriously ask: *Why?*

The short answer, for Augustine, is that genital sexual activity will cease in the resurrection of the dead because it is no longer needed. The theologian was one of many early Christian teachers, like Gregory of Nyssa, Clement of Alexandria, and Jerome, who could not imagine the continuity of genital sexual acts in the resurrection.[61] But they certainly did not agree with one another in detail about the nature of resurrected bodies in the eschatological life. For example, some of these theologians did not think that physical sex traits would endure in the resurrection of the dead (see chapter 4). Augustine disagreed. He believed that human beings will be resurrected as anatomically male or female according to God's original design and intent for humanity. That said, he made such comments without any awareness of sexual orientation or gender identity as many people understand these today.[62] The issue for Augustine was the purpose of sex. The theologian believed that genital sexual acts were only intended for reproduction. Thus, for Augustine, procreation is an earthly good, not a heavenly one. As a result, Augustine concluded that sex would be unnecessary in the resurrection of the dead— and that human beings will be healed of our lustful desires for one another.[63] In heaven, Augustine imagined that we will look upon one another and glorify God for the beauty of creation and the redemption of our bodies.[64]

We should pause now and consider Augustine's sexual ethic and eschatological vision in relation to one another. With respect to sexual ethics, Augustine approved of marital sex for the sake of procreation; but above this, the theologian praised virginity and celibacy. Notice, then, what is projected onto Augustine's eschatological horizon: an eternal embodied afterlife, in which sexual desire and activity are eradicated. Notice, also, that Augustine's pathway to heaven involves a life of abdicating sin—including sexual sin. This is not to caricature Augustine as someone who thought that the route to heaven required the absolute avoidance of sexual sin. Grace is fundamental to Augustine's theology. Grace heals the failures of humanity. At the same time, Augustine understood that human beings are called to cooperate with the grace of God and to avoid sin. As the theologian imagined it, that everyone would receive a judgment from God is a certainty. Whether God will cast anyone into hell is a decision that belongs to God alone. But within Augustine's eschatological formula it is also accepted that God would be just for condemning someone to hell for unrepentant sin.[65] And this could include sexual sin.

Thus, from a certain Augustinian point of view, the good of eternal celibacy is projected onto the eschatological life—not only as a statement of what will be, but also in relation to what is good of Christian ethics today. In other words, the celibacy of heaven functions to reaffirm the primary goods of virginity and celibacy on earth, as well as to constrain sexual activity to marital procreation as a temporary good for human living in the here and now. When seen in this way, a hermetically sealed loop of ethics and eschatology begins to appear. What is good on earth (morally and theologically) paves the way for a life in heaven. And, from an eschatological perspective, what life looks like in heaven functions to reify the shape and demands of morality on earth.

This is true not only for Augustine but also for a number contemporary Christian churches. For example, the Catholic Church agrees with Augustine that in the resurrection of the dead, human souls will be rejoined with bodies that are in a perfect state of grace. The *Catechism of the Catholic Church* explains, "In death, the separation of the soul from the body, the human body decays and the soul goes to meet God, while awaiting its reunion with its glorified body. God, in his almighty power, will definitely grant incorruptible life to our bodies by reuniting them with our souls, through the power of Jesus' Resurrection."[66] While the Catholic Church teaches that all people will experience the resurrection of the dead, only those found worthy—by God's grace—will live forever in the near presence of God. This requires the avoidance of sin and its reconciliation on earth. As with Augustine, this does not mean that those who have fallen into sin are guaranteed a place in hell. It does not even mean that God's grace will be limited to Roman Catholics. God's grace, we are told, is prodigal. But what the church does teach is that God is just in all judgments, including any judgment that *might* result in condemnation. While such a concern about sin is not limited to matters of human sexuality, it most certainly includes the practice of chastity (i.e., sexual virtue), whether through celibacy or marital procreative sex.

What is more, the Catholic Church teaches that the eschatological life will be defined by eternal celibacy. Like Augustine, the contemporary Catholic Church affirms that human beings will be resurrected in male and female bodies. But according to current church teaching, those bodies will not desire or engage in sexual activity. Pope John Paul II explored these ideas in his treatise *Theology of the Body*. The pontiff explained the possibilities of eschatological sex in these terms: "The union characteristic of man right from the beginning—belongs exclusively to this age. Marriage and procreation do not constitute, on the other hand, the eschatological future of man. In the resurrection they lose, so to speak, their reason for being."[67] Thus, for the Catholic Church, the eschatological vision of eternal celibacy can function to support the value the church places on virginity and celibacy today. The same eschatological vision of eternal celibacy also assists in tempering any exaltation of sex beyond its marital and procreative uses. In this sense, Catholic eschatology most certainly informs Catholic ethics. That is not to say, however, that the Catholic Church possesses a negative view of marriage or marital intimacy. Within Catholic teaching, theological perspectives are very often "both/and" in scope. In particular, while the Catholic Church affirms the celibacy of heaven and honors earthly celibacy (and chastity more broadly), it also very much celebrates the vocation of parenthood through sacramental marriage on earth. That sacrament is not seen as lacking in holiness when compared to earthly celibacy. Rather, marriage and celibacy are both instantiations of chastity, and both are honored and defended vigorously. Even so, within the Catholic theological imagination (of the Vatican), it is the path of celibacy that continues on in the resurrection of the dead.

Protestants, too, have a rather strong connection between ethics and eschatology. Many Protestants claim that all sin separates humanity from God, both in this life and in the next. For such Protestants, the theological category of *sin* very often represents the ethical category of *immorality*. Therefore, any person guilty of sin—apart from Christ's grace—is not only an example of immorality (on earth) but is also facing the full possibility of condemnation in hell. This includes matters of sexuality. Thus, when traditional Protestants affirm heterosexual marital sex as the only valid expression of human sexuality, they are not only commenting on moral values for the here and now, they are also commenting on what does (and does not) resonate with the grace of God and a sanctified life. Thus, for a variety of

Protestants, it is only the repentant sexual sinner who finds the grace of God and eternal rest among the righteous. In other words, good works may not get you into Protestant heaven, but bad works—apart from God's grace—will certainly send you to hell.

Among traditional Protestants, relatively little theological attention has been paid to the possibility of eschatological sex. As a religious tradition primarily focused on scripture, many Protestants have turned to biblical passages like Mark 12:18–27 to settle such questions. In that passage Jesus teaches that marriage will not endure in the resurrection. As the Protestant theologian David Jensen notes, "Throughout much of its history, the Christian church has assumed that Jesus' words about the disappearance of marriage in heaven have also entailed the end of sex. Resurrected persons become like the angels, sexless, unable to reproduce sexually, no longer tainted by the stirrings of the loins."[68]

What is more, for many Protestants, speculating about the fine details of the eschatological life is really just superfluous thinking. For example, the reformer John Calvin believed that a number of speculations about heaven should be disposed of quickly.[69] In fact, the reformer believed that those who are concerned with such matters can hardly be taken seriously—or may be people of malformed minds. Calvin talks about such eschatological questions with this warning; "For few out of a huge multitude care how they are to go to heaven, but all long to know beforehand what takes place there. Almost all are lazy and loathe to do battle, while already picturing to themselves imaginary victories."[70]

Calvin clearly sought to move people's thoughts away from the very eschatological questions this book explores about sex in heaven. Other Protestants have offered slightly more hospitable approaches to the question of eschatological sex. For example, Stanley Grenz, a twentieth-century evangelical theologian, affirmed that bodily sexual relations will come to an end in the resurrection. However, he also believed that aspects of the emotional connections of human sexuality might endure. He writes, "Jesus does not explicitly declare that sexuality will be absent, only that marriage will no longer be practiced. Human sexuality will no longer be expressed in genital sexual acts, and the sexually based drive toward bonding will no longer be expressed through male-female coupling. This is not to suggest, however, that the deeper dimensions of sexuality will be eradicated."[71] Thus, for Grenz, intimate bonding may endure in heaven, even if sexual acts do not—although the questions of how that happens and to what extent are left unanswered.

Presumably, traditional Protestants likely fall somewhere between Calvin and Grenz in their response to questions about eschatological sex. However, other Protestant theologians like David Jensen do not close the door as firmly (which will be explored in the next chapter). Arguably, the Protestant disposition to be "ever-reforming," according to a continual review of the scriptures, suggests that the Augustinian or Catholic conclusion may not be the final one.

CONCLUSION

As a whole, a variety of Christian communities have treated matters of sexual morality as hurdles or pitfalls to eternal salvation. As it turns out, in both Catholic and traditional Protestant theologies, sexual morality has been controlled by heterosexual, marital, procreative, monogamous, and/or celibate norms. Transgressions of these norms have not only been *moral* concerns among such Christians, but *eschatological* concerns as well. In particular, for many Christians, sin stands in the way of communion with God—in this life and in the next. To that end, Christians have continuously produced and revised sin-lists, which function to keep the faithful on the narrow path of righteousness, and which include a number of concerns related to sexual ethics. Christianity did not altogether eradicate sex from this life, but in its most traditional expressions, sex has been eradicated from the life to come.

However, even if the vision of a sexless heaven became the traditional view in Christianity (for both Catholics and Protestants), it is another thing to say that such an eschatological conclusion is the only one that can be articulated within a Christian framework. Clearly the Catholic Church has weighed in on the question of eschatological sex with the weight of the hierarchy's authority—and the decision has been to sustain the Augustinian view; namely, that sexual relations do not continue in the resurrection of the dead. Readers can respectfully understand why this view (and the authority of the church hierarchy) is meaningful and convincing to a number of Christians within this tradition. However, for a wide variety of other Christians, the conclusions of Augustine and the Vatican are not immutable. At issue is not only whether there are valid theological reasons for imagining eschatological sex as part of Christian heaven, but also the vital question as to what Christians value about sex on earth. If we take the Augustinian approach that sex is for the good of procreation, then we can more easily affirm why sex does not endure in the eschatological life. But when it can be shown that (on earth) there are other formulas for sexual ethics that include goods outside of marriage or procreation, we have reasons to explore how these goods might continue in (or be emblematic of) the eschatological life. In the next chapter, attention will be given to those theorists who have imagined not only more inclusive sexual ethics for the here and now, but also those who have begun to conceive of ways to imagine the continuation of sex in Christian heaven.

CHAPTER FOUR

NEW VISIONS FOR SEX IN HEAVEN

> Change can be frightening, and the temptation is often to resist it.
> —*Klaus Schwab*

While the idea of eschatological sex is not a new one, embracing it as a hope of heaven *would* be new for many Christians today. To that end, suggesting the possibility of sex in heaven may strike many Christians as gross speculation, heresy, or willful perversion. As Patricia Beattie Jung writes in her book, *Sex on Earth as It Is in Heaven*, "By and large the earliest Christian traditions had little, if any room for sex in their speculations about heaven. Sketching a vision to the contrary will take both imaginative boldness and a willingness to refute the best objections to such an account."[1] That kind of imaginative boldness has begun to be produced in the academic literature of Christian theology and ethics.

Scholars who have dared to suggest the possibility of sex in heaven have published their arguments in an assortment of collections and books. Many of these have emerged in the early part of the twenty-first century. In this chapter, the insights of David Jensen, Margaret Kamitsuka, and Patricia Beattie Jung will each be explored. These scholars have considered the possibility of sexual relations enduring in heaven. All of them write to an audience thinking about such possibilities within a broad Christian framework. What they provide are ways of thinking about eschatological sex from which other proposals might be imagined. Their arguments also reveal a variety of theological debates related to Christian eschatology more generally, and issues of gender and sexuality more specifically.

OPENING THE DOOR

In the fourth chapter of the Book of Revelation, the prophet John wrote these words, "After this I looked, and there in heaven a door stood open! And the first voice which I had heard speaking to me like a trumpet, said, 'Come up here, and I will show you what must take place after this.'"[2] As interpreters of the New Testament have looked through that open door, they have strained to see details of what life might be like in the heavenly realm to come. These interpreters have seen many things. Some Christians see the life to come as purely and eternally devoted to the worship of God, exclusive of relationships with other heavenly saints. Some scholars have called this a *theocentric* view of heaven.[3] Other Christians look through the door and see a realm in which God is certainly loved and worshipped, but also a place of reunion with family and friends (at least, those who are among the redeemed). Some scholars have described this as a *domestic* view of heaven; or inclusive of the communion of saints.[4] Another set of hopeful Christians believe that *all* of humanity will eventually find ourselves in the near presence of God—healed and transformed by the irresistible love of God. Other Christians can only see a sparsely populated heaven, with a remnant of "true believers," or, a finite number of people predestined by God for eternal bliss. One Protestant theologian, David Jensen, has looked through the door to heaven and considered the possibility of human sexuality enduring in the life to come.

Eschatology and Sex: Ancient Views

In his book, *God, Desire, and a Theology of Human Sexuality*, David Jensen considers the intersection of "eschatology and sex."[5] Neither wanting to deny the possibility of sex in heaven nor say too much about it, Jensen's reflection on eschatological sex is ordered so as to "leave the question open."[6] But if the question of eschatological sex is left open, any conversation about what that might be like requires us to think about important matters of sexuality and gender—which Christians have theorized in different ways, both in ancient and contemporary times.

With respect to ancient concerns about sexuality and gender, Jensen notes that there were competing perspectives among Christians. For example, Gregory of Nyssa argued that physical sex was the result of the fall of humankind into sin. According to Gregory, before the fall, God had created human beings "androgynously in a nonsexed angelic mode."[7] This view stands quite contrary to the paintings we sometimes see of an anatomically male Adam and an anatomically female Eve. Thus, for Gregory of Nyssa, because physical sex was a result of the fall, humanity is destined to return to the perfection of androgyny in the life to come. But to be clear, Gregory of Nyssa's vision of restored androgyny is not scripted with multivalent gender-queer possibilities. Rather, Gregory of Nyssa saw eschatological androgyny as a condition in which genitals, sexual attractions, desires, and pleasures would be eradicated in exchange for glorifying God.[8] As David Jensen notes, Gregory of Nyssa's view is one that points toward "a new existence beyond gender, beyond sex."[9] While some theorists today might think of being "beyond" gender or sex as a libertine matter of morphological freedom, Gregory saw it as a matter of moving past our sinful state, which for him, was indicated by the presence of genitals and sexual desire.

In contrast with Gregory of Nyssa, Jensen describes Augustine's fifth-century view that male and female bodies were not only made so in creation, but remain so in the eschatological life, albeit in a state of eternal celibacy. At issue for Augustine (as discussed in chapter 3) was his conviction that the one worthy fruit of sexual activity is procreation, within a faithful, sacramental marriage between a man and a woman. For Augustine, the fall of humankind into sin had not caused us to become gendered (physically), but rather, it had resulted in our sexual inclinations becoming wayward and ordered toward sinful activities. Thus, for Augustine, the restoration of humanity in heaven will not be a matter of removing the differentiation of physical sex. Instead, Augustine saw the sexual urge as that which will be purged in the resurrection. Jensen describes Augustine's view in this way: "Though male and female abide in the eschaton, men and women do not have sex, but participate in blessed communion eternally, as persons devoid of lustful desire."[10]

In response to this celibate view of the eschatological life, Jensen believes that Augustine claims too much. Jensen writes, "Why would sex be left behind? It is tempting as Jo Ind reminds us, 'to make an idol out of sex, especially as sex can, at its best, bring us the nearest many of us get to heaven in this lifetime.' But banishing sex from heaven is as problematic as claiming it to be heaven, for it removes the ambiguities of sexual life from their fulfillment."[11]

To that end, Jensen thinks it is more reasonable to say that "Christian hope envisions the transformation of all life, all bodies, but we don't know exactly what this will mean for our gendered and sexual bodies."[12]

Fixed Identities?

But even as Jensen finds that Gregory and Augustine's claims from antiquity are too narrow, he notes that contemporary liberal and conservative Christians often make a similar mistake. In particular, Jensen observes that many traditional *and* progressive arguments about gender and sexual diversities are often reduced to questions about "fixed" human nature. On the one hand, conservative Christians draw on the narratives of Genesis 1 and 2 in order to argue that God's intention for gender and sexual activity has always been ordered toward complementarity, emphasizing the reproductive pairing that only male and female bodies can achieve biologically (apart from technological interventions).[13] Departure from this norm, conservative Christians say, is a transgression, not only of biological nature, but of God's creative intent as well. In this view, there is only one natural expression of gender and sexual activity, defined by heterosexuality, and then, in marital union between *cisgender* men and women.[14] When such Christians believe that it is only heterosexuality that is written in the fabric of reality by the hand of God, the same Christians then draw on the moral language of unnatural sex, disordered inclinations, and perversions of nature when responding to any other gender or sexual diversity. In the face of gender and sexual diversities, Jensen notes that conservatives are left with two options: "to endorse a strictly defined toleration of LGBT persons or their rehabilitation as heterosexual."[15] What that looks like in practice is often the rhetoric of "loving the sinner but hating the sin," or efforts at conversion therapy to destroy homosexual inclinations and/or gender identities that are deemed transgressive (or sinful).

In response to the conservative view that humanity is naturally heterosexual and cisgender, Jensen observes that many liberal Christians have often resorted to a competing claim of fixed identities. For example, from a more progressive view, the meaning of the creations stories in Genesis 1 and 2 is not that men are exclusively made for women and women for men, but instead that complementarity is found in authentic human relationships rather than biological function.[16] For such liberal Christians, gender and sexual diversities are real and innate, and they exist as fixed realities upon a spectrum of sexualities and gender identities—something that should be celebrated as God's creative handiwork. For example, the gay man is gay because God has made him that way. The lesbian is a lesbian because God has put in her a unique capacity for love and eroticism with women. Bisexual people reveal the capacity for love and communion through sex more diversely. What is more, transgender people demonstrate that physical sex and gender identity are far more diverse and divinely artful than simple male-female bifurcation.

In response to both views, Jensen writes, "Despite their wide differences in terms of understanding human sexuality, many conservative and liberal approaches share a common notion of relatively fixed sexual identities. What conservatives construe as problematic sexuality, liberals cite as cause for celebration. But the identities are firmly in place.... Whatever the case, however, [they say] we should not betray our nature. On this, both conservatives and liberals agree."[17] But for Jensen, such conservative and liberal claims to fixed identities are as problematic as the rather absolute claims of Gregory of Nyssa and Augustine from antiquity. Jensen isn't saying that sexual orientation and gender identity lack grounding in biological, genetic, and/or neurological processes, nor is he necessarily championing the postmodern embrace of social construction found in much of queer theory (although he thinks that queer theory offers substantive insights). More importantly, Jensen believes that *prioritizing* fixed sexual and gender identities is contrary to the Christian understanding of being people in the process of supernatural transformation—the end results of which are eschatological and extraordinary. He writes, "Who we are, understood eschatologically, is not a fixed thing. The human person is always on the way to fulfillment, as God draws us toward God's very self in grace. The fundamental truth of Christian life is not a stable series of markers of personhood, but the instability of all categories in light of grace."[18]

For Jensen, the current markers of humanity are not nearly as important as our eschatological identity, which one day will usher in a new way of being human—the shape and nature of which, no one yet knows. Even so, Jensen says, Christians can have a small sense of what that means through one's baptismal identity. Citing the apostle Paul's letter to the Galatians, Jensen reminds the Christian community that one's identity is ultimately not gay or straight, nor trans or cisgender; but instead, that "as many of you as were baptized into Christ have clothed yourselves with Christ. There is [therefore] no longer Jew or Greek, there is no longer slave or free, there is no longer male or female; for all of you are one in Christ Jesus."[19]

The Episcopalian queer theologian Patrick Cheng has intuited something similar. In his book *Radical Love,* Cheng acknowledges that Christian baptismal identity is actually a queer identity. It transgresses human categories insofar as it sublimates all other categories that have been treated as fixed (e.g., male and female; gay and straight, etc.).[20] Furthermore, baptismal identity points the Christian toward an eschatological horizon of polymorphic modes of being in relation to God and others, through bonds of prodigal eternal love.[21] David Jensen describes the connection of baptismal identity and eschatological life in another way. He writes, "Christian eschatology does not claim that male and female, straight and gay, do not matter at all; only that they do not matter as the ultimate truth of life. In the eschaton, difference remains, but not as a reality that divides and alienates us from each other.... Baptism turns division toward the healing of relations, suggesting a desire for communion that intensifies in heaven, a desire that encompasses sex and intimates marriage."[22]

Sex in Heaven: The Possibilities

Jensen does not preclude the possibility of sex, gender, and intimate relationships (or something like these) manifesting between heavenly resurrected bodies. His reasons for holding this position are many. First, and with respect to scripture, Jensen notes that while Christ makes the claim that marriage will not endure in heaven (at all, or as it has existed on earth), Jesus does not outright deny the possibility of sex in heaven. The assertion that the end of marriage entails the end of sex is an assumption of the interpreter. For many Christians that assertion might be made because they stand (knowingly or not) on the shoulders of Augustine and his views on sex, and not necessarily on the basis of what the biblical texts themselves suggest.[23]

Second, Jensen acknowledges that sexuality and eroticism have been drawn upon by Christians to describe eternal union with God—and thus eroticism in heaven is not wholly contrary to Christian faith. For example, the Book of Revelation describes the relationship of Christ and the redeemed as a marriage consummated in heaven. What is more, other theologians have interpreted the sexual escapades in the Song of Solomon (from the Hebrew Bible) to be spiritual metaphors for union with God. Furthermore, Christian mystics have also drawn upon eroticism to describe the God-human relationship. Jensen quotes the medieval mystic Mechthild of Magdeburg, which bears repeating here:

> Then the bride of all delights goes to the Fairest of lovers in the secret chamber of the invisible Godhead. There she finds the bed and the abode of love prepared by God in a manner beyond what is human. Our Lord speaks:
> "Stay, Lady Soul."
> "What do you bid of me, Lord?"
> "Take off your clothes."
> "Lord, what will happen to me then?"
> "Lady Soul, you are so utterly formed to my nature
> That not the slightest thing can be between you and me . . .
> These are your noble longings and your boundless desire.
> These I shall fulfill forever
> With my limitless lavishness."
> "Lord, now I am a naked soul
> And you in yourself are a well-adorned God. . . ."
> Then a blessed stillness
> That both desire comes over them.
> He surrenders himself to her,
> And she surrenders herself to him.
> What happens to her then—she knows—
> And that is fine with me.

Jensen comments, "Here sex is not incidental to the communion Christians long for; sex expresses some of the longing of Christians in pilgrimage, as they are re-formed by grace. But our sexual identities here are also transformed: we all become, in a queer twist, brides of Christ."[24] That is to say, if Christians draw on the traditional (patriarchal) language of the marital love relationship between Christ and the redeemed (i.e., as bridegroom and bride), one's identity as a Christian is therefore as a bride to Christ—which for many people would be a transformation of sex and gender roles, indeed.

Third, Jensen champions the good of "play" in sexual activity, as that which might endure (in some form) in the resurrection of the dead. In contrast with Augustine, Jensen does not affirm that sex is only (or best) ordered toward procreation. This is a position that is not unique to Jensen, but it is a newly established one in Protestant Christianity—especially with their embrace of artificial contraception in the early twentieth century. Generally speaking, Protestants are not opposed to the pursuit of other sexual goods, such as intimacy apart from procreation. They merely disagree about what kind of bodies and which kinds of relationships are permitted such delights.

Jensen believes that Christians should include play in the list of goods that we associate with sexual activity.[25] For Jensen, play is a good in God's creation (generally speaking) that can be expressed through sexual relations. As one of many human goods, play (or recreation) will be redeemed and included (in some fashion) in the resurrection of the dead. And if sex is also redeemed, then there may be room to leave open the possibility—and the question—of how the joy of sexual play might have its place in the eschatological life.

Erotic Unions

Jensen is not saying that eschatological eroticism will necessarily be through genital touching (as many know it now). But neither is he denying that possibility. At issue for Jensen is that human sexuality includes more than just the experience of genital sexual activity. For Jensen, genital sexual relations are often symbolic and communicative of more than just physical pleasure. Thus, when traditional Christianity denies the place of sex in heaven, that assertion also erases a wide variety of relational goods that sexuality can facilitate or symbolize. Jensen appears to appreciate the insights of the evangelical theologian Stanley Grenz when it comes to exploring some of the deeper dimensions of eroticism in human relationships. Agreeing with Jensen, Grenz suggests that sexual relationships should not be reduced to the concept of genital activity. Grenz believes that human eroticism should be about holistic communion, and that such communion is God's intent for human sexuality. As Grenz reflects on eschatology, however, the theologian argues that the eroticism heaven will offer is something that will transcend a genital experience. This does not mean that Grenz thinks all aspects of sexuality will disappear in the eschatological life. Rather, Grenz argues that the deeper aspects of sexuality "will be expressed in the communion that is God's love. It does not disappear, but is fulfilled, though its typical expressions will look different from our current experience of sex on earth."[26] In particular, Grenz believes the eschatological life will be "the end of genital sex, but the fulfillment of sexual desire"—insofar as the deeper dimensions of that desire really orders us toward the fulfillment of loving communion.

Grenz is calling Christians to make certain distinctions between the continuities and discontinuities between life on earth and the eschatological life. With respect to eroticism, in the here and now, human sexuality is often thought of in terms of physical/genital stimulation and pleasure. But in transcending that definition, human sexuality can reveal deep desires for relationality and communion. To that end, while life on earth might allow one to enjoy physical pleasures, heaven will fully fill our erotic capacity for deep and stable union with others. That insight is meaningful to Jensen. He observes that in some cultures, sex is over-genitalized, made instrumental and devoid of concern for human communion. When this happens, we can imagine that the instrumental use of sex—being narrowly focused on genital experiences—can lead to any number of negative outcomes, including a lack of sexual satisfaction, confusion, anxiety, and sometimes violence. To that end, Jensen appreciates Grenz's more holistic view of sexuality. What is more, Jensen appears to agree with Grenz that the eschatological life will fulfill sexual desire in a more comprehensive sense—as a matter of union and wholeness. Nevertheless, Jensen questions the hard line of saying that genital sex will be absent, arguing that "if sex, as Grenz suggests, also expresses the longing for communion, it seems odd that genital sex is automatically excluded from eschatology."[27]

Jensen's Contributions

Thus, what David Jensen has provided for Christian theology is an open-ended agnosticism about eschatological sex. It is an agnosticism that doesn't dare describe what *will* be in any narrow sense of eschatological predictions. At the same time, Jensen sees no valid reasons why sex, sexuality, and gender would be exterminated in the eschatological life. As a result, he appears to accept that the resurrected life could be sexual in ways that are recognizable to us now; and he appears to accept that the continuation of sexuality and gender might take on such a transformed and mystical state that our language about gender and sexuality only hint at what erotic delights await humanity. To that end, Jensen has opened the theological door to heaven (or is at least helping to prop it open) in order for others to consider a wide variety of ways for conceiving eschatological sex within the Christian imagination.

RESURRECTION: A HEALING OF THE WHOLE HUMAN SELF

Christian reflections on eschatology are often informed by a long-standing belief in the resurrection of the dead. Resurrection is not a matter of simply reanimating or resuscitating mortal flesh. Resurrection refers to the re-creation of the embodied self, in which mind, spirit, and body are transformed into an incorruptible eternal existence. According to traditional Christian theology, the resurrection of humanity will occur at the end of time. But even if that is so, the nature of a resurrected human is never fully explained within the New Testament texts. As a result, church leaders and a wide variety of theologians have had to speculate on what eternal life will look like if *bodily* resurrection is part of that future.

Within the New Testament narratives, only Jesus of Nazareth stands out as a character study (albeit a brief one) of a resurrected being. On the one hand, Christ's resurrected body appears to suggest a continuation of embodied existence (as human beings know that now). He eats, cooks, touches, talks, and listens.[28] Even the holes in his body seem tangible enough to be penetrated by the curious fingers of Thomas.[29] On the other hand, Christ's resurrected body demonstrates some radical discontinuities with natural human life. He moves through solid locked doors.[30] He disappears like a ghost.[31] He is unrecognizable to some of his disciples (perhaps suggesting a shape-shifting ability).[32] What is more, his resurrected body appears capable of transcending time and space as it is depicted in the scenes of his ascension, from the earthly plane to the heavenly.[33]

Christians are encouraged to look to Jesus as "the pioneer and perfecter" of the life of faith.[34] And yet, looking at the character portraits of the resurrected Jesus in the New Testament raises as many questions as it answers. When it comes to resurrection, no one really knows for sure what that kind of existence will be like. Christian theologians have offered many descriptions. In a long line of such interpretations, religion scholar Margaret Kamitsuka offers a distinctively unique reading about life in the resurrection. It is one that attends to the healing of the whole human self. In particular, Kamitsuka believes that resurrected humans are in as much need of psychological healing as we are physical. To that end, Kamitsuka argues that a vision of heavenly healing should include a *psychodynamic* perspective. When it does, it also provides for critical reflection on gender and sexuality as a dynamic part of Christian eschatology.

Bodies in the Resurrection

Recognizing that doctrines of resurrection have featured prominently in Christian discourses about eschatology, Kamitsuka believes that it is important to establish "what kinds" of resurrection possibilities Christian eschatology can envision. She names two positions among Christian theologians. The first is a view that champions belief in eternal life but disputes the belief that "*bodily eternal life is intelligible.*"[35] The second view is "the position of those who defend the intelligibility of bodily resurrection—a position that places divine intentionality at the center of the issue of resurrected bodies."[36]

Kamitsuka ultimately privileges the latter view, that bodily resurrection is intelligible. However, she fleshes out why others object to this view. On the one hand, some believe that bodily resurrection suggests that the human spirit will experience an imperfect communion with God until that spirit is rejoined with a resurrected body. But the idea of a "less than perfect" communion with God (in heaven) contradicts the idea that life in heaven is whole and glorified. One way to solve this problem is to suggest that eternal life does not begin until the final resurrection of the dead. In this case, when you die, you cease to exist. But as some theologians have suggested, if the self is eradicated at death, then "you" won't be resurrected. Instead, some kind of eternal replica of you (remade as an eternal body) goes on to live in glory.[37] To solve this problem, it has been suggested that the resurrected body is a spiritual body that is created upon death. But even this proposal arouses a theological question: *Why would we have an eschatological body at all?* Citing the theologian John Morreall, Kamitsuka rehearses the objection to bodily resurrection: "If one begins with a definition of the beatific vision as a 'direct experience of an imperceivable God,' then bodies are completely superfluous. Not only would they not add anything, but 'it is hard to understand how an embodied person enjoying the beatific vision would even know that he [sic] was embodied."[38]

Responding to these theological objections, Kamitsuka turns to theologians like Thomas Aquinas and Richard F. Creel, both of whom suggest that belief in a resurrected body is not a claim to the *depths* of happiness that one will experience with God, but the *extent*.[39] Kamitsuka argues, "[The fact] that God would allow the blessed corporeal delights is a sign of 'God's largess.' Unlike in the mortal world, the saints in heaven would experience desire without frustration, discomfort, or suffering: 'Being hungry or thirsty is not incompatible with being happy as long as we can readily secure good food or drink.'"[40] Said another way, the happiness of heaven is indeed a matter of being in God's presence, but *how* resurrected people will experience happiness with God might very well be, in part, through heavenly delights that a resurrected body can enjoy—whether eating, drinking, friendship, or the like.

Quite possibly it could include sexual delights, too. That theological assertion is certainly disputed among traditional Christians. However, if resurrected bodies might enjoy physical pleasures—as a means through which happiness with God can be experienced—then Kamitsuka believes sexual pleasures can be imagined as part of that blessed experience. But such a suggestion requires Christian thinkers to once again consider questions about sexuality and gender within an eschatological context. Margaret Kamitsuka thinks we do so well by informing our eschatological questions with insights from feminist and queer theories.

Essentialist and Constructionist Perspectives on Gender and Sexuality

At issue for Kamitsuka is the way Christian theologians talk about the nature of gender and sexuality. As David Jensen noted, there are some who assume that gender identity and sexual orientation are fixed or essential features of the human person—the result of complex biological, genetic, and neurological factors. This *essentialist* view of gender and sexuality does not deny that environment, nurture, and social influences shape one's sense of self to some extent. However, the essentialist view prioritizes the innate features of sexuality and gender identity over social interactions. Thus, for essentialists, sexual orientation and gender identity are grounded in *what* we are, not *how* we are with others. In contrast with the essentialist view, some feminist and queer theorists suggest that the experience (and performance) of gender identity and sexuality are produced through social relations. When understood in this way, gender and sexuality are social constructions. Human beings might have some basic sexual inclinations and perceptions of a sexual self, but apart from social relations, those inclinations and perceptions of self have no real meaning, nor do they take any kind of meaningful shape. Thus, for those who hold to a *constructionist* view of sexuality and gender, it is really social forces that shape the contours of our identities and desires. As we participate in society, constructionists say that we are shaped by the explicit and implicit ways in which societies promote ideals of what is normal and what is deviant. It is against these ideals, or with them, or through them that each person fashions (both consciously and subconsciously) concepts of gender identity and sexuality. As these identities unfold, our desires for others are likewise shaped. Thus, for constructionists, the foundations of gender identity and sexual orientation are inextricably bound in *how* we are as social creatures, not *what* we are biologically.

Such competing views can shape how Christians talk about eschatological sex. For example, one option is the Augustinian approach, which argues that physical sex and gender are essential features of humanity (i.e., that we are either male or female)—not only in this life, but also in the life to come. Furthermore, the Augustinian "essentialist" view of physical sex and gender also assert that sexual desire and activity will not continue in heaven, because marriage and procreation no longer have a place (recall chapter 3).

A second approach also relies on an essentialist view of gender and sexuality, but it rejects the sexual asceticism of Augustine's vision of heaven. Kamitsuka cites the gay theologian Ronald Long, who is convinced that gender and sexual diversities are sacred because they are innate and God-given. To be made the way we are now (essentially, wonderfully, and diversely) is not something that will be eradicated in the life to come. To the contrary, Long argues that sexual orientation and gender identity will endure in heaven—and they will be celebrated. By resurrecting LGBT people as LGBT in the life to come, Long believes that millions of lesbian, gay, bisexual, and transgender people will be vindicated at the final judgment and confirmed in their being throughout eternity. Thus, for Long, eschatological sex will look (at least) something like what humans experience now. It will be in close approximation to our categories of sexual orientation and gender identity. Heaven, he argues, will be "a place of differentiated sexual attraction—a place marked by personal identity, familial recognition, and bodies 'inflected by gender.... [For example,] if there will be gay male bodies in proximity to gay male bodies in heaven ... there will be gendered erotic desires.'"[41]

Contrasting with these essentialist views on gender and sexuality, Kamitsuka notes that constructionist approaches to eschatology are certainly possible. Citing Elizabeth Stuart as one example, Kamitsuka writes, "Stuart argues that in heaven, cultural constructions, inevitably distorted by sin, will be erased. The saint's eschatological genderless body is foreshadowed in baptism, when the believer becomes 'an ecclesial person.' All cultural identity markers—gender, race, kinship, nationality—become relativized and 'non-essential.'"[42] Taking this view, the continuation of sex may be possible in heaven, but some social constructionists do not bet on it. Three reasons present themselves. First, if gender is eradicated, then whatever eschatological sex will be, it will not be a continuation of what it is here. Second, if a theocentric view of eschatology is presented, it can change one's orientation from domestic relationships to divine contemplation (eternally). Third, New Testament descriptions of heaven seem to suggest that "clinging" to one another in erotic relationships—as many humans do now—is not something that will continue in the life to come.[43]

However, Kamitsuka believes that a fourth option can be imagined. According to this view—her own—a Christian thinker can embrace a constructionist view of gender and sexuality while still accepting that erotic relations might continue in the life to come. Kamitsuka suggests that one can "grant that heaven—to the extent that it can be theorized at all—[can] be theorized as discursively structured for the saints whose gender is 'performed.'"[44] That is to say, in heaven it very well could be that gender identity, expression, and sexual activity are all creative performances of the endless possibilities of what it means to be an eternal being in relation to other eternal beings. In fact, Kamitsuka states that her theological hope for heaven "is that the transformed 'spiritual' bodies of the blessed (1 Corinthians 15:44) will be able to effect novel and non-hegemonic gendered and sexual performances."[45] But even if so, one might ask why people in the resurrection would seek one another for such kinds of relationships. Kamitsuka suggests that it is in erotic relationships, especially in heaven, that psychological wounds might be healed.

Heaven, Abjection, and Psychological Healing

Kamitsuka considers the psychodynamic theories of Julia Kristeva. Of all the sources of pain in this world, Kristeva argues that people must come to terms with the suppressed trauma of abjection from one's mother. As Kamitsuka explains, "Abjection is the term Kristeva uses in her effort to emphasize the impact of the child's violent split from the maternal body at birth and the infant's subsequent gradual separation from the mother's body, which is the primary source of nurture, bonding, nourishment, pleasure, and nascent desire."[46] According to Kristeva, within each of us is a "'deep well of memory' of that early quasi-borderless, maternal experience that cannot rise to the level of object but instead remains at the level of 'primal repression.'"[47] Thus, it is from an ineffable oneness that we were all forcibly separated at birth. That trauma, the feeling of abjection, is deep within all of us. According to this theory, abjection is a wound that inevitably leads to melancholy. Kristeva defines this as "the mood and state of those suffering from the inability to cope with the largely unarticulated loss of the maternal and with assimilation into the symbolic, phallic world."[48]

In other words, when the subconscious pain of abjection is not therapeutically addressed, we find ourselves unable to adequately deal with our feelings of isolation, which intensify in a social world of relationships marked by distance and separation. As a result, we search for something, or someone, to heal that original wound. One way in which human beings try to heal the pain of abjection, as Kristeva suggests, is through sexual relationships. It is in genital relations with others that, to some extent, we seek oneness again. But so long as the wound of abjection is not healed, sexual encounters will "only erotically defer the process of mourning the painful experience" of abjection itself.[49] The only way to heal this wound, according to Kristeva, is through "functional mothering," which as Kamitsuka explains "becomes a basis for a new ethics."[50] The reader may not be familiar with this terminology. *Functional mothering* is a practice that encourages people to learn to take pleasure and seek wholeness in extending "care for another."[51] If abjection from our mothers is our original wound, then a return to motherly oneness is our path to healing. To do so is not to crawl back into the womb. It is to create a kind of motherly "oneness" again through the practice (and pleasures) of intimate tender care. Functional mothering orients us to people as distinct human beings who are in need of us to care for them (just as we are in need of care ourselves) through the union of loving interpersonal relationships.

When set within a Christian theological framework, Kristeva's psychodynamic insights about abjection raise at least two questions for Kamitsuka: first, whether abjection is an expression of sin; and second, whether abjection will be instantaneously healed in the resurrection of the dead. Kamitsuka says, "Abjection is not sin; it is a repression-turned-psychic-wound."[52] As a wound, it is in need of healing. However, if it is not wholly healed on earth (which seems a dim possibility) then its healing belongs to heaven. But that, too, raises a question. What does healing in heaven look like? Kamitsuka argues that "unless we are willing to say that God wipes out memories of the blessed, then the blessed will carry with them their wounded unconscious" into heaven.[53] But for Kamitsuka this does not mean that the eschatological life will be an eternity of carrying subconscious wounds. Rather, Kamitsuka believes that Kristeva's theory "provides an image to help us imagine a heavenly situation where sharing one's melancholy with a caring other becomes part of a journey toward pleasurable openness to the needs of others. [And] from this perspective, the blessed in heaven would require interpersonal community and time to share deeply."[54] Thus, in this view, heaven is a place where healing occurs through process.

For Kamitsuka, this heavenly interpersonal community of healing might also include erotic love. She writes, "What if, in heaven, the immediate presence of the divine so infuses the blessed that they are able to share deep psychic wounds with each other and thus experience the eros of mutual [healing pleasure]? Such eros would reverberate, we can imagine, to other interpersonal erotic pleasures, including [experiences of] sex."[55]

This leads Kamitsuka to also consider that "we can theologically hypothesize an eschatological situation with resurrected bodies experiencing [sexual desire] unencumbered by any lingering psychic wounds."[56] Or, said another way, the reason why eschatological sex might very well belong in heaven is that it would function as one way of celebrating the healing of our earthly wounds—with special attention to the psychological pains that are the origin of so many human tears and longings. What is more, it would not need to happen along essentialist lines of gender and sexuality, but rather as dynamic performances creatively explored throughout eternity.

Kamitsuka's Contributions

Kamitsuka's contribution to theory on eschatological sex is manifold. She provides intelligible ways for thinking about bodily resurrection that are not limited to gender essentialism, nor to the vision of a sexually ascetic heaven. Likewise, Kamitsuka challenges Christian theologians to take seriously constructionist views of gender and sexuality, as well as the psychological aspects of life, the wounds of which heaven will be able to heal. However, the healing that Kamitsuka imagines is one that encourages Christians to think of heaven in a new way. For Kamitsuka, heaven is not a place where all traumas will be magically undone. Instead, it is a state of being in which we humans participate in our own healing through loving interpersonal relationships in the presence of God. These are important contributions to eschatological reflection. They encourage contemporary Christian thinkers to move beyond theological theories from antiquity—and they challenge us to have holistic views of healing. What is more, Kamitsuka also helps the Christian community to imagine why sex in heaven is more than just an eschatological reward for good behavior or right faith on earth. If Kamitsuka is right, then eschatological sex will not only be a heavenly delight, it will also be a pathway for celebrating the healing of the whole human self.

TRANSFORMING TRADITION

The audacity to challenge tradition can be read as heroic work or villainy. It only depends upon who's telling the story, when, and where. From the perspective of those challenging tradition, the story can be one of interrogating power so as to make room for new perspectives or to champion the voices of the disenfranchised. From the perspective of those being challenged, critiques of tradition can feel like an assault on what has long been established as good and reliable for human flourishing. When it comes to challenging religious tradition, the stakes are even higher. This kind of challenge calls into question what has otherwise been enshrined as immutable and divinely established.

Admittedly, challenging church tradition on sexual ethics and eschatology is a knotty endeavor—and the knot is made up of different cords. One cord has to do with being taken seriously. For example, in certain places (whether in the public square, denominational meetings, at cocktail parties, or in the academy), "sex in heaven" may be dismissed as a novelty concern. Indeed, it can be difficult to convince some people that the subject of eschatological sex is worth the time of our exploration and analysis. But in truth, eschatology and sexual ethics are serious matters. In particular, the relationship between sexual ethics and eschatology has much to do with how people of faith are living their lives now; what they value and how they explicitly (and implicitly) shape cultural norms concerning gender and sexuality within their communities.

Another cord in the eschatological knot is the *ecclesial* one. For much of the history of the Catholic Church and traditional Protestantism, the Augustinian approach to gender, sex, and eschatology has been assimilated and perpetually assumed. In other words, the eschatological vision of eternal celibacy has been sustained for a very long time. Thus, to bring moral and theological debates about gender and sexuality from earth to heaven may very well seem to be a perverse assault on heaven's gates. In particular, to suggest there is sex in heaven is to visually fill the city of God with acts of carnal pleasures—whether inside of the heavenly mansion that Christ has gone to prepare for us, or outside on the lawns of paradise. That image is not going to sit very well with those Christians who have internalized an Augustinian view of sex and eschatology. But here we are, exploring just as much—something that requires at least a small dose of courage.[57]

Of the existing reflections on eschatological sex that function well as a comprehensive critique of traditional Christian thinking on such matters, Patricia Beattie Jung's book *Sex on Earth as It Is in Heaven* stands out. Whereas David Jensen represents a theological view that opens the door to the possibility of sex in heaven and Margaret Kamitsuka exemplifies what it means to engage in eschatological reflection with (often overlooked) critical insights into gender, sexuality, and psychodynamic theory, Patricia Beattie Jung mounts a reasoned theological argument as to why the Augustinian vision of heaven—which is still very much alive in many Christian churches—is in need of revision. We will consider four pieces of Jung's argument: first, her hermeneutical engagement with New Testament texts on sex in heaven; second, her direct responses to Augustine and other early Christian theologians with respect to the eschatological life; third, her constructive argument about the possibility of sex in heaven; and fourth, her insights about eschatology and Christian sexual ethics in the here and now.

The Bible and Eschatological Sex

As noted in chapter 1, the Bible is a primary source of theological and moral authority for Christians. When turning to New Testament texts, eschatological sex is not a primary concern, but the idea of it does appear. Of all of the texts in the New Testament, the Synoptic Gospels (Matthew, Mark, and Luke) narrate a rather explicit disputation about sex in the resurrection of the dead. More precisely, Matthew, Mark, and Luke each narrate Jesus discussing the place of marriage in the resurrection of the dead—a relationship (on earth) in which sex was a commanded component within the Jewish law. We have seen this scriptural concern in previous chapters of this book. The Gospel of Mark captures the scene in this way:

> Some Sadducees, who say there is no resurrection, came to [Jesus] and asked him a question, saying, "Teacher, Moses wrote for us that if a man's brother dies, leaving a wife but no child, the man shall marry the widow and raise up children for his brother. There were seven brothers; the first married and, when he died, left no children; and the second married the widow and died, leaving no children; and the third likewise; none of the seven left children. Last of all the woman herself died. In the resurrection whose wife will she be? For the seven had married her.
> Jesus said to them, "Is not this the reason you are wrong, that you know neither the scriptures nor the power of God? For when they rise from the dead, they neither marry nor are given in marriage, but are like angels in heaven. And as for the dead being raised, have you not read in the book of Moses, in the story about the bush, how God said to him, 'I am the God of Abraham, the God of Isaac, and the God of Jacob'? He is God not of the dead, but of the living; you are quite wrong."[58]

As Patricia Beattie Jung points out, there is much going on in this text—and much of that is in the theological and historical contexts in which this passage is situated.

In particular, the text says that it was the *Sadducees* who had come to speak with Jesus. In the first century, the Sadducees represented a school of Jewish thinking that rejected the idea of a general resurrection of the dead.[59] To that end, Christ's dispute with the Sadducees is not simply over marriage in the resurrection, but more broadly, whether there will be a resurrection of the dead at all. The reader should note two comments that the Gospel of Mark narrates for Jesus. First, Jesus disagrees with the Sadducees on the subject of the resurrection. In particular, the scene presents Jesus affirming that there will be a resurrection of the dead. Second, Jesus teaches that in the resurrection there will be no marriage and that humans become like angels. With respect to this second point, Jung notes, "Some conclude that Jesus is here teaching that there will be no sex in heaven. This leads others to argue further that this means—at least ideally—that there should be no sex on earth."[60]

Given that many of Christ's teachings represented ruptures with Jewish traditions (as they had developed in his time), it is not unreasonable to suggest that his ideas on marriage meant to critique some existing models of domestic life and erotic personal relationships—whether in this life, and perhaps into the eschatological life, too. Christ's theology of domestic relationships is never fully explained in the New Testament. In truth, he approaches marriage in at least two ways: he describes marriage as a covenant of equals to be respected (e.g., Matthew 19:3-9), and yet he also indicates that marriage will cease in the resurrection of the dead. But what that means theologically and ethically is remarkably uncertain. Jung describes Christ's comments on marriage and the resurrection this way: "Certainly at least some (patriarchal? abusive?), if not all, forms of marriage will not continue, but that does not necessarily mean that in the life to come we will be asexual, nor does it mean that sex in glory will not be steadfast." Thus, according to Jung, for any Christian to cite Christ's response to the Sadducees as a sure indicator that there will be no sex in heaven is reading far too much into the text.

However, for many Christians, it is Christ's example of celibacy that establishes a sexless life as the idyllic expression of the Christian life—whether on earth (now) or in the life to come. The assertion that Christ meant to prioritize a celibate life for the kingdom of God is a statement that Jung finds incongruent with other canonical New Testament teachings. Consider first Christ's own celibacy.

Jung does not deny that Jesus, in his New Testament descriptions, appears to have lived a celibate life. In truth, there are no explicit scriptural references to Jesus having been married or having any other kind of sexual partners. But according to Jung, while Christ does appear celibate in the New Testament texts, the celibacy of Christ is a "preferred but not required lifestyle."[61] For Jung, Jesus may have preferred celibacy in order to better inaugurate and build the kingdom of God on earth. That is a fair observation. Worldview and community building efforts sometimes do require sacrificing other earthly goods. If this is true, then even if Jesus was celibate, his celibacy did not mean to privilege it as the best way of being human in the kingdom of God. In fact, the New Testament narratives about Jesus show him celebrating or welcoming people who are in various sexual relationships. This includes his time at a wedding (John 2:1–11), his framing of marriage as a covenant relationship (Matthew 19:3–9), and his welcoming of prostitutes (Matthew 21:31). Nowhere in these passages does Jesus call for people to cease being sexual beings.

That is not to say that Jesus "accepted anything." As Jesus is presented in the New Testament texts, he urged people to avoid transgressing the boundaries of covenant relationships, and he condemned the objectification of people as mere sexual objects to be taken and used.[62] But even so, nowhere in the New Testament does Jesus teach—as an absolute rule—that it is better to be celibate than sexually active through genital relations. Thus, for Jung, even a celibate Jesus does not make *that* Jesus antisex.

However, some Christians will argue that Jesus did indeed privilege celibacy in his teachings on eunuchs. As literally defined, eunuchs are men who have been castrated. Recall from chapter 3 that there were some men in Christian history who maimed their genitals in order to be eunuchs for Christ. They did so while taking the words of Matthew's Gospel very literally. Recall that this text narrates Jesus as saying, "There are eunuchs who have been so from birth, and there are eunuchs who have been made eunuchs by others, and there are eunuchs who have made themselves eunuchs for the sake of the kingdom of heaven. Let anyone accept this who can."[63] This passage is indeed peculiar.

Looking at this teaching more closely, Jesus made these comments about eunuchs after denying Jewish men the unilateral rights of divorce and remarriage that were permitted by the Torah.[64] His disciples were astonished by his teaching and replied to Jesus, "If such is the case of a man with his wife, it is better not to marry."[65] Christ responded to his disciples' shock with his commentary about eunuchs. That is a little odd. Perhaps Christ meant that it would be better to live like a eunuch if a man wasn't able to treat his wife like an equal partner. Given Christ's concern for women and other marginalized people (as depicted in the gospels), such egalitarian ideas could have been in Christ's mind—but about that we cannot be completely certain. All we can know for sure is that the Gospel of Matthew connects Christ's teaching on marriage, divorce, and remarriage with a relatively positive regard for eunuchs. Jung, however, suggests that this may not be a reference to (or preference for) sexual asceticism. Situating the character of the eunuch in a broader first century historical context, Jung writes:

> Eunuchs were associated with the gender characteristics and roles of both males and females. In the ancient Mediterranean world, eunuchs were generally not viewed as celibate or virginal. Rather eunuchs were seen as passive (that is, "mounted") sexual partners, who like females and slaves, both male and female, could (and did) give sexual pleasure through fellatio, cunnilingus, and manual sexual activity.
> ... Far from ascetic, the sexual lifestyle of most eunuchs was presumed to be morally dubious by some and held in suspicion by many. Though not capable of reproduction, and usually not of coitus, eunuchs were nevertheless viewed as "highly sexed," if not promiscuous.... Some powerful women viewed eunuchs as ideal lovers and/or marriage partners precisely because such unions would relieve them of the prospect of childbearing.[66]

Thus, for Jung, Christ's reference to eunuchs in the kingdom of God cannot be so easily interpreted as a reference to sexless people, or as a norm of celibacy.

If we reflect on Christ's teaching about eunuchs alongside his teaching about the lack of marriage in the resurrection, new interpretive possibilities arise. Namely, it may be that even if marriage ends in the eschatological life, something more like the life of a eunuch begins. In particular, Christ's vision of a marriage-less heaven could indicate something more like the eunuch's unique existence on earth. More specifically, the eschatological life will no longer be bound by the dictates of religious marriage laws on earth. The eunuch, in a limited way, shows us how. Jung says it a bit differently, explaining, "Jesus is emphasizing what risen life will *not* be like. It will not be a continuation of life as we know it.... [like the religious laws that concern] the orderly transfer of property, the protection of widows, and the propagation of the species—[these] will disappear in the life to come."⁶⁷ But as we shall see, Jung believes that something else of human eroticism may continue.

Christian Theologians and Eschatological Sex

Whereas the New Testament literature offers no explicit promise of eschatological sex—nor any denial—Jung notes that a number of sex-negative views arose among early Christian theologians. Even so, their denials of sex in heaven were not uniform. Whether discussing sex on earth or in heaven, Jung correctly explains, "there was no single view of sexuality in the early stages of Christianity."⁶⁸ For example, Tertullian held the belief that bodies would be resurrected male and female, albeit robbed of sexual desire or activity.⁶⁹ Clement of Alexandria, however, took a position much like Gregory of Nyssa, teaching that the distinction between men and women will disappear in the resurrection of the dead—whether in the constitution of the resurrected body (i.e., a lack of genitals) or in the affective life (i.e., the lack of desire) for one another.⁷⁰ What is more, the early Christian theologian Origen is often read as denying a physical resurrection of the dead; and as such, he believed that the spiritual bodies of the "resurrected" would lack gender or sexual desire.⁷¹ The theologian Jerome would change his mind on the shape of human life in heaven. Jerome first "declared there would be neither sexual intercourse nor sexual differentiation (gender) in the risen life. But in his later writings, he partially reversed this view, noting that people might have their sexual organs, but they would feel no desire and would not use them."⁷² Chrysostom on the other hand could only imagine "a genderless vision of risen life in Christ."⁷³

Eventually, as Jung describes it, the Christian tradition came to emphasize the teachings of Augustine on the resurrection of the dead—and this would more or less settle (for the church, anyway) the disagreements articulated by other early Christian theologians. It is for this reason, then, that Augustine stands out as the privileged theological voice describing the eschatological life. As this chapter (and chapter 3) has already explained, Augustine believed that human beings would be resurrected as male or female, according to what their physical sex had been on earth. But because Augustine relegated sexual activity to marriage for the sake of procreation, the theologian denied that sexual desire and activity would continue in the resurrection of the dead. At best, gendered bodies would serve only to evoke praise for the beauty of God's redeemed creation.⁷⁴

In response to Augustine's eschatology, Jung offers a most helpful critique. In particular, she questions how the theologian can admit to the enjoyment of some corporeal pleasures in the resurrection, but not sexual ones. Citing Augustine, Jung captures a peculiar eschatological teaching of the theologian. In particular, Augustine asserted:

> The bodies of the righteous, then, such as they shall be in the resurrection, shall need neither any fruit to preserve them from dying of disease or the wasting decay of old age, nor any other physical nourishment to allay the cravings of hunger or of thirst; for they shall be invested with so sure and every way inviolable an immortality, they shall not eat save when they choose, nor be under the necessity of eating, while they enjoy the power of doing so. For so also was it with the angels who presented themselves to the eye and touch of men [*sic*], not because they could not do otherwise, but because they were able and desirous to suit themselves to men by a kind of manhood [*sic*] ministry.[75]

Jung responds, correctly, that the theologian's admission to eating and drinking in the resurrection opens a line of critique to his sexual asceticism. Jung says, "Sexual desire could have been imagined as serving purposes distinct from those associated with any sense of a temporal need for reproduction. It certainly could be distinguished from lust.... Like the capacity to feast in non-gluttonous ways, Augustine could have imagined sexual desire as graciously enjoyed in the life to come, apart from lust and any earthly concerns about the survival of the species."[76]

But considering what Augustine could and should have done, with respect to his articulation of eschatology and sexual ethics, does not change the tradition the theologian established.[77] Arguably, it is upon the shoulders of Augustine that so many Christians stand, and upon which they condemn the idea of sex in heaven; or at best, find it a topic of mere theological novelty. Thus, Jung believes that revising the Christian tradition from the Augustinian perspective now falls to contemporary Christians. In rather poetic terms, Jung invites Christians to that task: "Thankfully, as is so often the case in Christian community, what one is unable to do, another takes up. Melodies that cannot be sung by one member are carried by brothers and sisters in other parts of the choir. What Augustine perhaps could and should have constructively imagined about life in the world to come, now falls to us. We honor him and all the faithful before us when we take up the challenge of reimagining life abundant in the new creation."[78] So as not to be ambiguous about what that might look like, Jung offers her own vision of sex in heaven.

The Purposes of Sex, Revisited

The crux of Jung's argument about eschatological sex is really a question of what sex is for, morally and theologically. If Christians take the Augustinian view that sex is only for biological reproduction in order to procreate a child within the context of heterosexual marriage, then it would seem that sex ceases in heaven. But if there are any other valid ends of sexual activity, which are untied to procreation or marriage, then such might endure in the resurrection of the dead. Jung says it this way, "The question of whether there might well be sexual desire and delight in heaven also depends upon whether one thinks sexual activity can be love making. Though taken for granted at least rhetorically in our culture, such a holy purpose was not traditionally associated with sexual activity."[79] Jung further suggests, "once this potential [of love making] is recognized, the notion of sex in heaven becomes more plausible."[80]

Jung rehearses a number of ways in which Christian theologians have sought to revise Christian thinking on sexual ethics so as to include love making as a moral good apart from procreation. Those arguments need not be repeated here in any detail. What they share in common is a conviction that procreation is "a" good of sexual activity, but not the only good. Supporting this view are compelling interpretations of Christian scripture, revised thinking in natural law, and critiques of church theologians (including Augustine).[81] While some Christian thinkers will need to continuously engage these debates, Jung sees beyond them and embraces a Christian view of gender and sexuality that is freed from many (if not most) of the traditional restraints of Augustinian sexual ethics. This allows her to say, "As I imagine risen life, though still identifiable and distinct, embodied persons will be ever more open and available to one another. There will be a mutually porous quality to relationships, wherein we are each both permeable and penetrating." She appears to mean this in both physical and interpersonal terms.

In particular, Jung's vision of heaven is one that accepts a wide variety of ways for living out a resurrected life. With respect to gender, Jung accepts that heaven will not necessarily eradicate physical sex, nor gender identity, whether that is expressed as male, female, transgender, intersex, or something else entirely. She writes, "All manner of such sexual differences—intersex, male, and female—may become more fluid, or they may remain fairly stable. They may well be matters of comparative indifference to the life of faith in Christ. Certainly they will no longer be sources of alienation and discrimination. What is retained about gender differences must surely be only what enables communion; what is 'left behind' will be whatever obstructs it."[82]

That said, a question remains; namely, how do diverse resurrected bodies share a life of loving communion that is both "permeable and penetrating of one another"? Jung imagines that such loving communion could take many forms. For example, she accepts that some may find it in celibacy. For these people, the permeable and penetrating relationship is (most notably) with God: being lost and then found in the glory of God forever. Alternately, some may find that celibacy provides a means of communing with other resurrected beings on levels that transcend physical sex. Jung says, "Detailed speculations about the heavenly future of celibacy are perhaps best left to those among the faithful who have lived out this sexual vocation and tasted of the ways their experience of sexual desire has been sanctified therein. But I would humbly suggest that celibacy's extraordinary witness to the open, all-inclusive nature of God's love might well be included and further sanctified in the new creation."[83] Or, we might imagine (something Jung does not explicitly state) that those who have taken vows of celibacy on earth might come to enjoy the pleasures of sex in heaven—revealing that earthly vocations need not limit the possibilities of the eschatological life.

But if resurrected human beings are able to have sex, what kind will it be? Jung says, "Whether all this means people will engage in coitus, fellatio, cunnilingus, genital rubbing, or the like, I care not to speculate."[84] What is more important to Jung is that any vision of eschatological sex should be about the quality and character of the intimacy we share with others. She writes, "our experience of erotic desires—which might well include but not be exhausted by sexual desires—are and might well be even more transformed by God's grace. God desires that we be increasingly inclined toward intimacy and drawn into one another's arms in ways that are genuinely humanizing."[85]

Sex on Earth as It Is in Heaven

Such a view of heaven, Jung believes, should shape the sexual ethics of Christians on earth. In particular, if Christians allow the eschatological imagination to inform ethical reflection, then the Christian community can better live on earth as it is (or will be) in heaven. For Jung, this means reforming sexual relationships according to the qualities of the reign of God.

Central to Jung's vision of sexual ethics is the embodiment of love in human sexuality, which is infused and informed by the grace of God. She names three types of love: *eros*, *agape*, and *philia*. Drawing on the moral theologian Edward Vacek, Jung defines agape as "love for the sake of the beloved"; eros as "love for one's own sake"; and philia as "love for the sake of the relationship."[86] Unlike some Christian theologians, Jung believes that all three of these expressions of love can embody the love of God and "our participation in the life of God."[87] At issue for Jung is that apart from participating in the life of God, human beings participate in sin. Our thoughts, actions, and feelings can so depart from the ways of God's reign that we end up alienating ourselves from others and from God. However, when we allow *eros*, *agape*, and *philia* to participate in the life of God, Jung believes that these forms of love help human beings to overcome sin—including sin in erotic, sexual relationships. She writes, "*Philia* corrects personal tendencies toward aloneness. *Agape* corrects erotic tendencies toward selfishness and *philia*'s tendencies toward exclusive special relationships. *Eros* corrects agapeistic tendencies toward self-abnegation. Each way of loving bears an important witness to the nature of authentic intercommunion."[88]

Even so, love (in any of its forms) can be marred by sin. For Jung, therefore, this means that the Christian community should pay attention to how our desires of love are experienced, including sexual desire. Such a statement may sound peculiar. After all, desires seem to happen to us. Indeed, what we desire sometimes feels out of our control. This is why, perhaps, many cultures have spoken of Cupid's arrow. Pierced through the heart by that god's influence, our desires are made to conform to his will. Or said in more contemporary terms, sometimes we simply desire what we desire. Passion rises, and we feel what we feel.

Jung believes that the Christian community needs to think more carefully about the experience of sexual desire when contemplating sexual morality. In particular, Jung says that people of faith not only need to think about *what* it is they are doing, but also about the ways in which the very experience of erotic desires might be schooled by habits of thoughts, actions, and feelings.[89] Jung argues:

> We have some capacity to nurture and shape, and consequently some moral responsibility for, not only our sexual activities and practices but our sexual feelings as well. To be blunt, I am saying

we have some influence over "what turns us on" (and off). While also powerfully involuntary, our sexual desires are to some limited extent malleable, capable of being nurtured as well as repressed, and disposed toward this or that, good or bad end. We can grow in our understanding of what attracts us and become somewhat (again in a limited sense) responsible for those attractions.[90]

In other words, as Jung suggests, people need to think about reforming some experiences of sexual desire.

The prospect of reforming sexual desire is one that can raise some immediate concerns. For example, in the name of reforming sexual desire, lesbian, gay, bisexual, and transgender people have been put through regimens of so-called reparative therapy. In these "therapies," people have reported receiving electroshock therapy, ice baths, humiliation, mortification of the body, and forced sexual activities. No professional academy of medicine, psychology, or psychiatry accepts these methods as valid—and all agree that "reparative therapy" for sexual orientation and gender identity is dangerous. What is more, there are many other scenarios in which reforming sexual desire has meant artificially limiting a person's sexual expression. Particular sexual activities such as sex with contraception, masturbation, and oral sex have all been condemned at one time or another, with accusations that lust (i.e., sinful desire) has motivated these activities. Moreover, various relational configurations have been targeted as illicit or unnatural because they have not conformed to some very specific norm.

Clearly it is important to be careful about how one defines reforming sexual desire. For Jung, the proposition of reforming sexual desire is nuanced. On the one hand, she is not saying that every sexual desire that humans experience can be controlled or eliminated (nor that it need be). On the other hand, she is saying that we do have the power in us to fashion good habits (i.e., virtues) when responding to our sexual desires. Apart from cognitive disability, we can (and do) make choices about what we do and do not indulge in. Jung writes, "One way we can shape our experience of sexual desire is by pondering it. Nearly all human beings for that matter have the ability to step back from and reflect on our sexual affections and thus make judgments about their appropriateness."[91] Notice what Jung is saying: that by practicing that pause, human beings (as rational creatures) can reflect on what we desire, what that desire is ordered toward, and if it is good or wise to pursue it.

That said, it is important to remember that Jung situates the reform of sexual desires within a broad Christian context. For Jung, when *eros*, *philia*, and *agape* are informed (or infused) with God's grace, such interrelated experiences of love should guide the Christian community into a better state of chastity (the traditional name given to sexual virtue). Indeed, chastity (guided by the light of prudence) is precisely the virtue that serves to help human beings live and do well in response to our desires for the pleasures of touch in sexual relations.[92] Chastity prepares us to pursue sexual relations well or to refrain altogether. To that end, chastity contributes to human flourishing—and from a Christian view, it contributes to righteousness. That said, Christians do not agree about exactly what chastity permits. As Jung describes the problem, "Sexual desire requires both restraint and nurture.... But that is exactly the heart of the matter, isn't it? How does one kindle the fire—stimulate erotic desire—without schooling it in ways that are lustful?"[93]

To be sure, Christians do not need a vision of sex in heaven in order to define and practice chastity on earth. Sexual virtue can be distilled from biblical interpretation, natural law perspectives, and/or church tradition. Nevertheless, a vision of sex in heaven could certainly help. In particular, a vision of sex in heaven provides a *qualitative* description of sex in a state of grace. As Jung has argued, it is not necessary for Christian communities to describe what sexual activities take place in heaven. We only need to think about how the grace of heaven would inform the quality of those erotic eschatological experiences. Translating the quality of those experiences from heaven to earth is precisely how Jung believes that eschatology can inform ethics.

For Jung, this means paying attention to what we allow to inform our sexual desires and activities. What we habituate ourselves to can form a stable disposition. What is more, what we permit ourselves to experience repeatedly gives a certain kind of "muscle memory" to the power of the will. Jung's hope is that Christians will cultivate stable dispositions of good character when responding to desires for sex. For her that includes habituating fidelity to relational commitments, eschewing violence and manipulation of any kind; openness to gender and sexual diversities; and the recognition that not every sexual impulse needs to be fully actualized. What is more, when it comes to being schooled in the ways of sex, Jung believes that the Christian community should be aware of the ways in which pornography has the capacity to distort the heavenly vision of sex—and by doing so, to negatively inform sexual desire, choices, and activities. (We will explore Jung's concern about pornography in more detail in chapter 6, when revisiting how to live on earth as it is in heaven.)

Jung's Contributions

What Patricia Beattie Jung has provided us, then, is a comprehensive argument as to how Christians might claim the possibility of sex in heaven, while being respectful of the longer Christian tradition. In addition, Jung has demonstrated that the relationship between eschatology and ethics is much closer than what some might otherwise imagine. By turning from eschatology to ethics, Jung opens up possible lines of discourse for articulating or revising sexual ethics on earth. She does so by challenging tradition without letting go of the call for chastity. To that end, if David Jensen and Margaret Kamitsuka represented theologians who opened the door to questions about sex in heaven, Jung has shown the Christian community how to step through that door and start exploring—in more detail—the real possibilities of eschatological sex.

CONCLUSION

Together, David Jensen, Margaret Kamitsuka, and Patricia Beattie Jung identify a range of possibilities about eschatological sex within a broad Christian context. Jensen provides an agnostic openness to sex in heaven. He treats the subject as a critical question with which to be engaged, not as a matter to be either wholly embraced or wholly rejected. Kamitsuka provides insights from feminist, queer, and psychodynamic theories. These reflect critical analyses of sexuality and sexual ethics that are often missing from traditional Christian reflections on sexual morality. Jung provides a more complete analysis of the Bible and church tradition concerning the possibilities of sex in heaven, while also developing a constructive moral argument about the qualitative character of eschatological sex. Each is an important argument that makes a significant contribution to the study of eschatology and sexual ethics. Each is compelling in its own light.

That said, the reason why each scholar must qualify their arguments with admissions of "this might be the case" or "that could be the case" is because each one seems to be asking a rather predictive question: *Will there be sex in heaven?* No theologian could possibly know for sure. One can have beliefs about an afterlife, but what that life will be like (if there even is one) can only be seen through that dark glass of theological interpretation.

There is, however, another approach that can be taken. It is the argument of this book that Christian thinkers can move past speculation about the afterlife and shift the emphasis to the construction of material metaphors about the life to come. When Christians speak in metaphors about heaven, they are not saying what will be. Instead, they are describing what the afterlife will be *like*. It is a technique that is employed by Jesus in the New Testament gospels when he speaks in parables and metaphors. While it is impossible to say what heaven will absolutely be like in every (or any) detail, metaphors of heaven can be deployed as creative ways of describing the likeness of heaven. By using metaphors in this way, an argument by analogy can be constructed and intelligibly defended.

In the next chapter, I argue that sexual metaphors for heaven can be creatively articulated by drawing on traditional resources of religious authority. For example, when readers turn to the Bible, they will find a wide variety of material metaphors used to describe heaven: streets of gold, a mansion of many rooms, a celestial feast, a new and eternal city, and so forth. Admittedly, some Christians who read the Bible literally believe that these descriptions are not metaphors, but rather eschatological rewards to be conferred on the righteous. By bracketing a literal reading of eschatological texts, it is possible to read the physical descriptions of heaven as metaphors that only serve to indicate the quality of life in heaven. By distilling what those qualities are and then finding sexual examples of them, it will be possible to name sexual metaphors for heaven. These will in no way be promises of what will be. But as potent material metaphors of heaven, these metaphors can function as eschatological images from which to inform Christian sexual ethics today.

CHAPTER FIVE

SEXUAL METAPHORS FOR THE ESCHATOLOGICAL LIFE

> There is a continuity between this temporal life and eternal life, not in mode but in substance.
>
> —*Hans Schwarz*

"In heaven there is no beer." At least that is the lyrical assertion of one particularly boisterous German polka. It is often heard in pubs and at sporting events. When played, strangers in the crowd become familiar while singing and drinking along. But if you put your beer down long enough to consider the polka's meaning, the song boasts what heaven will be like (or not like, for that matter), and in turn, what should matter in the here and now. The lyrics may be familiar to some readers:

> In heaven there is no beer.
> That's why we drink it here (Right Here!)
> and when we're gone from here,
> our friends will be drinking all the beer!

The song is meant in jest, but it reveals a rather ascetic view of religion that is still present in the collective imagination; namely, that enjoying worldly pleasures isn't something one should expect in the life to come.

The eschatological logic here is "tipsy," but nevertheless it communicates a kind of ethic. In particular, if heaven is a place without beer, then the joys and delights of the afterlife will be quite different from the pleasures of earth. Thus, to enjoy beer here is to "get it in while you can." A beer-less heaven means that there will be a significant discontinuity of values between earth and heaven. At best, beer (or whatever food or drink you prefer) is a temporary good. It neither denies you entrance into heaven (hopefully), but neither will it be continued there. In this sense, the pub song reveals a kind of despair about the asceticism of the world to come: drink now because you'll be sober for eternity. Or, perhaps, the song is a sly admission that this life is all there is for human beings. If true, then the Book of Ecclesiastes gives good advice that there is nothing better for people to do but to "eat, drink, and enjoy themselves" while they can.[1]

But in truth there is a point here. What people say (or sing) about heaven opens and closes possibilities about the life to come and how one should live life here. To look at the polka lyrics a little more closely, these might be seen as steering people toward the idea of a *theocentric* heaven. This view of eschatology is one shared by a variety of Christians. They believe that the experience of heaven will be the ecstasy of nothing else but enjoying the direct vision of God forever (whether as perfected resurrected beings or as purely spiritual beings devoid of a physical body). Theocentric thinkers tell us that in the direct presence of God, no human relationships or bodily pleasures can compare. This vision of heaven is one of mystical communion with God, in which the worship and enjoyment of God eclipse all else. However, as we have seen in previous chapters, the theocentric vision is not the only Christian view of heaven. Those who envision heaven as a reunion of friends and family see a *domestic* or *social* afterlife, in which there are relationships and corporeal delights. These include things like loving relationships between the communion of saints, as well as material rewards of eternal feasts and streets of gold. Theologians and believers who hold this view see the goodness of God enjoyed not only in the eternal gaze of God, but also in graced relationships, perfected environments, and certain bodily pleasures.

It is the social vision of heaven that most clearly can entertain the possibility of eschatological sex between redeemed human beings. If human relationships and feasting can be enjoyed in a domestic version of heaven, then so too sexual pleasures might have their place as mediums of God's goodness and grace. As described in the last chapter, the suggestion of eschatological sex in this sort of domestic heaven has already made its way into some contemporary Christian theology. However, positive statements about heaven are almost always problematic. In particular, the use of finite language to describe the infinite will at some point always fail to grasp the ineffable subject at hand.

There is a reason why theologians must qualify so many of their statements about heaven. They realize that if they say too much, any theological prediction about heaven will far exceed their powers of foreknowledge. If they say too little, then they surrender eschatology to agnosticism or obscurity. But saying too little would also deny that there are at least some things that can be suggested about heaven from reflection on scripture, experience, and sacred tradition. The safest bet, here, is simply to quote the apostle Paul, who said that "now we see in a mirror dimly, but then we will see face to face."[2] Or, a riskier yet still modest wager is to say only what *might* be—which allows the theologian to offer a rendering of heaven that comes without guarantees. The riskiest bet of all is to make absolute predictions about the life to come—the results of which require death for verification.

However, there is another option that allows for creative descriptions of heaven without making predictive promises. That option is to admit that any description of heaven is, at best, a metaphor. This allows Christian communities to understand heaven in terms of what it *might* be like qualitatively, not what it is, or will be, in actual form.[3] But even if Christian descriptions of heaven are articulated as metaphors, this does not mean that eschatological metaphors lack any real meaning for the here and now. Describing the quality of heaven in metaphorical terms can serve to stimulate the moral and theological imagination to reflect on what is worth pursuing on earth. In other words, even metaphors about life in heaven can help the Christian community to better think about what it means to live on earth as it is in heaven. To that end, it will be argued in this chapter that any physical or material description of the life to come is best conceived as an eschatological metaphor. This argument will apply to eschatological sex as well.

THEOLOGICAL RESOURCES FOR MAKING ESCHATOLOGICAL METAPHORS

Admittedly, talking about the afterlife is tricky business. To the theologically minded, it is the serious work of interpreting scripture and sacred tradition. To the skeptic, it is the fiction of creative (or delusional) believers. For the suffering, it is a potential hope for a better world. However it is approached, talking about heaven is fraught with difficulties. But so is all engagement with religious ideas and phenomena. This is a call for intellectual and theological humility.

That said, there is no question that Christianity has preserved a variety of ideas about life after death. As noted in previous chapters, when Christians talk about heaven it can mean anything from a spiritual heaven that exists now, to the realities of some future apocalyptic event at which the dead will be resurrected to everlasting life. In truth, Christian communities leave many of the fine details of the eschatological life to mystery. But whatever is sketched of heaven is bound to raise some questions and critiques.

For example, the domestic view of heaven envisions feasting, friendship, streets of gold, mansions, and maybe even sex. But descriptions of a domestic heaven should cause Christians to ask a number of questions. Why would human beings in heaven need to eat? What would an interpersonal relationship look like if time and space have no meaning? Why would we still care about gold or the size of our heavenly house if God is the greatest reward? Would we even want to have sex while in a spiritual state of eternal bliss? If we did, would it be according to our earthly orientations and identities? Or would heavenly sex transcend biological urges and social constructions of desire?

Likewise, the theocentric vision of heaven should also arouse some critical questions. For example, if heaven is nothing else but gazing at God forever, then why have an earthly experience of diverse relationships? Or if heaven is only the single relationship between the righteous and God, then why make the prodigal "love of neighbor" such a key ingredient on earth? So, too, if heaven really is radically different from earthly life now, then why do some Christian scriptures describe it in continuous terms? A theocentric view of heaven may appear more transcendent and mystical than what a domestic heaven can boast, but its sheer otherworldliness can read as privileging spiritual existence over physical existence, a kind of dualism that Christianity turns away from in its embrace of doctrines like creation, the incarnation of Christ, and the bodily resurrection of the dead.

Apophatic and Cataphatic Theologies

Clearly, whatever might be suggested about heaven is in need of healthy critique. That critique need not come in the form of outright denying an afterlife. There are other options. For example, among the resources of Christianity is the critical approach of *apophatic* theology.[4] Christian apophatic theology takes seriously that descriptions of God and eternity will always be inadequate insofar as the finitude of language fails to capture the fullness, wonder, and mystery of the divine. The Christian mystic Pseudo-Dionysus is one of the theologians who embraced the apophatic way. For example, when writing about the divine source of all things, Pseudo-Dionysus says, "Darkness and light, error and truth—it is none of these. It is beyond assertion and denial. We make assertions and denials of what is next to it, but never of it, for it is both beyond every assertion, being the perfect and unique cause of all things, and, by virtue of its preeminently simple and absolute nature, free of every limitation, beyond every limitation; it is also beyond every denial."[5] This example of apophatic theology demonstrates that any positive claims about God must be negated in order to honor the utter mystery of divinity. Consider another example. If Christians say that God is love, apophatic theology is a reminder that God is not love if by love Christians mean any limited human understanding of that term. Such negation of theological assertion is a practice that could be applied to all forms Christian theology.

So, too, apophatic theology does not allow Christians to make any *absolute* positive claims about the eschatological life. For example, if Christians claim that there will be some kind of continuity between human sexuality in this life and in the life to come, apophatic theology urges them to take seriously the possibility that in the mystery of the eschaton, "bodies" and "sex" will fail to hold the same meaning that they do now. This must be the case, if for no other reason than the fact that current notions of bodies and sex are predicated upon finite realities such as separation and togetherness—realities that surely will not persist (in the same way) when existing in the time and space of eternity; in union with God and the company of heaven.

The theologian Patrick Cheng describes the ineffability of the eschatological life in another way. Cheng writes, "The doctrine of last things may be the queerest doctrine of all because it is the ultimate return to the radical love from which we originally came. That is, if radical love is defined as a love that is so extreme that it dissolves all boundaries, then the ultimate dissolution of identities is what will occur at the end of time."[6] Cheng is correct. Anything Christians say about heaven must submit to the apophatic thresher lest eschatological thinking become reduced to the finitudes of human imagination or the puerile exercises of expecting literal material rewards for a life of "keeping the rules" or "believing just the right thing" on earth.

However, even if heaven "ultimately dissolves all boundaries and identities," Christians nevertheless come to the task of engaging in eschatology as done by people who have a particular identity and a meaningful sense of self. Our identities and sense of self arise from the very bodies we inhabit, as well as our ever-changing human relationships. These identities are meaningful because the human experience is shaped by a glorious tangle of biological realities, sensory inclinations, intellectual capacities, and social interactions. As relational creatures with powers of apprehension, inclination, and intellect, how human beings respond to forces within and without powerfully shape our concepts of the self, including who we are and what we value. To that end, when people engage in eschatological thinking with references to life now, many do so in order to find ways to connect their identity—whether in terms of sex, gender, orientation, race, ability, economic status, geography and so forth—in relationship to God and all things eternal. This is why domestic and material descriptions of heaven have been important to so many Christian visions of eschatology. In other words, domestic and material descriptions of heaven—such as reunions with loved ones, mansions, streets of gold, feasting, and sex—build bridges of understanding from the knowable to the ineffable.

To that end, while Christians should appreciate that apophatic theologies rightly humble all theological and moral claims, it is not necessary to privilege apophatic theologies over those that seek to illuminate theological questions about heaven through relatable terms. This is the kind of work that belongs to *cataphatic theology*—another resource within the warehouse of Christian thinking. Cataphatic theologies describe eternal things in positive terms, sometimes through metaphors, in order to liken the unknown to life as humans know it now. There is, of course, an extreme to be avoided when engaging cataphatic theologies. In particular, it is the error of assuming that cataphatic descriptions of the divine are themselves complete. They are not. But cataphatic theology is nevertheless employed because it can provoke meaningful contemplation about the reign of God. In truth, creative cataphatic theologies can motivate Christian communities to ponder the mysteries of God in no less significant ways than what icons, music, scriptures, sacraments, and liturgies do. It is possible, therefore, to speak meaningfully of a domestic heaven that includes eschatological sex through cataphatic theology, especially as a matter of metaphor.

Sexuality is fertile ground for producing meaningful theological metaphors, if for no other reason than the fact that sexual desires, pleasures, and scenarios can illuminate concepts of ecstasy, goodness, love, fulfillment, and flourishing. This is not a new (or even progressive) idea. For example, the Song of Solomon is a book of the Hebrew Bible that explicitly describes a sexual relationship between King Solomon and one of his many brides. While there have been disputes about whether the Song of Solomon is pornographic, a number of traditional Christian thinkers have argued that the eroticism of this text works well as spiritual metaphor for the relationship between God and the redeemed.[7] To that end, it is not a controversial statement that Christian theology can be improved when it draws upon the subject and contents of human sexuality. Or, said another way, Christian theology can be sexual theology. But as the Protestant theologian James Nelson has commented, "This is not to claim that sexual theology will provide an all-encompassing approach to the Christian task. It is to say, however, that this is another needed approach with which to grapple with the meaning of God's purposes, presence, and action for our lives at this particular time and place in history."[8] The suggestion here is that Christianity might benefit, not only from a sexual theology, but also from a sexual eschatology.

Admittedly, sexual metaphors do have their limitations. For far too many people, sexual relationships have been locations of violence, abuse, and shame. Where sex has been experienced in such negative ways, the thought of eternal asexuality or celibacy may be a preferred option. In truth, asexuality and celibacy may very well have cataphatic value as metaphors for the eschatological life. And yet, in the face of traumatic sexual violence and abuse, Christians might still hold to the theological hope that in the life to come, the wounds of sexual violence will be healed by the eternal love of God, as experienced in loving union between the communion of saints. If this is true, then cataphatic descriptions of sex in heaven might still be meaningful to many members of the Christian community.

But even if Christians could agree that sexual metaphors for heaven are valid, it remains to be seen what kind of sexual relationships or activities would serve well for those metaphors. On this matter it is almost certain that there will be disagreement among Christians. Some suggestions will be offered here nevertheless.

SEXUAL METAPHORS FOR HEAVEN

In the spirit of naming metaphors for heaven, any number of sexual varieties can and should be considered. Contemporary Christian ethics are no longer solely represented by heterosexual, marital, procreative, or monogamous norms. Those norms are present in some denominations and individual congregations, but not in all. Such churches may believe that their standards represent biblical or historic Christian teaching, but that's a debate for another time. What these churches cannot deny is that Christianity, as a global religion of many traditions, boasts a variety of views on gender and sexuality.

This includes conservative, progressive, and radical perspectives (all terms that are relative to each other). Therefore, to search for sexual metaphors for heaven within a broad Christian context is to allow the imagination to consider any number of possibilities, inclusive of a wide variety of sexual and gender diversities. But these possibilities must be intelligible, somehow, in relation to the Christian resources that shape Christians' theological thinking.

One resource worth returning to is the Bible, and in particular, the Gospel of Luke and the often-cited text in which Jesus comments on marriage in the resurrection of the dead. Recall that Luke 20:27–36 describes a scene between Jesus and a group of Sadducees. Because the Sadducees did not believe in the resurrection of the dead—and wanting to inquire about Jesus's own views—they asked him to whom a woman would belong in the resurrection of the dead if she had been married to seven different brothers (a tricky question, given the traditional Jewish obligation for a man to marry his brother's wife if she was widowed and childless). The Gospel narrates a stark response from Jesus, who replies, "Those who belong to this age marry and are given in marriage; but those who are considered worthy of place in that age and in the resurrection from the dead neither marry nor are given in marriage."[9] This curious response from Jesus seemingly affirms a belief in the resurrection of the dead. However, it also transgresses the marital norms that were consistent with ancient Judaism. In particular, marriage was more or less an expectation for first-century Jewish men. In fact it was a religious duty for most Jewish men to fulfill (a duty that is expressed in greater detail within the Talmud).[10] Notice, then, that Luke's Gospel not only eradicates the idea of eschatological marriage, it also critiques the practice of marriage in reference to those who are *worthy* of the resurrection. By doing so, Luke's Gospel challenged the customary expectation for being married, as well as its normative place in the center of Jewish life. And yet, it does not necessarily eradicate sexual activity from this life or the next.

The assumption that sex will not endure in the resurrection because marriage does not persist is simply an imposition on the text. As we have seen in previous chapters, some theologians have insisted on a sexless eschatological life because of the final wording of this passage, in which Jesus says, "but those who are considered worthy of a place in that age and in the resurrection from the dead neither marry nor are given in marriage. Indeed they cannot die anymore, because they are like angels and are children of God, being children of the resurrection."[11] For some, the reference "they are like angels" has carried with it a sexually ascetic ideal. Recall the insight from David Jensen, who explains, "Throughout much of its history, the Christian church has assumed that Jesus' words about the disappearance of marriage in heaven have also entailed the end of sex. Resurrected persons become like the angels, sexless, unable to reproduce sexually, no longer tainted by the stirrings of the loins."[12] But in truth, such a reading of angels is a curious one to sustain. The understanding that angels are sexless overlooks a biblical narrative that suggests otherwise. Specifically, Genesis 6:1-2 describes divine beings (i.e., angels) taking human mates and even producing hybrid children with them. Thus, whatever else Christians might say about becoming like angels in the resurrection of the dead, an angelic or eschatological life does not insist upon the expurgation of sexuality.

What is more, if the theologian Raymond Lawrence is correct in his analysis of this passage, then "Jesus' remark . . . that there will be no marriage or giving in marriage, might mean that in the kingdom of God, holy promiscuity will prevail."[13] Lawrence's comment is provocative but not without support. The eradication of marriage invites us to consider the eschatological life as one in which redeemed human beings are not limited by exclusive relational boundaries. Rather, the eschatological vision of Luke 20:27-36 is one in which humans are free from the bonds (or bondage) of marriage, and thus free to experience dynamic relations with all who are redeemed. In this vision of the resurrection of the dead, nonexclusive relationships prevail. And here's the rub: it would seem that Christians are already accustomed to thinking about the eschatological life in polyamorous ways like these. In other words, many descriptions of heaven depict it as a state of being in which humans live in eternal love with God and with *all* the company of heaven, indiscriminately. Traditional Christianity has simply lacked any sexual metaphors to express the love and joy of such dynamic relationships.

Promiscuity

It might be assumed that Christians have disregarded sexual metaphors for heaven because they have largely favored a *theocentric* vision of eternity (an afterlife of an uninterrupted gaze of God, absent social relations), or perhaps because they disdain sensual pleasures as a lower sort, whose animalistic features are absent in the glories of heaven. That is sometimes true (for particular theologians and churches), but it is not altogether true. Recall that Christians have historically likened the eschatological life in domestic and physical terms, describing it like an epic feast, in which the sensual pleasures of the tongue, mouth, and belly are completely fulfilled with food and drink.

Such a description means to indicate that heaven is a place of fulfillment and abundant life. In this sense, even traditional Christian descriptions of heaven draw on sensual metaphors that tend toward the prodigal and the excessive (feasts, a mansion, streets of gold, and so forth). If we were to imagine a sexual metaphor to express the same sensual and prodigal realities of love, fulfillment, and abundant life, we could say that the eschatological life is one that will be promiscuous. One might even ask: How could it not be? As Laurel Schneider has argued, the central figure of Christianity—Jesus of Nazareth—is himself an expression of prodigality and promiscuity more generally conceived. Schneider explains:

> It is impossible to say, on the basis of the surviving narratives, that Jesus preferred categories of people to the actual people who crossed his path.... If anything, the narratives of Jesus of Nazareth suggest that the divinity which his flesh reveals is radically open to consorting with anyone. It follows no rules of respectability or governing morality in its pursuit of connection with others, many others, serially and synchronically, passionately, and openly.... This kind of excess of intimacy and disregard for propriety is the definition of promiscuity in sexual terms. Jesus is a "promiscuous boy" (to borrow Furtado's phrase) whose entire teachings might be reducible to the refrain "don't get mean."[14]

Thus, if Christians hold to a theological principle that Jesus of Nazareth reveals the reign of God, and further, that Jesus reveals the prodigal orientation of God's love and desire to consort with any and all people, then when we draw on sexual imagery to describe the eschatological reign of God (in such terms), at least one description of eschatological sex will be promiscuous sex.

Christians might imagine, then, that the life to come can be likened to a place of great heavenly feasts as well as great sexual freedoms—each expressions of the prodigal nature of God's love and desire for human beings to enjoy the pleasures of abundant life. When thinking about heaven in these terms, the eschatological life might be described as a place where the lover will be able to enjoy the uninterrupted pleasures of sex and sexuality, whether alone, with another, or with many others. In this heaven there will be no frustrations over finite feelings of jealousy, anxieties about attractiveness, worries about physical performance, fears about sickness or disease, or feelings of sexual alienation. This heaven is a place where the lion not only lies down with the lamb and where warriors beat swords into ploughshares, but also where promiscuous sex is one part of the "excess of intimacy and disregard for propriety" that embodies the love of the reign of God. In this vision of heaven, no one is told they cannot go back for seconds at the heavenly feast, and no one is told to deny themselves the pleasures of sex. In short, promiscuity is freed from all the complexities, conditions, and finitudes that sometimes wound human beings on earth.

To claim that eschatological sex can be conceived as promiscuous sex is to remove the moral stigma of promiscuity itself. To share oneself with others as an expression of healing vulnerability, mutual pleasure, grace, solidarity, and love of humanity is an otherwise celebrated thing to do. However, to do so with many others through sexual engagements has been wholly condemned by the institution that we now call "traditional Christianity"—and the moral values that traditional Christianity enforces. Those values, however, are not necessarily the direct inheritance of Christ's teachings. Suspicion about promiscuity (or really anything not marital or procreative) is something that was innovated and developed by people claiming to sustain the teachings of Christ and the apostles. Consider, again, the historical insights highlighted in previous chapters. For example, it was the Christian sexual ascetics of the second century who disdained many aspects of sexual desire and activities beyond procreation. Gregory of Nyssa believed that sexuality was a result of the fall of humankind into sin. Augustine found all sexual desire to be the equivalent of the sin of lust—and even warned that certain forms of sexual expression within marriage were "forgivable faults." The institutional church of the fourth century and onward sought to chastise sexual desires toward marital, monogamous, and procreative sex as a matter of doctrine. Medieval Christian theologians invented the category of sodomy, defining it as any nonreproductive sex act. With sodomy as a new category of concern, penance and punishments for sexual sins proliferated. With such views making up the general framework for sexual ethics, Christianity became a faith tradition associated with the denial of most sexual pleasures. That Christians should continue to stand on the shoulders of Augustine or other theologians of antiquity is clearly something now resisted by a wide variety of Christian denominations, congregations, scholars, clergy, theologians, and individual believers.

Therefore, to say that promiscuous sex is a valid metaphor for sex in heaven is also to say that the way in which Christians conceive of sexual morality is in much need of reform and renewal. Recall from chapter 1 that there is a relationship between eschatology and ethics. What we say about heaven from our experiences on earth is to affirm that there are some earthly goods that seem apt descriptions of heaven. So, too, we can acknowledge that the relationship between eschatology and ethics is reflexive. This means that what we can imagine about heaven could creatively inform and transform codes of morality now. The suggestion here is that promiscuity is an eschatological metaphor that is not only valid for the life to come, but may be helpful for thinking anew about Christian sexual ethics in the here and now.

Admittedly, promiscuity is not without its problems. For example, some people have had negative reactions to it on the basis of bad firsthand experiences. We should take these experiences seriously in order to inform our moral analyses of promiscuous encounters. On the other hand, some people have had negative concepts of promiscuity artificially imposed on them. To say that negative judgments about promiscuity have been artificially imposed on some people is only to recognize that heterosexual, marital, monogamous, and procreative norms for sexual activity have too often been proselytized as absolute moral truth. Perpetuating these norms without room for conversation or alternative ways of thinking about sexuality has sometimes caused real trouble for those whose morality has been shaped by traditional religious communities. Clinical psychologists have seen this firsthand. For example, David J. Ley writes, "One young man I saw a few years ago, was an 18-year-old college student, deeply afraid that he was addicted to masturbation. He was only masturbating once a week, but because he'd grown up in a family where any sex outside of monogamous marriage was sinful and condemned, his quite normal sexual behavior was experienced with deep shame and fear."[15] Ley goes on to comment, "Sadly, when people within religious communities seek help for their sexual concerns, they are most often told to suppress or 'battle' their sexuality, or sent to pseudotreatments such as sex or porn addiction programs, where their sexual desires are portrayed as a form of sickness. Shame creates a feedback loop of pain, fear, dysfunction and self-hatred, which is the true root of most sexual problems."[16]

Within many traditional constructions of Christian sexual ethics, promiscuity is nothing else but the *sinful* enjoyment of sex with more than one person. The degree to which people have absorbed traditional teaching on this matter may shape how they reflect upon (and experience) their sexual liaisons. For example, there are some people who may think that they are OK with promiscuity in theory, but who cannot escape the feeling that their sex lives are dirty (and name it as such) due to religious indoctrination. That is to say, it is entirely possible for people to never fully enjoy certain experiences of sex because their minds are narrowed by the rote condemnations engrained within. What is more, another unfortunate consequence of traditional Christian teaching on sexuality is that it fails to prepare people for how to navigate the real world of human sexuality. Ley comments, "An entire generation of people are encountering crippling sexual shame and pain, as they wrestle with their sexual desires and interests, in a world for which they were unprepared.... Unfortunately, the vagueness and broadness of the sexual constructions in the purity movement [have] left people confused, and often feeling that they must reject even normal, healthy sexual urges."[17]

Of course, such a comment raises an important question as to whether promiscuity is normal and healthy; and the moral question, whether promiscuity is good. If the word "normal" is defined as that which is statistically frequent, then yes, enjoying more than one sexual partner is most certainly normal among many populations of adolescent, young adult, and adult human beings.[18] In fact, some theorists have suggested that without sexual promiscuity, humankind would not have survived and flourished as we have, both socially and reproductively.[19] That said, the question as to whether promiscuity is healthy is contingent on multiple factors like the partners involved, their physical health status, their mental health status, the sex acts involved, contraceptives and prophylactics used (or not used), and the potential mental and physical outcomes of the sexual experiences had (pregnancy, pleasure, anxiety, infections, joy, delight, friendship, emotional attachment, and so forth).

The stereotype among many Christian communities is that promiscuous people are dangerous carriers of disease and mindless about morality and human flourishing. So let's be honest: sometimes promiscuous people give evidence to that stereotype. When that happens, the experience of sexual promiscuity can produce genuine negative reactions, which may cause a person to see sex with multiple people as unwanted or better left untouched. However, let's also be rational: having sex with more than one person in no way guarantees that trouble will come. You will not get a disease from every person you have sex with. A woman will not always get pregnant every time she has sex. You will not lose your sense of morality or your faith in God because of promiscuity—nor even if you have made some mistakes in sexual relationships.

To say this about promiscuity within a Christian context, some people of faith will demand some biblical evidence for such claims. Such evidence is available. For example, it is the promiscuity of polygamy—not monogamy—that is the traditional practice of sexual relationships in the Bible (albeit with all the trouble of patriarchy). King David is one such case study of a promiscuous person of faith. If you are unfamiliar with his story, do pause here and read about his many lovers and wives and his bold pursuit of adultery, while still being "a man after God's own heart."[20] Or consider the many New Testament statements about eunuchs and prostitutes entering the kingdom of God. These are referenced without any word on whether such characters ceased to be sexual beings.[21] The New Testament does call for monogamy in at least one place, but there it requires monogamy for those who want to be bishops of a church (presumably because there is not enough time to take on the responsibilities of a church and more than one spouse).[22] Thus, whether we are reflecting on promiscuity biblically or practically, all we can realistically say is this: within the realities of harmful consequences and good ones, the performance of promiscuity must be mindfully pursued. Promiscuity exists as one way of engaging in sexual relationships. To do so well, the light of eschatology can be an important guide.

One way in which eschatology frees us to think about promiscuity more generously is that its context is heaven; namely, the grace of heaven allows us to imagine promiscuity without the complexities, conditions, and finitudes that cause human beings trouble on earth. In heaven we can leave those troubles behind. What that leaves us with is the opportunity to think about what goods can be shared and communicated through sexual relationships with multiple people. In particular, sexual promiscuity can serve as a representation of the indiscriminate love that heaven envisions, the gospel commands, and that Jesus demonstrated in his willingness to touch (and be touched by) many people—regardless of body or status.

Arguably, the love of the gospel motivates each person to see another as someone to be welcomed, healed, held, and helped—and to do so by giving from the very best of ourselves. In New Testament Gospel narratives we see this love expressed through much physicality. It is seen in the good Samaritan holding, cleaning, and restoring the body of a stranger; in the kissing and rubbing of Christ's feet with the tears, oil, and hair of a "sinner"; in the power of a woman's touch as she reached out to Christ's body for healing; in Christ's saliva mingled with dirt and massaged upon blinded eyes; in Christ stripping himself of clothing in order to hold and clean the feet of his disciples. These are not the only physical expressions of love that are seen in the New Testament Gospel narratives, but they all demonstrate the indiscriminate nature of Christ's love, as Laurel Schneider so well described it. What is more, some of these are examples in which divine love is expressed through *episodic* encounters. That is an important insight that should not go unnoticed. The love of God may indeed be steadfast, but that does not also mean that divine love cannot show up in the chance encounters of life. Arguably, Christianity affirms that the sacred incarnates whenever and wherever divine love is offered in any multitude of forms. The argument here is that sex can be one of those forms—and that the sexual encounter need not be expressive of long-term, domestic commitments to exhibit qualities associated with the prodigal love of God.

If we draw on sex as a metaphor to communicate that indiscriminate and physical love of the gospel, then promiscuous sex works well. Seen in this way, the promiscuity of heaven will not be mindless sex or sex for the sake of feeding our ego. In heaven, promiscuous sex will be the intentional sharing of human love and hospitality through intimate, exquisite, playful, healing, and indiscriminate bodily relations. In heaven, every member of the communion of saints will have that option of sexual fulfillment, whether alone, in pairs, or in larger celebrations of love. That love will not be exclusive between any set of people but shared among the whole company of heaven. It will not be a necessity of heaven, nor a compulsion, but rather an opportunity to embody communion and unconditional love through the bodies of heaven that reflect the glory of God. To participate in eschatological promiscuous sex would be to allow the grace and love of the reign of God to fill every part of us, but especially through our sexual dimensions. That proposal should really be no more shocking than the traditional Christian eschatological vision of God's love and heavenly fulfillment expressed through eating or housing arrangements (e.g., in heavenly feasts and the heavenly mansion with many rooms). Sex simply furnishes another medium through which to celebrate the love of God fully expressed.

The Psalmist sings that "the heavens are telling the glory of God."[23] In the Gospel of Luke, Jesus says that if humans are silent about him, "stones would shout out."[24] In heaven, there will not be one aspect of the redeemed human being that does not also have the capacity to declare the glory of God and show the love of God for all. One of those capacities is human sexuality—and in heaven that sex would not be limited to any one person, nor would any sexual expression fail to express the love of God. For example, the delights of oral sex, intercourse, masturbation, mutual masturbation, sexual role-play, and group play all would actualize God's prodigal love (to name a few examples). So, too, the vision of heavenly sex could include LGBTQ and heterosexual examples, not to mention fulfillment for all sorts of bodies of various shapes and sizes. Indeed, anything we might imagine that has the ability to demonstrate mutual love, consensual play, justice, and human hospitality are visions that might capture the promiscuous sex of heaven.

Monogamy

But even if promiscuity is one valid metaphor for eschatological sex, it is certainly not the only one. Monogamy is another option. Although monogamy has long been a key ingredient in traditional Christian sexual ethics, suggesting that monogamous sex will exist in heaven requires dislocating monogamy from marriage, or reconceiving the concept of marriage altogether in an eschatological form. Recall, again, that multiple New Testament Gospels narrate Jesus's teaching that there is no marriage or giving in marriage in the resurrection. Therefore, if the assumption is that the absence of marriage means the absence of sex, then traditional monogamous sex would be replaced with eternal celibacy. One way around this vision of a sexless heaven (without indulging the visions of promiscuity) is to suggest that monogamy need not be conceived within a marital context. The Christian ethicist Patricia Beattie Jung has made a suggestion in this direction. Recall that Jung writes, "Certainly at least some (patriarchal? abusive?), if not all, forms of marriage will not continue, but that does not necessarily mean that in the life to come we will be asexual, nor does it mean that sex in glory will not be steadfast."[25] If Jung's comments represent a defensible interpretation of Christ's teaching, then Christians should regard it as a good thing. Namely, in heaven, a better version of human relationships will prevail.

If that is the case, then people who have been committed to monogamy on earth might see the possibility of being monogamous in heaven (even if conventional institutions of marriage fail to endure in the life to come). In heaven, monogamous partners will make love in graced perfection, as an expression of God's love between them. That is one possibility. In fact, the eighteenth-century Christian mystic Emanuel Swedenborg taught that earthly spouses would find each other again in heaven. Swedenborg believed that those spouses who truly enjoyed their love on earth would stay together forever. However, he also realized that not every marriage is a truly happy one. To that end, he taught that those who were not perfectly matched on earth would be free to find new spouses for eternity. He also believed that these heavenly marriages would be inclusive of sex. Swedenborg wrote, "Partners enjoy intercourse with each other just like intercourse in the world, only happier and richer, though without having children. Instead of that, or in place of it, they have spiritual offspring—loves and perceptions. This happens for those who enter heaven."[26] Swedenborg's vision of better relationships in the afterlife speak to deep needs of love and fulfillment. As Christians thinkers, what both Swedenborg and Jung offer is a vision of sex in heaven that in turn can motivate married or monogamous Christians to explore how their relationships on earth reflect (or not) the graces of heaven. Such would apply to the sexual aspects of their relationship as well. In particular, spouses and partners might reframe monogamous sex (now) as a meditation on heaven, in which the ideal of perfectly graced eschatological monogamy could help couples grow emotionally and spiritually in their physical expressions of shared love and intimacy.

That said, when Christians turn to other biblical narratives about heaven, it appears that there is actually another marriage that will supersede the ones on earth. In particular, the redeemed of heaven will be married to Christ, like a bride to a groom. In the Book of Revelation, the prophet John describes that peculiar scene:

> Then I heard what seemed to be the voice of a great multitude, like the sound of many waters and like the sound of mighty thunderpeals, crying out, "Hallelujah! For the Lord our God the Almighty reigns. Let us rejoice and exult and give him the glory, for the marriage of the Lamb has come, and his bride has made herself ready; to her it has been granted to be clothed with fine linen, bright and pure"—for the fine linen is the righteous deeds of the saints. And the angel said to me, "Write this: Blessed are those who are invited to the marriage supper of the Lamb." And he said to me, "These are true words of God."[27]

According to many traditional Christian theologians, the bride depicted in this scene is not just one person but the entire community of the redeemed. The Lamb is Christ. In other words, in Christian heaven, all will be presented as a bride to Christ—who is the eternal husband.

The Book of Revelation never depicts an explicit scene of sexual consummation between the bride and groom, but it might well be implied. In the era in which this text was written, marriage was sealed not simply by a contract but by marital lovemaking. Thus, it would make little sense to draw on the imagery of marriage without the sexual connotations thus implied (even if as a metaphor). Furthermore, in chapter 21 of Revelation, the prophet John receives another vision of heaven. He describes it in these words, "Then one of the seven angels who had the seven bowls full of the seven last plagues came and said to me, 'Come, I will show you the bride, the wife of the Lamb.' And in the spirit he carried me away to a great, high mountain and showed me the holy city Jerusalem coming down out of heaven from God."²⁸ Note the peculiar unfolding of this vision. John is told that he is going to be shown the wife of the Lamb, but is then shown a city. The city is described in prodigal terms: large, luxurious, and without defect. If the city *is* the bride (which is one view), then the consummation occurs as the Lamb (the husband) dwells within the city—the husband within his wife. However, if the people living in the heavenly city represent the bride of Christ (and the city is something prepared for her), then the domestic relationship of the husband (the Lamb) and the bride (the redeemed) is still intimated by their shared dwelling space.

In marital terms, monogamy is the practice of being married to one person at a time. When expressed in sexual relations, it means taking only one sexual partner at a time. Thus, if the only marriage in heaven is between Christ and the redeemed (collectively), then eschatological monogamy belongs to the marriage of the bride of heaven and the Lamb, who is Christ. That said, the monogamy of heaven appears more polygamous when the finer details are examined. In particular, it appears that it is only each member of the redeemed who love Christ monogamously; in turn, Christ loves and is married to each member of the bride of Christ. That is not unlike some of the polygamous marriage arrangements one can find in antiquity, or, among some contemporary religious and cultural practices.²⁹ Thus, if read literally, Christ the heavenly groom has a harem in heaven.

However, if we accept the collective understanding of the bride of Christ metaphorically, then monogamy prevails as the imagery. If that marital metaphor includes a sexual component, it would mean that monogamous sex in heaven would be nothing else but physical union between the bride (the redeemed) and Christ (the husband) as an expression of covenantal love. But when that metaphor is applied to the *individuals* of heaven, it actually ends up challenging traditional Christian sexual ethics (either in optics or substance). In particular, by retaining gendered language about Christ as the husband and the redeemed as the bride, it sets the men of heaven as being brides of Christ, who—within the construct of sexual monogamy—are to receive their husband within themselves in the eternal life to come. Just the suggestion of this penetrative posture will be difficult for some Christian men to accept, especially for those who have spent a lifetime defending gender roles that have much to do with receptive and penetrative sexual positions. Imagine the surprise of the Christian man who has been resolute in his view that men should only penetrate women and never themselves be penetrated; that they must never even think in those terms. But in the resurrection of the dead, in the monogamy of heaven (at least, in this metaphorical iteration), male brides of Christ are "bottoms" for Jesus. They receive the Lord in themselves as a bride receives her husband. Absent a vagina, penetrative sex (in the very literal sense) puts the male bride of Christ in a position that has otherwise been designated as sodomy by traditional church teaching.

These are not purely statements of parody. This is a real concern for some Christian men, who either need or want to reassert their heterosexual individuality on earth and in heaven. For example, in a 2018 online article, "Don't Be Gay for Jesus: Understand Why the "Bride-Groom' Metaphor Doesn't Work for Individuals," the anonymous "News Division" of *Pulpit and Pen* goes into some detail about why Christian men calling Christ their husband is incorrect.[30] The article begins with this (homophobic) statement: "Okay, men. We need to have a talk. Stop being gay."[31] After a few initial (sexist) comments explaining that "it's understandable that women are 'led-on' by theo-erotic versions of God," the authors of *Pulpit and Pen* express dismay that some men (evangelicals, in particular) would call Christ their husband.[32] The theological argument here (while offensive in rhetoric) is at least worth considering. In particular, *Pulpit and Pen* encourages Christians to read the eschatological wedding not as an individual relationship between Christ and Christians, but instead as a covenantal relationship between God and the people of God. The authors write:

> The Covenant people of God—Israel of the Old Testament and the Church (serving as the Spiritual Israel) in the New Testament—is the bride. They are the bride collectively. No one member of the bride is the bride.... The simple principle is this: Jesus is not a polygamist. He doesn't have one billion (or so) individual brides. He certainly doesn't have brides who are dudes.... If you are a man, Jesus is not your groom, and you are not his bride.... It makes us all look stupid when our Christian leaders refer to Jesus as their significant other. It makes us look gay when men do it, calling themselves a bride or calling Jesus their husband. In the age of "gender fluidity" and chaos in the realm of human sexuality, we really don't have the luxury of being imprecise on this issue.[33]

Pulpit and Pen may have a very important theological point about the collectivity of the eschatological marriage between Christ and the redeemed. Unfortunately, it is lost behind offensive rhetoric about women and LGBTQ people. That said, their comments also expose the remarkable anxiety that some Christian men have about any conceptualization of being a bride of

Christ—so much so that these authors are explicit in their fear that it makes them "look gay." While such concerns may not dominate all Christian discourse on eschatology, the reader will find that the question is not really a rare one in certain sectors of evangelical and fundamentalist discourse.

Admittedly, to note that men will be brides of Christ (individually or collectively) is certainly not the most substantive statement that can be made about monogamous sex as eschatological sex. Perhaps all it does is to expose some potential flaws in heterosexist, patriarchal thinking—as well as some anxieties among some Christians about sexual identity in the life of the world to come. To be sure, there are other ways of thinking about monogamous sex as eschatological sex. In particular, if Christian communities retain the heavenly metaphor of marriage to Christ and place it within a *theocentric* vision of heaven, then eschatological monogamy can be read as mystical union with God through Christ. In this view, the redeemed enjoy not only the eternal gaze of God forever, but also eternal intimacy with their ultimate beloved. In this case, the concept of eschatological monogamy would function as a metaphor for the joy and devotion of union with God for all eternity.

The reader should note that employing sexual intimacy as a metaphor for union with God is hardly new. As previously noted, the Song of Solomon is an erotic text of the Bible that theologians have often spiritualized in order to approximate the relationship between God and the people of God. So, too, many texts of the Hebrew Bible use the language of a sexual relationship to describe the relationship between God and Israel—including the times when that relationship breaks down. For example, Ezekiel 16:8 reads, "I passed by you again and looked on you; you were at the age for love. I spread the edge of my cloak over you, and covered your nakedness: I pledged myself to you and entered into a covenant with you, says the Lord God, and you became mine."[34] Isaiah 54:5 reads, "For your Maker is your husband, the Lord of hosts is his name; the Holy One of Israel is your Redeemer, the God of the whole earth he is called."[35] What is more, in reference to Israel and God, Hosea 2:7 says, "She will pursue her lovers, but not overtake them; and she shall seek them, but shall not find them. Then she shall say, 'I will go and return to my first husband, for it was better with me then than now.'"[36] Such metaphorical descriptions appear frequently in the Hebrew Bible. Thus, to shift that sexual biblical imagery to the eschatological life is not so much a stretch of progressive theology as an application of an ancient theological genre to heavenly life.

If Christians employ the metaphor of union with God as a monogamous union in a theocentric heaven, this sets the stage for thinking about what goods monogamous sex can communicate. In particular, the image of eternal monogamy with God takes seriously that knowing and being known is an ongoing experience that has no ending point. In this sense, the concept of heavenly monogamy would reveal that relationships are vocations of attending well to one another. The vision of eternal monogamy would also reveal that we can never know a person simply on the basis of a particular point in the relationship, but rather that we must attend well to the beloved as they and we change with the passage of time (and eternity). In this sense, monogamy limits engagement with others not so much to be exclusive and cut people out (or to deny our many attractions), but rather to invest deeply into the life of another soul. When eschatological monogamy is captured by the marital imagery between God and humanity, then the vision is really one of embracing the mystery of an eternally unfolding relationship of love. That kind of eschatological vision might inspire Christians to think carefully and creatively about pursuing monogamy in the here and now. Indeed, it may help Christians become better partners and spouses, whose vocation is to attend fully to their beloveds.

Celibacy

But monogamy is not the only alternative metaphor to the vision of a promiscuous heaven. Celibacy stands as a third option worth considering. To suggest as much is not to retreat from the work of sexual liberation, nor is it to do an about-face and embrace a negative view of sexual desire or experiences. Instead, it is to recognize that human beings have many ways to navigate life. One such way is to intentionally abstain from sex in order to channel erotic power through other endeavors. Sister Carol Bernice of the Community of the Holy Spirit is one such example. Her story appears in an important text that collects the lived experiences among queer people, *Queer Christianities: Lived Religion in Transgressive Forms* (edited by Kathleen Talvachia, Michael Pettinger, and Mark Larrimore). After having raised children and then accepted herself as a woman who loves women, Carol also felt herself called toward a religious life. While attending a retreat, Carol was not only aware of her sexual orientation, but suddenly also, her interest in a life in a religious community. She writes, "I was inquiring of the sisters if I, too, could become a sister. They did not say no. I look back now and think I had my vocation handed to me on a platter. There it was, clear and shining before me: a life of devotion in the company of women. That they were engaged and energetic, beautiful and intelligent and on fire with the Holy Spirit was all the more cause for rejoicing."[37]

As she describes it, Sister Carol Bernice's choice to become celibate was not from a fear of the erotic, nor was it a compulsion because no other option was available. Before taking vows, Carol had taken a woman as her beloved. They were together for seven years before her partner died. Reflecting on that experience, Sister Carol writes:

> Our life together and her death have provided me with a virtual treasure trove of formative experience and guiding principles upon which to base a life of poverty, chastity, and obedience. I learned from her that we live and die for each other.
>
> You say to my heart, "Seek my face" and so it is your face I seek!
>
> This is verse 8 from Psalm 27, and whenever it comes up in the round of the Divine Office, I am reminded of that time in my life. I was curiously at peace with the prospect of [her] imminent death and totally, joyously alive in those moments of communion with her. I experienced a whole and holy sense of communion both with my beloved and dying partner and with the eternal Beloved with a capital "B." ... I knew I wanted more and more of that and opened myself to what I now recognize as the promptings of the Holy Spirit. Never had I been so open, and let me tell you that, in my experience, openness is the key to total happiness.[38]

Thus, for Sister Carol, the movement into celibacy was not to run from erotic intimacy, but to find it more deeply in celibate community with women, and especially in union with God. Which is to say, concepts of eroticism can be quite shallow if they only focus on genital/sexual encounters.

Sister Carol discloses that, "Never have I felt like I have given up something—only gained. I do not feel less whole as a person, that is to say, I do not feel less sexual. In my body I have a deeply rooted felt sense that my sexuality is simply flourishing.... With the poets I can sing the body electric and rejoice in the dearest freshness deep down things. For me, celibacy affords the openness to each and all which makes for kindness."[39] When described in this way, celibacy provides another route to express the love of the reign of God indiscriminately, with big, bold, and prodigal giving of oneself to others.

That celibacy does not indulge in genital relationships makes it no less erotic. Consider Sister Carol's words again: "With the poets I can sing the body electric and rejoice in the dearest freshness deep down things."[40] Someone cynical might be tempted to say that this experience of eroticism through celibacy is really just coded terms for a deficient sex life. But such a judgment is just as problematic as the heterosexual person telling the gay or lesbian person that they are incomplete because they do not experience heterosexual sex. Christians need to consider that the eroticism of celibacy provides a mode of living that does not artificially close off, shun, or shame the sexual dimensions of life. Rather, celibacy provides for an erotic bond of union between others and God that is far more expansive than genital relations.

To speak of celibacy as a metaphor for the eschatological life, therefore, is to imagine an experience of heaven that transcends genital relationships. That celibate heaven would not disparage genital relationships as bad, boring, or taxing. Rather, a celibate heaven would celebrate that heavenly bodies are capable of union with God and one another in far more transcendent intimate ways. To see the glory and goodness of God in celibate human relationships is to understand that God is immanently present through authentic relationships—especially those that are devoted to service of others, contemplation, and care for the collective. Celibacy, in this sense, opens a person up to as many embodied expressions of gospel love as promiscuity might, but it does so in a way that is not limited to physical sexuality, as it is (now) commonly experienced. In heaven, celibacy amplifies the "body electric" and makes every human or divine encounter a joyous one that enlivens and delights the entire body (in ways that orgasms might not rival). Thus to imagine a celibate heaven is to prioritize the sharing of deep love between people in ways that transcend genital sexual experiences, when sharing eternal life with God and the communion of saints.

This view of heaven might also inspire some to pursue celibacy in the here and now. Sister Carol Bernice offers one example. Others might feel led in the same direction. But "feeling led" seems to be the key here. Anyone might experiment with celibacy from time to time—and in truth, experimentation is sometimes an important way to figure what one really wants. However, if a person feels that celibacy is being forced on them, or if the experimentation with celibacy leads to frustration and a lack of electrifying erotic bonds with God and others, then celibacy may well not be for them. But for those who are called in the direction of celibacy, it can open up empowering ways for living in community, as well as manifesting the love of the reign of God on earth.

CONCLUSION

To say that celibacy, monogamy, and promiscuity all might work as eschatological metaphors is not to say that these are the only metaphors. There could be as many eschatological renderings for gender and sexuality as there are experiences of these on earth. Each would hold value for thinking not only about the quality of heaven, but also for matters of Christian ethics in the here and now. In fact, whatever one says about heaven has the capacity to shape values on earth. Thus, to say that celibacy, monogamy, and promiscuity are valid metaphors for heaven is also to say that each may have some insight for navigating sexual morality in the here and now. In the next two chapters, we will explore in what ways these visions of heaven might be embodied on earth. But we will also consider in what ways our seeking to live the life of heaven can be frustrated by the realities of our human limitations and complexities.

CHAPTER SIX

AN ESCHATOLOGICAL SEXUAL ETHIC, PART 1

The Gifts and Fragilities of Monogamy

> The soul wanders in the dark, until it finds love. And so, wherever our love goes, there we find our soul.
>
> —Mary Zimmerman, *Metamorphoses*

It was the theologian Hans Schwarz who said, "One can already experience heaven on earth when one finds happiness, does good things, and experiences joy in day-to-day life. But heaven on earth is only present in a form which can be misunderstood and is insufficient, since everything in this world is ambiguous."[1] These comments reflect a theological attitude that is present in many Christian communities. It is a spiritual orientation affirming that the reign of God is *already* here as a result of the coming of Christ and the presence of the Holy Spirit. Even so, it is *not yet* fully here in terms of the restoration of all things by divine grace and love. Therefore, when Christians seek to live on earth as it is in heaven it is largely with an expectation that real good can be achieved, but perhaps not perfect good. That perfect good is an eschatological hope. Nevertheless, it is a hope that can inform the here and now—even if Christians also tend to expect that the imperfections of earth will complicate everything.

A MORALITY OF ALREADY/NOT YET

The Christian recognition that some good is achievable on earth embraces the possibility of outlining a meaningful morality. But it does so without claiming to define or embody it perfectly. In many ways this resonates with the work of critical realists (recall from chapter 1), who seek to articulate practical moral goods, while at the same time recognizing the need for critical reflection on (and a revision of) all moral judgments. In Christianity, eschatology helps to both promote and humble moral claims. The vision of heaven can pull at the person of faith, inspiring a longing for true good and ultimate meaning. Even so, many Christians affirm the words attributed to the apostle Paul: that our vision of heaven is—in the here and now—one that we can only "see through a mirror, dimly." Thus, if the reign of God is 'already and not yet,' then visions of heaven can both affirm particular goods of this world and also motivate critiques—the kind that identify where heaven is not yet present. In this sense, eschatology can (and perhaps should) motivate people of faith to look with a critical eye on all established and conventional systems. If the world is not yet fully filled with goodness, and if sin (e.g., alienation, privilege, and prejudice) finds a way to corrupt human relationships and systems, then existing codes of morality also suffer from the effects of sin. In other words, everything is always in need of revision. That includes codes of sexual morality, too.

An eschatological perspective may be helpful in our attempt to review and critique existing codes of sexual ethics within Christianity. There are many ways of doing this. One eschatological approach (as seen in chapter 3) is to assert something like Augustine did: that there is no sexual activity in heaven because sex is only for procreation on earth. That assertion is one that some Christians see as the normative vision of heaven, and they hold to it with a sincere belief. But as Patricia Beattie Jung has argued, the theological assertion of a sexless heaven is not the only view. As she has explained it (see chapter 4), there are good theological reasons to believe that sexuality might continue in the eschatological life. In other words, Jung imagines that even if procreation does not continue in the eschatological life, humans will still be able to make love in the fully realized kingdom of God. That said, Jung comments,

> Whether . . . people will engage in coitus, fellatio, cunnilingus, genital rubbing, or the like, I care not to speculate. Whether men will ejaculate and women ovulate, again I care not to speculate. . . . Mine

is a claim about God's sanctification of and the potential sweetness of our sexual fires. What precise shape sexual desire will take and how we will come to such delights might well prove quite surprising, as is often the case even now.[2]

Some Christians may feel more comfortable with Jung's inclination that we need not be specific about what kind of sex may take place in heaven. But recall the story that started this book—the one about the rabbi making love to his wife while his apprentice hid under their bed to learn about the ways of sex. The apprentice needed to learn all of this because it would one day become a part of his own religious obligations within marriage. For the rabbi's apprentice, it wasn't enough to glean, generally, that something was going on in that bed above him. Therefore, he came out from under his rabbi's bed to be better informed. So, too, let's now think of Christian heaven in similar terms.

If sex in heaven is something even generally interesting to the Christian imagination, it might benefit our theological reflection to come out from hiding under the bed of heaven and see what could be going on; namely, it is possible to imagine a variety of sexual relations that are *metaphorically* emblematic of certain goods of heaven. Sexual metaphors for heaven dare to communicate what other material metaphors for heaven currently do—for example, streets of gold, feasting, and so forth. In other words, these material metaphors suggest that heaven will be a place of fulfillment, enjoyment, and extravagant welcome. Naming these metaphors is one way that Christians have sought to help bridge the gap between the ineffable (heaven) and the relatable (now). But as noted in the previous chapter, naming sexual metaphors for heaven does not at the same time seek to be predictive about what will be. It merely embraces heaven as an ideal state of being, and then seeks to describe (by approximation) what the joys and fulfillment of that ideal state might be like through relatable terms, including sexual ones.

Still, a question remains. Even if sexual metaphors for heaven are not predictive, can they nevertheless function to inform a Christian sexual ethic on earth? The answer, proposed here, is a qualified "yes." If there are good reasons for imagining a wide variety of sexual relations as emblematic of the goods of heaven, then those metaphors may speak to the pursuit of what is good on earth. The same is true of *any* metaphor for heaven. However, because the Christian imagination is captured by an "already/not yet" understanding of the reign of God, any sexual metaphor for heaven will be complicated by the "not yet" realities of earth. Because heaven is not yet fully on earth, even the best sexual descriptions of heaven will be incomplete (somehow) in the here and now. In the last chapter, *promiscuity, monogamy*, and *celibacy* were each named as noncompetitive sexual metaphors for heaven. It is time now to see if (and if so, how) those metaphors might be realized on earth, as guides for Christian ethics.

In this chapter, the reader is invited to consider an eschatological sexual ethic with respect to the gifts and fragilities of monogamy. The possibilities of promiscuity and celibacy will be discussed in the next chapter. Monogamy has long controlled Christian sexual ethics, so much so that it is often assumed rather than deliberated. An eschatological analysis of monogamy will allow the reader to consider why monogamy is indeed a good choice for some people. But it will also reveal that even the good of monogamy is complicated by the already/not yet realities of Christian eschatology. The effort here is to offer a realistic account of how monogamy might be pursued with excellence—and yet an admission that it will likely never be pursued perfectly. That is to say, even if Christians dare to name monogamy (and as it will be discussed later, promiscuity and celibacy) as a metaphor for heaven, we cannot expect that any ideal of heaven will be lived out perfectly on earth. Many Christians tend to demonize promiscuity, praise monogamy, and treat virginity and celibacy as spiritually pure states. Christian eschatology can disturb all of these typical Christian attitudes, thus revealing that there are certain sexual goods that Christians have been slow to name as well as imperfections with any model one might choose, including those that traditionally have been praised.

THE GIFT AND FRAGILITY OF MONOGAMY

"They lived happily ever after" is often the short epilogue given to stories about true love. In most cases, "happily ever after" refers to a life of love and devotion between two people who forsake all else in the bliss of monogamy and marriage. That is not just the sentiment of fairy tales and romantic comedies; it is also the goal of traditional Christian sexual ethics. In other words, traditional Christianity has long taught that monogamous marriage is the perfect state for lovers to inhabit if they wish to engage in genital acts of sex. Such lovers must, at the same time, be heterosexual and (historically) open to procreation.[3] However, Christian eschatology provides good reasons for critiquing marriage and sexual monogamy as *absolute* goods. Christian scripture itself suggests that marriage does not persist in the resurrection of the dead. In Matthew 22:23–46 and Luke 20:27–36, the gospel writers report Christ's assertion that in the resurrection, there is no marriage. Thus, even traditional Christianity has treated marriage as a temporal good and not as an eternal one. Most Christian communities have simply assumed that with the absence of marriage in heaven, sex will disappear as well. But that line of thinking requires a belief that sex should only occur in marriage, as a matter of theological and moral correctness. That assumption, however, has already been well critiqued by various Christian theologians and scholars of religion more generally. Marriage may be a place where sexual virtue can be practiced, but it is not the only location for sexual morality to be achieved. Monogamy, too, may be a good relational choice for many, but it in no way guarantees goodness in sexual relations. That is to say, the number of people a person has sex with is not, in itself, an indicator of moral goodness or perversity. Morality has to do with the quality of relationships, and not necessarily the quantity or configuration.

Nevertheless, in the last chapter it was argued that even if marriage does not persist in heaven, some version of monogamy might function well as a viable metaphor for the eschatological life. In this view, the monogamy of heaven is not a simple or crude rule about "only having sex with one person forever." Rather, the monogamy of heaven is a much more *qualitative* matter. There it would represent an intentional and mutually supportive relationship with another person, fully infused with grace. As such, the grace of heaven makes room for a person in their entirety: celebrating their strengths, filling in for their weaknesses, healing their wounds, forgiving their errors, and sustaining their flourishing forever. That's one way of imagining it. However, the monogamy of heaven as depicted by Christian scripture isn't so much between humans as it is between humans and God. Whether one draws on the eschatological imagery of the marriage between the Lamb and the Bride (Christ and the redeemed), or from other biblical descriptions of God's persistent love (as a spouse) for the people of God, the one monogamous relationship that endures in heaven is between God and humanity (with the one caveat that humanity functions as a collective whole—and that where God's love persists for each person, something like polyamory is yet another metaphor for heaven).

The image of eternal monogamy with God takes seriously the understanding that knowing and being known make up an ongoing experience that has no ending point. Heavenly monogamy with God reveals that relationships are about attending completely to one another. Moreover, the metaphor of monogamy between God and humanity suggests that in human relationships we can never know a person simply on the basis of a particular point in the relationship, but rather that relationships are ever changing. Relationships require us to be attentive to the beloved as they and we change with the passage of time (and eternity). What is more, the eschatological monogamy between God and humanity is an example that cannot be reduced to sexual imagery, even if sexual consummation can be imagined in the description of the marriage between Christ and the redeemed.

Arguably, the eschatological metaphor of monogamy can both challenge and reform the way in which monogamy is understood and practiced on earth. In truth, a problem with marriage and monogamy is that they can be practiced poorly—especially when they cause people to treat partners like possessions. When this happens, it is sure to create conflict. In other words, if something is "mine" and not "yours," then the afflictive emotions of jealousy and wrath can be easily aroused. That is especially true when it is perceived that "my" property is in danger of being "taken" by you. If this is the primary attitude that people bring to monogamy, it will be problematic.

At its best, monogamy represents a mutual and dynamic commitment between two people to love one another as a vocation. As a vocation, monogamy can be a lifelong study and celebration of human intimacy: physically, sexually, emotionally, and relationally. As the couple progresses through one stage of intimacy, they are bound to discover another, and still another—tending and savoring each new discovery shared together. Monogamy further provides a kind of companionship that not only delights in the good times, but is also a solid foundation upon which one finds stability and comfort during the many challenges of life. Monogamy, so defined, requires treating one's partner, not as property, but as a lifelong companion with whom to seek mutual love and flourishing. When *sexual monogamy* is included in that partnership, it is probably best understood as contributing to that couple's overall relational intimacy—even as it is also about the episodic enjoyment of human eroticism. Indeed, years of research affirm that it is not rigid sexual monogamy that allows a couple to flourish.[4] Rather, when a couple's sexual activity is reflective and expressive of their overall relational intimacy, it is then that sexual relations can contribute to their relational flourishing.

Nevertheless, no relationship is perfect. Couples can commit themselves to the kind of ideal monogamy described here, yet still struggle to achieve it. From a Christian eschatological perspective, this should be anticipated. We know that the love of heaven is not yet fully realized on earth. In truth, partners fail to realize the fullness of monogamy in many ways. For example, when partners commit to being an emotional support for one another, they still take on other friends as emotional mates. This is all well and good. But sometimes, and perhaps for complex reasons, a partner may find that they turn more toward a friend or a coworker than their partner or spouse at home. When that imbalance of emotional sharing reaches a threshold where it begins to harm the marriage or partnership, there can be pain and confusion. At the same time, such transgressions need not spell the end of the relationship. Couples seeking to heal such emotional imbalances are often able to talk about resetting some boundaries, recommitting to one another, forgiving past mistakes, and moving on with a renewed sense of relational commitment.

Likewise, people who have set a goal of sexual monogamy sometimes find themselves in complex situations that make imperfect the promise (or ideal) of monogamy that they had previously embraced. The already/not yet nature of Christian eschatology should seemingly prepare Christians for that reality too. And yet, in Christian communities, perfection in sexual relations is often demanded. When this happens, sex becomes remarkably stigmatized, or else it is treated as an idol on the altar of Christian perfectionism. Because sexual relations have so frequently been stigmatized (if not idolatrized), sexual mistakes are often taken to be less forgivable than emotional transgressions—or somehow more emblematic of a lack of love than of other problematic issues in the relationship.

When people make sex the *make-or-break* dynamic of a relationship, it is important to understand why. Some people do so not with an agenda to stigmatize sex, but rather to affirm how important sex is in terms of intimacy, trust, and love. Such a statement should be appreciated and felt deeply. Sex can indeed contribute to intimacy. Sex does require trust, especially if one is mindful of all of its potential consequences (both those that might make us better and those that do not). And sex can certainly be expressive of love. When sexual relationships are grounded in these concerns, any transgression of sexual monogamy is profoundly painful. The wounds of that transgression will go deep.

But there are also good reasons to investigate whether intimacy, trust, and love are really all that motivate challenging and complicated feelings in the face of infidelities. While it is true that love, sex, and intimacy are intentional connections that people can—and do—make, it is not true that such noble commitments are perfectly practiced. For example, a person who embraces the language of monogamous love and yet assumes the posture of owning their partner (and treating them like property) probably isn't reflecting the love of heaven. In fact, having a possessive attitude will very likely produce persistent problems in a relationship. *Belonging* to a partner is not the same thing as owning a partner. Belonging to another is about trust and dynamic fulfillment. It is not about having someone on a short and tight leash. To that end, if a sexual transgression occurs, the real pain of broken trust can be compounded with other emotions that the property-mind creates—for example, feelings of jealousy, possessiveness, and wrath. This can also motivate considerations of retaliation, which can (and often do) override efforts at restoration.

From a Christian eschatological perspective, jealousy and retaliation are not expressive of living on earth as it is in heaven. The only way to embrace jealousy and vengeance as heavenly goods is to interpret God as a retaliatory deity as depicted in doctrines of hell, or, as a supernatural being of small ego who experiences jealousy like so many humans do. Some Christians do, in fact, see God that way. Indeed, some people of faith will show us passages in scripture that describe God as being a jealous god—and therefore assume that if the vocabulary of divine jealousy is in the scriptures, then it must be a good thing. But such a view is a rather literal one (whether deployed by believers or skeptics). It avoids a more complex analysis of why the concept of divine jealousy might have been used in the ancient scriptures at all.[5] For example, the biblical language of God's jealousy may have more to do with exploring and establishing concepts of faithfulness, justice, and covenant and why these are important relational dynamics—not as literal claims to the emotional range of God.

The most generous Christian reading of God, which is arguably the hope of the gospel, is the one that understands God as above petty egoism, whose love is restorative and unconditional. With this God—and in the heaven this God sustains—jealousy and wrath (as afflictive and alienating emotions) have no place. If this is true, then jealousy and possessiveness are really frailties to overcome, not inclinations to indulge or to confuse with love. And yet, we live on earth and not fully in heaven. Here, we must learn to respond well to the pain of human frailties and transgressions—not only in life generally speaking, but in our partnerships and marriages too. How we do so might be improved upon from an eschatological perspective.

This perspective asserts that one's partner or spouse is someone who (just like you) is not yet living in the full grace of heaven. If they were fully graced, they could love you as you deserve to be loved—and you could do the same for them. In truth, all human relationships participate in the eschatological realities of the already/not yet. To that end, the belief that perfection is the starting place of monogamous relationships really has no place in Christian morality. Indeed, believing that perfection is both the starting place of relationships as well as that which must be sustained is surely going to lead to disappointment. From a Christian eschatological perspective, monogamous relationships on earth neither start nor finish with perfection. But what they can do is aim toward relational goods that provide for an increase in happiness and grace. At their earthly best, monogamous relationships are vocations that progressively increase in goodness and mutual care. But if they are relationships that *progressively* get better, that also means that in the here and now, these relationships will likely face any number of mistakes or finitudes: emotionally, relationally, financially, sexually, and/or socially. People will never know what kinds of struggle their relationship might face. But there will be struggles. There will be wounds. The reign of God is already and not yet—and that "not yet" is the hard part. To say so is not being pessimistic. Nor is to encourage people to stay in abusive relationships. The point here is that a Christian eschatological view requires us to evaluate intimate relationships in light of both human goodness and the human propensity to make mistakes.

That said, when couples make vows to sexual monogamy, it is a mutually affirmed *rule*. It is meant to shape and define the relationship. That commitment to monogamy often reflects multifaceted values, including love, romance, mutuality, boundaries, accountability, and trust. Keeping to these commitments allows monogamous couples to live with feelings of relational closeness and security. Monogamy allows a couple to focus on one another as a vocation of love. Thus, transgressing sexual monogamy is indeed a failure of a commitment—whether that commitment was made in a marriage ceremony or in quiet conversation between lovers. To be blunt, infidelity is an injustice if the agreement of monogamy was a noncoerced choice. But why does it happen? Why do so many studies show that so many people—including Christian couples—are incapable of keeping to the monogamous rule they once embraced? Why do otherwise good people find themselves in situations where sexual transgressions become a struggle? According to at least one study, approximately half of all monogamous relationships experience incidents of infidelity (of some kind, whether emotional, sexual, or both; sometimes these infidelities are revealed and sometimes they are kept private).[6] That number invites careful analysis.

Since this is a work of Christian ethics, the primary resources for exploring the gifts and fragilities of monogamy should not be the unbaptized attitudes of one's wider culture—like the unrealistic narratives of some romantic comedies, or the afflictive emotions of jealousy, vengeance, and wrath. Instead, a Christian exploration of monogamy and its limitations requires deploying the principles of the faith itself. While Christians will disagree about what should count as these principles, here they include gracefully confronting sinfulness, the hope of healing transformation, and the exercise of mercy. Such a Christian view takes seriously the pain and injustices of infidelities, but so too it also seeks to undo all sorts of deficiencies in traditional Christian sexual ethics. This includes dismantling the idolatry of sex, which when socialized or catechized produces a rather extreme reaction to sexual mistakes.

Clearly there are extremes to avoid here. On the one hand, carefully exploring why sexual infidelities occur is not an effort to justify bad behavior. People need to take seriously the idea that sex does matter. It's more than just the pursuit of bodily pleasure. As rational creatures, we situate all of our choices within some framework of what is ultimately worth seeking, navigating how the various pleasures (and pains) of life contribute to our flourishing or our frustration. These are moral concerns that reflect larger ethical frameworks. So how any of us approach the enjoyment of sex is important—recognizing that sexual mistakes can also become habits of vice if left unattended by careful reflection. On the other hand, the altar of Christian perfectionism has likely produced too many harsh judgments concerning issues of monogamy and infidelity, and those need to be critiqued as well.

The Christian view offered here is that a "one-size-fits-all" approach to sexual ethics is not very helpful, and that issues of confession and restoration are often quite complex. Sometimes there is great ambiguity when it comes to why people choose what they do. To draw on another Christian metaphor, sometimes the wheat and tares grow up together, making it difficult to distinguish between what should be harvested and what should be weeded.[7] Sometimes people pursue good things but do so at the wrong time, with the wrong people, or without adequate communication—not with an agenda to do wrong, but perhaps wishing to achieve some measure of imperfect happiness. A few lusty steps away from the road of promise and virtue may not seem like a grave error. But sometimes a few steps of error, when left uncorrected, can lead one to feel lost in a deep, dark woods.

Therefore, to explore the imperfections of monogamy will require straightforward conversation in order to attend to justice, but also compassion for the sake of mercy and restoration. The reader is encouraged to think carefully about one's own reaction to the cases presented. As we will find, transgressions of monogamy sometimes occur because people are not always able to see the difference between apparent good and actual good. When the mistake involves sex, feelings of shame, condemnation, and pain arise for a variety of reasons (sometimes out of genuine contrition, sometimes because of exposure, and sometimes because of the judgment of others). So, too, some people who are accustomed to making harsh moral judgments refuse to see genuine complexities in the lives of people who have made mistakes, sexual or otherwise. But as Christian eschatology articulates so well, all human relationships are instantiated in the here and now, within the already/not yet schema of the reign of God—and as such, relational mistakes should be anticipated (in some fashion). Such a statement is not meant to indulge pessimism, nor to encourage suspicion of loved ones. Rather, the Christian vision of the reign of God simply admits that the fullness of grace is not yet fully present. But even if it is not yet fully present, it is already here as people embody (even if imperfectly) the way of Christ and the values he advocated. What that means is that unrealistic standards of perfection—as well as vindictive attitudes of judgment—have no place within a Christian ethic. A Christian approach to analyzing relational mistakes embraces a both/and approach. Namely, we dare not excuse what is unjust (in our hearts or in argument); but neither can we fail to exercise compassion for the sake of healing the mistakes that can wound us.

Infidelities and Their Causes

Sin

So why do so many people wrestle with infidelity? One answer is that in the "already/not yet" realities of Christian eschatology, human sinfulness damages the integrity of our intimate relationships. From any number of Christian perspectives, categorizing infidelity as a sin will be widely affirmed. Sin is the state of being alienated from God, from one another, and from nature. However (and unfortunately), naming sin has often been a rhetorical strategy to demonize or condemn people in the totality of their being. Such a view of sin tends to produce anxiety and fear. It usually functions to alienate people in ways that have produced poor relationships, misunderstanding, prejudice, and even violence.

Due to the ways in which the rhetoric of sin has been used to demonize and alienate people, it is tempting to rid oneself of the concept. But within a Christian theological worldview, it is possible to speak of sin not as a nail to hammer, but rather as a wound to heal. In truth, Christians can reclaim the concept of sin without thinking of it as a matter of being utterly depraved. In particular, if sin is that which causes alienation, then sin represents things like selfishness, bad choices, carelessness, unreflective behavior, and hubris.

Sin might also be thought of as the complicated effects that ripple out from the bad choices of others—which can (and do) cause misunderstanding, hurt, envy, jealousy, impulsiveness, apathy, systematic injustices, and so forth. Sin, therefore, is many things. Sometimes it manifests itself in thoroughly bad choices to knowingly harm others. But it is also more complicated than that. Namely, sometimes sin can manifest in choices that aim toward some actual good, but falls short due to various contextual realities. So are sexual infidelities sinful? Yes; the breaking of mutual commitments can cause alienation and emotional harm. But are all infidelities the same? No; sometimes pain and complications in life cause people to seek comfort in ways that could otherwise be good but are not particularly good given the existing relational contexts. What is more, not every infidelity is a premeditated course of action pursued with villainous zeal, even if every infidelity manifests an injustice of some kind. And no, it would not be correct to label something like promiscuity or polyamory as sin when these are pursued intentionally and without commitments to monogamy. With these qualifications in mind, it is not judgmental to say that when a mutual monogamous promise is broken, something of sin is at play. But from a Christian perspective, if sexual infidelities are sins then they are also in need of grace and healing. That kind of a claim requires a little more explanation. In particular, it may be helpful for one's moral and theological education to reflect on various species of infidelities in order to know how best to respond to each case.

Concupiscence and Lust

To begin with, let's not complicate the obvious. Sometimes infidelities occur because human beings choose to sublimate reason to appetitive sensory inclinations. That's the formal way of saying that sometimes a person is so overwhelmed by sexual desire that any thought about what is actually good to pursue is jettisoned for what "seems to be good" in the moment. Some Christian theologians have called this the indulgence of *concupiscence*: allowing the arrow of sensory desire to guide one's decisions instead of keeping reason (especially faith-informed reason) as one's governor. In fact, some Christian theologians have understood that concupiscence is the result of the fall of humankind into sin: either designating sexual desire as the result of the fall, or, sexual desire as especially problematic because of humanity's fall from grace (recall chapter 3). But these are certainly not the only Christian views about sexual desire, or the best ones for that matter.

In particular, there is a difference between the experience of sexual desire itself and how human beings shape their responses to it. First, let's consider the experience of sexual desire generally speaking. For complex biological, psychological, and social reasons, a large number of human beings find certain other human beings really attractive, in a sexual sense. In these moments, people are not only having intellectual experiences of conscious attraction. There are objective bodily changes happening, too. This includes blood flow speeding up, sex organs swelling, heart rhythm increasing, and a rise in hormone-driven bodily feelings. Arguably, these natural bodily feelings aren't sinful—but rather, they are how human sexuality operates in order for anything else to happen. But when those feelings are experienced in the direction of someone who is not one's monogamous mate, the ways in which people respond to those attractions and sensations are important matters of sexual ethics.

Some Christians believe that experiencing sexual desire toward anyone who is not your spouse or significant other is innately wrong. In Christian ethics, *lust* is usually the name given to "disordered or inordinate sexual desires" (which, admittedly, are slippery concepts deployed by certain theologians, and then with various rhetorical strategies).[8] The perspective advocated here is that lust should not be defined as the experience of sexual desire itself (generally speaking). Doing so perpetuates the idea that sexual desire is somehow innately or especially problematic. That's precisely the kind of attitude that has malformed Christian thinking about sexual ethics for centuries. Rather, if we maintain lust as a category for Christian ethics, then we need to distinguish between sexual desire as a generally good thing and lustful experiences of it as the problematic (or sinful) instantiations to transform and heal. Admittedly, that kind of statement invites a number of critical questions. One question might be, what distinguishes some sexual desire as problematic (or a sinful instantiation) from sexual desire that is generally good? At bare minimum, the Christian law of unconditional love is a helpful arbiter. Namely, we can distinguish between sexual desires that are ordered toward mutual sexual expression and those that seek to exploit or harm others. In this sense, generally good sexual desires are experiences of sexual attraction towards others with whom basic requirements of mutuality and nonmalfeasance are possible. Lust, on the other hand, would certainly be represented by sexual desires that dehumanize others, or desires that intend malevolent harm. But lust might also be a kind of excess, for example, indulging a generally good sexual desire in ways that knowingly violate relational commitments.

Thus, when sexual attraction emerges, people have an active (and moral) choice to make: to indulge in that attraction or not. That human beings will experience sexual attraction to other people is likely a given. Commitments to monogamy do not shut off the sensory powers of sexual perception and attraction. Therefore, what people do with those attractions is a matter of morality. For example, the utter objectification of another person as a mere instrument for self-gratification would certainly not pass any test of Christian morality. Namely, finding someone sexually attractive does not negate the requirement of unconditional regard for that person.

Likewise, sometimes people are so moved by sexual desire (even without objectifying another person) that the apparent good of sexual satisfaction is pursued in transgression of a preestablished commitment to sexual monogamy. When that happens, sexual desire can transform into the lusty pursuit of sex with the wrong person at the wrong time and for the wrong reasons. That is not to say that feelings of sexual desire or the enjoyment of sex with many others are innately wrong. The moral challenge here is learning how to respond well to sexual desires, not only generally, but especially when other relational promises have been made. For example, experiencing a fantasy about someone who is not one's partner or spouse may be relatively harmless. Fantasies—as a matter of imagination—only become problematic when they are entirely objectifying, or when they disproportionately command our mental attention and harm the quality of our relational intimacy. That said, indulging an erotic fantasy by pursuing sexual relations in ways that transgress monogamous vows would more clearly be a violation of a partnership or marriage. As creatures with powers of sexual desire, capabilities of fantasy, and relational choices to make, we have much to negotiate in terms of sexual morality. Given that most people will experience sexual attractions for others who are not their partner or spouse, one's moral formation really can benefit from habits of virtue designed to guide people through such experiences.

Within a Christian ethic, one will not only need stable character traits to navigate such realities, but also the shaping power of neighborly love. The love of neighbor that Christ commanded bids people to consider what is in the best interest of human well-being, dignity, and mutual respect. The commandment to love is not only an earthly rule; it is also reflective of the life to come in the fullness of heaven. As applied to sexual ethics, this commandment encourages the Christian to see beyond the desires of the moment and expand their vision of care in a far more inclusive way. Namely, when a person wants to lead with love, it is necessary to pause and reflect on what is actually expressive of Christian love in a given situation. As a result, the commandment to love (and the reflective pause it generates) can help the Christian to apprehend that the sensory desires for sexual pleasure and fulfillment are but one set of goods among many. That is not to say that Christ's love commandment cannot be fulfilled in short-term sexual relationships. But when it comes to keeping to monogamous promises, the commandment to love reminds the Christian of one's long-term, meaningful commitments.

Likewise, the same commandment should be the resource that helps to heal when mistakes are made. Love seeks healing and restoration, not vengeance or destruction. That said, where lustful moments result in infidelity, the healing of Christian love may look different in each case of it. Whether infidelities are disclosed or not, all people involved need the healing power of love. Christian love is multifaceted here: it seeks to comfort and protect the offended. It seeks to renew the one who has transgressed. So, too, such love might be able to restore a relationship where trust has been broken. At other times love may look like a merciful separation if the memory of the violation creates only ongoing strife and division. The reader should consider, then, that there is a difference between extending forgiveness for lust and infidelity and the restoration of human relationships. In some cases, restoration may not come until the fullness of heaven is made known. One cannot underestimate how violations of monogamy can manifest profound human pain (in many forms). Likewise, we should not underestimate love's powerful potential to restore relationships. Indeed, in some cases love may help Christians to name and to heal the human failings borne of lust. One should not discount that a Christian response to the transgression of monogamy might somehow dare to include the words (and practice) of Jesus, who said to a woman apprehended for adultery: "Neither do I condemn you. Go on your way, and from now on do not sin again."[9]

Narcissism

Lust may indeed be a cause of infidelity, but it should also be said that there are some people who simply do not care about what they do or how what they do hurts others. Whether this is a matter of habituated selfishness or personality disorder, there is (arguably) a profound difference between those who are apathetic about their behaviors and those who struggle (morally, emotionally, and relationally) with lust and the choices they make in light of it. There is no need to deny that some people seem undisturbed by their own duplicity in their pursuit of pleasures or possessions. Such people are remarkably unmoved by anyone's concerns but their own. When they pursue infidelities, it is not with complex feelings of desire and remorse. Rather, such infidelities are pursued with what appears to be a pure lack of regard about their active lying, the potential harmful consequences, or the bad habits at play.

This is no caricature. Such selfishness and apathy toward others fit a range of characteristically narcissistic behaviors. One psychologist writes, "If you've been in a relationship with a narcissist, you're probably already aware of the characteristic behaviors associated with this personality type: The partner hogs the mirror, constantly asks for favors, and seems to care little about what you think."[10] When that narcissism expresses itself in sexuality, it includes "sexual entitlement (feeling that you deserve to have the kind of sex you want), lacking sexual empathy (failing to know what your partner wants), and being sexually exploitative (using people to satisfy your needs)."[11] Perhaps not surprisingly, psychologists have found that being a sexual narcissist "increases the likelihood that people will cheat on their partners."[12] For such a person, lies are told to cover other lies. This is done in order to maintain a lifestyle in which they can pursue their pleasures whenever they want, however they want—regardless of other relational commitments they have made. To be caught in their web of narcissism and lies can feel like hell. Many narcissists do not see the purpose of honesty or even compassion, because it is "their life, not yours." Such people are indeed in need of grace, but it may be of the redemptive and restorative kind that only heaven can bring.

Sex, Sociality, and Nonmonogamous Self-Discovery

However, in other cases, people sometimes struggle with infidelities for more complex reasons. For example, people may assume that monogamy is their only choice, or they are pressured into committing to monogamy out of veneration for tradition, or they yield to social expectations. In these cases, people may feel like there is no other option but to accept the dominant model of monogamy for sexual and romantic relationships. By way of comparison, a similar kind of social-moral suppression happened to many LGBTQ people in recent history, especially when it was not possible to be "out" without being condemned, marginalized, or even killed. For example, the archives of modern LGBTQ history reveal a rather common scenario of gay men taking wives, lesbians taking husbands, and transgender people hiding their identities from their cisgender partners as a matter of practicality when (and where) there simply were no other public options. And yet during these times (and in places yet today), queer people have found one another in order to have sexual encounters and romances outside of their socially prescribed "heterosexual" marriages.

Today, many people can look back with some compassion on these cases of infidelity, with comments like, "Well, what else could they do?" With more understanding about gender and sexual diversities, many people are now able to extend quite a bit of moral generosity to complicated sexual relationships of the past (or in other locations), especially where sexual orientation and gender identity were (or are) at play. For example, the 2005 Ang Lee film *Brokeback Mountain* explored precisely these social realities. The protagonists are two men who fall in love with each other but go on to have heterosexual marriages. The film captures the pain of their female spouses, but it also champions the plight of these men. The audience is made to feel quite a bit of remorse that the men could not be who they were because of the times and places where they were living. We are further made to feel that the characters truly did love one another in spite of committing infidelities against their wives.

In the same way that many LGBTQ people have had to navigate secret relationships, in cases where broader social understanding is not firmly in place, so too we need to consider that some people may drift from the monogamous norm for more complex reasons. At issue here is that a monogamous agreement may represent a cultural expectation rather than a deep personal commitment. It is not wise to dismiss how powerful the mechanisms of culture are in regard to the articulation of moral norms. In particular, it is probably very likely the case that a number of people adopt monogamy because it is the dominant cultural model. In many places, little space is provided to question that norm. Indeed, how many times in our moral education (from youth to adulthood) do we sit down to consider the strengths and weaknesses of monogamy in comparison to other relational configurations? Such an education would provide for an impressive opportunity for reflection in order to make empowered choices. Unfortunately, for many people, education about what they truly desire in sexual relationships is relegated to a curriculum of trials and errors, self-discoveries of delight, as well as mistakes that endure.

Monogamy should be a conscientious choice, not an assumed good. But making space for people to consider their options isn't always available. On the conveyer belt of life, it is understandable that people often adopt cultural norms (such as monogamy) and then assume that those norms will make them happy. Absent a real opportunity to think these things through, people who feel cajoled into "rule following" may privately have different preferences or values about sexual relationships. This possibility should encourage us to pause in our judgment about why people drift away from monogamy.

In some cases, it might be a faulty assumption to attribute it to an utter disregard for morality.

For example, as rational creatures we can (and do) value sex for a multiplicity of reasons. Yes, sex feels good. But it can also serve as a form of personal affirmation and social connection; a form of emotional relating and relaxation, and even an oasis from the struggles of the world. Monogamy steers two people to enjoy those sexual goods together—*but only together*—for a lifetime. However, it is not at all clear that sex need only be in such a setting to benefit from such goods. Recognizing that sexual pleasure can also facilitate positive social connections may be just one reason why some people may opt for more open relational configurations. In truth, human sexuality may have much to do with sociality and not exclusive romantic bonds.

As some anthropologists tell the story, the origins of humanity were not in a garden (per the story in the Book of Genesis), but rather in tribal communities as hunter-gatherers. Within this social context, sexual monogamy was (allegedly) unknown. Sex was shared for mutual pleasure and social cohesion. This also provided the utilitarian benefit of successful procreation. No child brought into the world in such a social context was ever parentless. In fact, the absence of sexual monogamy meant that every child belonged to every member of the tribe. At the same time, the positive procreative outcome wasn't the reason our ancient relatives were having sex. Unlike other animals, human beings have never required a mating season to get together. We're attracted by far more complex attractions and curiosities.[13]

Apparently, our ancient ancestors were better at accepting something that many modern folks cannot: *it feels good to touch each other.* And when you can enjoy one another, you're more likely to bond with that person. Imagine that happening, however, not just between two people, but between members of an entire tribe. Thus, if certain researchers are correct, human beings have not only enjoyed sex as a matter of desire and fulfillment, but also as a symbol of social solidarity.[14] In a similar way that human beings now hug, rub shoulders, shake hands, and kiss to show connection, our ancient ancestors may have shared genital pleasures. To that end, if the enjoyment of sex transcends sexual orientations—and, in fact, is part of how we express sociality—it may go a long way in explaining why people sometimes reach across the line of monogamy and touch other people. It could very well be thousands of years of inclination coursing through our human veins—an inclination to "reach out and touch someone" in order to show bonds of affection and mutual trust. That feeling is not sinful. But where people commit to sexual monogamy, the otherwise good inclination to have sex for sociality then represents a rupture of another promise that has been made.

Thus, perhaps before one assumes monogamy as their relational goal or takes formal vows to it, one's relational needs and goals should be discerned and explored with more honesty—including efforts to talk about monogamous and nonmonogamous arrangements in the wider public square. Unfortunately, attempts to talk about nonmonogamous sexual options have sometimes been shut down as "sick, immoral, or sinful," deferring instead to conventional scripts about monogamy. Monogamy can indeed be good. But where it is used as a tool to denigrate other possible options, it is no less offensive and rude than heterosexist attacks on those people who experience other forms of eroticism and relational love.

Thus, perhaps the reason why some people find themselves struggling to adhere to sexual monogamy is that monogamy isn't really the relational model that works best for them. Many people who are polyamorous or have open relationships report being very happy. The response to that might be, "Fine. Go be nonmonogamous with someone like that." And, indeed, maybe such people should. But how one comes to an awareness of their nonmonogamous orientation might very well be a difficult process, especially in a society that venerates monogamy as the model of moral purity. Surely there can be some generosity extended to people as they discover who they are and how they best flourish. We can do so while at the same time respecting the pain of those people whose trust has been transgressed. Those who have suffered from infidelities will tell us that the pain is indeed real; that the violation can be life altering; and that moving forward with broken trust is neither easy nor something to just "get over." Such pain should not be overlooked nor underappreciated. In truth, such pain can haunt a person for a lifetime—even as they try to heal and move on.

But sometimes pain is amplified by indulging false narratives. If there are, in fact, real, complex reasons why infidelities occur, then it benefits us to know them and to name them—even if that is a difficult dissection of a given relationship or incident of infidelity. Beyond the narcissist who cares little about the life and love of others, many human beings wrestle with infidelities for reasons that go beyond "not caring" or pure selfishness. One matter that Christian ethics has not yet adequately addressed is that there may be natural inclinations within human beings to draw on sex with others—many others—in order to build and sustain sociality. The existence of that inclination does not mean that monogamy should be dismissed as a good choice for many people. But it also means that some infidelities—and some nonmonogamous choices more generally—might stem from a deeply human need for connection, and not utter disregard for morality. Thus, while an infidelity remains a transgression because of an existing monogamous commitment, what sometimes motivates the desire for taking other sexual partners may not be sinful itself.

Falling in Love

What is more, sometimes people transgress sexual monogamy because they fall in love with someone else. When that happens, people are caught between even more complex forces of passion and commitments. However, this does not (necessarily) mean that a person no longer loves the partner or spouse with whom emotional and sexual monogamy was first claimed or assumed. Arguably, it is untrue that romantic love can only be felt for one person at a time. Many readers might dispute that claim. But we have to think about the experiences of humanity as a whole. For example, a person could live much of their life only knowing the love of one person—and as a result, believe that they are truly monogamous. But then the unexpected happens. For example, a new job takes you and your spouse to a new city, where you meet new people—and you find yourself falling in love with someone new. Or, as John Portmann has thoroughly discussed in his book, *The Ethics of Sex and Alzheimer's*, it very well could be the case that you fall in love with someone else while your partner or spouse (whom you also deeply love) can no longer recognize you, but lives on with a debilitating illness.[15]

Many people are socialized with the romantic narrative that it is only a matter of time until they find "the one"—and that this will be the only person they will love forever. That kind of socialization amounts to a false education in human relationships. For each of us, there are many people in this world that could be "the one." So when you meet one of them, it not only feels real, *it is real*. It only gets complicated if you meet more than one "one" at a time; or meet another "one" after having secured a relationship with someone else. This is not an effort to justify the infidelities or affairs that arise from the passion of romantic love. But it certainly aims to contribute some understanding to such painful realities. People are not villains just because they fall in love. Falling in love is a capacity of being human. We must learn how to respond to these emotions in ways that are both honest and just. Expecting people to do so perfectly is a tall order for such powerful emotions. Even so, people are capable of recognizing that feelings of romantic love do not obligate anyone to follow through with them, especially when doing so would amount to a transgression of existing relational commitments. Of course, it is easier for the one not experiencing those feelings to say so. Responding to these powerful emotions is something that requires fortitude—but it also requires grace. For many people, there are no dress rehearsals for the sudden or persisting feelings of love and attraction that show up at the wrong times in life. These feeling are not innately bad. But how people respond to them is important for the sake of relational justice and personal integrity.

Oddly enough, however, cultures that promote sexual monogamy sometimes have a penchant for celebrating stories of emotional and sexual infidelities—and do so as an indulgence of romantic fantasy. This too confuses our moral education and sends mixed messages about what we value about love and sex. For example, in the musical *Camelot* we watch with understanding (and maybe hope) as Sir Lancelot and Lady Guinevere work out their passion for one another, right under the nose of the king—Guinevere's husband. But if our partner or spouse were to do the same, there would be no adoring audiences telling us to try to understand. In real life, those "cheaters" get "kicked to the curb." *Camelot* also ends in devastation, but not without the approval of the audience with the understanding that Lancelot and Guinevere do love one another. *Camelot* is certainly not the only story to celebrate such dangerous love. We might also consider the tragically beautiful story depicted in the opera *Aida*. The Broadway iteration of this opera (which ran from 2000 to 2004) had audiences cheering on the star-crossed lovers, Radames and Aida—who are surely meant for one another, but whose relationship violated other marital plans and commitments.

If our partners or spouses admitted to the same, what would our response be? Can we cheer on Lancelot, Guinevere, Radames, and Aida while castigating and demonizing the "cheaters" in our lives? Clearly infidelities are complicated. Some of our enduring love stories have been trying to tell us this for a long time: in the tales of star-crossed lovers and sincere feelings of love even in the face of adultery. At the same time, there is no doubt that these infidelities are also painful and a breach of our confidence.

Sexual Addiction

Falling in love is not the only reason why people sometimes fall into infidelities. Sometimes the reason may be addiction or emotional desperation. In recent years, the psychiatric and psychological sciences have begun to address hypersexual disorder and those who struggle with sex addiction. That said, these classifications are works in progress. In other words, hypersexual disorder and sex addiction are professionally discussed as conditions that people live with, but they have not (as yet) been included as formal diagnoses in the most recent *Diagnostic and Statistical Manual of Mental Disorders (DSM-5)*.[16] Indeed, many specialists believe that more empirical study is needed before making hypersexual disorder or sex addiction formal classifications. But for those who believe it to be a real condition in need of treatment, symptoms of hypersexual disorder include:

> Sexual fantasies, urges, or behaviors [that] occur in response to dysphoric mood states (anxiety, depression, boredom, irritability) or stressful life events; [or] an individual engages in consistent but unsuccessful efforts to control or reduce their sexual fantasies, urges, or behaviors; [or] an individual engages in sexual behaviors while disregarding the potential for physical or emotional harm to self or others; [or] the frequency or intensity of sexual fantasies, urges, or behaviors cause significant personal distress or impairment.[17]

Of these symptoms, *emotional distress* and a *lack of control* are notable. These symptoms suggest that people who wrestle with hypersexual disorder have a psychological inability to exercise temperance in response to sexual urges. Thus, it is possible to say that such people may pursue multiple sexual relationships without intending to harm any other relationship of which they might be a part.

However, where hypersexual disorder is linked with depressive symptoms (as some research indicates is common), "people may avoid difficult emotions such as sadness or shame and seek temporary relief by engaging in sexual behavior."[18] The idea that people turn to sex to escape afflictive emotions is not new. Sex can provide a distraction from pain and stress. It can temporarily get our minds off of the problems we face. But when sex becomes a habituated coping mechanism, it can—according to some specialists—devolve into a form of psychological and emotional dysfunction.[19]

Why is all of this important? Mental health has long been stigmatized, and thus it is often treated as less important than matters having to do with physical health. Therefore, when we hear that some people may struggle with monogamy because of hypersexual disorder and sex addiction, there will likely be some who will only hear this as "an excuse" for bad behavior. No one is disputing that violating commitments and inflicting emotional and relational pain is, indeed, bad. But if hypersexual disorder and sex addiction are confirmed as legitimate mental health diagnoses, then the pain of hypersexual disorder and sex addiction needs to be treated, not demonized.

Emotional Desperation

Finally, there may be cases when people pursue sexual infidelities or affairs because of emotional desperation. For example, in some long-term relationships one of the spouses or partners may have shut themselves off from the other—emotionally, relationally, physically, or sexually. They may do so for complex reasons. The result is two very lonely people living parallel lives within the appearance of a shared domestic life. When that happens, the partner who has been shut out may try to give their mate the space and time they need to work through their issues. The partner or spouse who is shut out may be forgiving of the emotional and relational distance, even though such are transgressions of relational monogamy, too. But after a certain amount of such treatment, the partner who is trying to keep the relationship alive may find that they are so emotionally and relationally empty that they seek fulfillment and comfort in the arms of another. Such real-life tragedies find expression in some contemporary fiction. For example, they show up in one story line of the cinematic debut of *Sex and the City*. In it, the plot considers infidelity in the face of emotional distance between the married characters of Miranda and Steve. The viewers discover that Miranda has become emotionally and relationally distant to Steve—who eventually sleeps with another woman out of desperation for connection. At one of their therapy sessions, the following dialogue unfolds:

> *Miranda:* I don't know that I can trust that it won't happen again.
> *Therapist:* Steve, you're very quiet today.
> *Steve:* Miranda, I know I made it hard for you to trust me. But . . . you made it hard for me to trust you.
> *Miranda:* Me?!
> *Steve:* The way you treated me? And cut me out of your life like that? I mean, yeah, I broke a vow. But what about the other vows? Like promising to love someone for better or for worse. What about that? How do I know she's not going to punish me for the rest of my life?
> *Therapist:* You don't. And she doesn't know for sure that you won't have another indiscretion. All you can know is that you want to move forward and risk that the love you have for each other won't allow that to happen. And that's what we'll discover here.

Toward the end of the film, a resolution comes. Functioning as the narrator of the film, Carrie—one of the main characters—explains:

> *Carrie:* On the day of her decision deadline, true to form, Miranda had argued both sides of the case. [The scene shows Miranda, a lawyer, at a coffee shop mapping out a list of pros and cons about Steve on a legal notepad. She gets up and notices her reflection in the store window. Her cappuccino had left a milk mustache. She couldn't see that imperfection sitting there alone. The character realizes in this moment that as she sat litigating the strengths and weaknesses of another person, that she had many shortcomings and faults of her own.]
>
> *Carrie:* It suddenly dawned on Miranda that Steve's list might have had more cons than pros.

The scene then cuts to Miranda and Steve meeting on the Brooklyn Bridge, each forgiving the other and vowing to try again.[20]

Not every story will end this way—and some may find this vignette too sentimental or "Hollywood" to reflect reality. But the story does reveal how monogamy can fail on multiple levels, and further, that stigmatizing sexual mistakes over emotional mistakes may itself be a mistake. In the case of Miranda and Steve, both partners had transgressed the relationship: one emotionally and relationally, the other sexually. From their storyline we learn that when people are starving, they may very well eat from any plate. When they are thirsty, they may drink from any well. From the outside looking in, seeing a partner "cheat" (sexually) with another may look like a cardinal violation. But there are times when the transgression of sexual infidelity is the byproduct of emotional desperation, and not the cold-hearted calculations of a narcissist. To avoid this, or at least to work through it, many therapists report it is necessary to nurture the emotional connection in a relationship, upon which so much else rests or falls.[21]

Healing Relational Transgressions

There are many reasons why some people struggle with sexual monogamy. They can range from narcissism to poor self-esteem; from falling in love to indulging episodic concupiscence; and perhaps, even, to addiction. Understanding the reasons why infidelity happens is not an effort to endorse it. Nor is it to assume that everyone who "cheats" is a corrupt villain. When we look more closely at the causes of infidelity, there are multiple factors at play. In other words, character complexities of deficiency and excess can intersect with people's relational commitments, psychological dispositions, social intermingling, and erotic desires. Transgressions are bound to occur. We are fortunate if they do not.

The complexities of human character and the transgressions that arise from them can be situated within a narrative that makes sense of them. One narrative is offered by Christian eschatology. In particular, if it is true that the reign of God is not yet fully present, then there is nothing on earth—including our sexual relationships—that will not experience (in some way) the struggle and pain of sin. Sometimes that expresses itself in infidelities and affairs. At the same time, if the reign of God has indeed "already" arrived with the coming of Christ and the presence of the Holy Spirit, then there is also nothing on earth—including our sexual relationships—that cannot be redeemed by grace somehow.

Of course, sometimes the wounds of sexual infidelities are so great that it takes a lifetime for healing to come. In such cases, the reconciliation of particular relationships might not be possible on earth. Indeed, there are some things that only the fullness of heaven will be able to restore. We should be sensitive to that and not insist that every infidelity is just something to "get over." But it is also true that infidelity need not, in every case, be the reason why relationships die. If the Christian vision of the world as already/not yet is true, then couples who do choose monogamy may also choose to see any struggles with emotional and sexual monogamy as something to be worked out as part of their relational growth and as one part of the path of grace.

An eschatological vision allows Christians to admit that monogamy will not be perfect here. Even so, where imperfection exists, sexual partners can seek to manifest grace as an intentional effort to live on earth as it is (or will be) in heaven. What this means is that achieving forgiveness and reconciliation is often possible, even if it is difficult. Couples need not accept the narrative of sexual perfectionism that makes genital relations both the gold standard of faithfulness and the one unforgiveable sin. Instead of living on such a tightrope of anxiety and acrimony, couples can intentionally seek to live out their relational commitments while understanding that every bit of human life needs a safety net of grace—including their vocation toward love and intimacy.

The already/not yet expectation of Christian eschatology, therefore, softens rigid expectations of monogamy. This softening is not meant to discourage monogamy as a goal, but rather to acknowledge its fragility—and from it, to grow stronger. Too often, Christians treat sexual monogamy as unlike any other human experience. Perfection is expected of sex, while graciousness is granted toward emotional, relational, social, and spiritual needs for growth. That seems wrong. Eschatology reminds Christians that all aspects of life are in need of the grace of heaven. It is not yet fully present.

The suggestion, here, is that the eschatological image of the faithful relationship between God and humanity can be helpful, especially for couples who take on the vocation of monogamy. When we look to the eschatological horizon, we see that the relationship between God and humanity is not a story of earthly perfection rewarded with heavenly bliss. Instead, it is a story of a faithful return to one another in the face of (many) transgressions. It is a story of love besting vengeance and separation. It is a story of learning to see mistakes as wounds in need of healing, not evils in need of punishment and wrath. The monogamy of heaven isn't obsessed with sex as that which defines true belonging. Rather, the monogamy of heaven is an expression of loving faithfulness that defines and refines each and every part of the relationship—and it culminates in wholeness and peace.

To that end, Christian eschatology can encourage monogamous couples to ground relationships, not so much in perfection, but in a dedication to pursuing love, mutual support, and relational growth. This can be conceived as a matter of spiritual discipline. With practice, these disciplines can transform our understanding of romantic and domestic love. In particular, Christians might choose to model (with the grace of heaven) what it looks like to pursue human flourishing in monogamous loving relationships—while choosing to resist the afflictive emotions that arise from possessive and jealous attitudes. Without expecting perfection yet still seeking to honor boundaries and to cultivate genuine care for one another, couples might just find the meaning of unconditional love as they walk this path—choosing the gift of monogamy, so defined. Or, to say it more simply, perhaps the monogamy that should matter most is not sexual monogamy—even if that is important for many couples for a whole host of legitimate reasons—but instead, the mutual nurturing of genuine love and companionship that dynamic partnerships can (and do) provide.

CHAPTER SEVEN

AN ESCHATOLOGICAL SEXUAL ETHIC, PART 2

The Christian Possibilities of Promiscuity and Celibacy

... what we will be has not yet been revealed.

—*1 John 3:2*

In traditional Christian ethics, there has always been an approved alternative to monogamy—the path of celibacy. In fact, many formative church theologians in the early centuries of Christianity praised celibacy as a higher good than even monogamous marriage itself. What is more, in various sectors of Christianity today, there are purity movements that have continued to champion the cause of virginity and celibacy—even to the point where some Christians have advised couples not to kiss before marriage (though this kind of asceticism is by no means a majority view).[1]

Outside the domains of celibacy and monogamy, sexual expressions that are nonmarital, multipartnered, or even solo performances have largely been condemned. So, to suggest—as this book does—that promiscuity can function as a sexual metaphor for heaven, as well as an eschatological ethic for earth, is one that will likely be off-putting to any number of people. Some may dismiss the idea as the product of perversion and sin. If this is your reaction, don't turn away just yet.

Eschatology has a way of turning everything on its head and critiquing conventional models of living (recall from chapter 1 the example of 1 Corinthians 7 and its unique advice on marriage). It is possible, therefore, that even traditional ideas about sexual morality may be challenged by visions of the eschatological life. Remember, too, that traditional Christianity has long avoided sexual metaphors for heaven due to the influences of theologians like Augustine, who asserted that sexual relationships will cease in heaven because the procreative function of sex will no longer be necessary. And yet, a wide variety of Christians (both conservative and liberal) take issue with the procreative norm. Both conservative and liberal Christians have suggested that there are reasons other than procreation to have sex—they simply disagree about what they are. In the spirit of exploring how Christian sexual ethics might be articulated anew, this chapter considers how the sexual metaphor of promiscuity in heaven might be pursued on earth—including sex with friends, polyamory, and pornography as iconography of heaven. In turn, we will consider celibacy once again. In particular, we will look at the potential joys of a celibate life, as well as the problems of compulsory celibacy (especially the alleged connection between compulsory celibacy and sexual abuse). But as with monogamy, we will see that whatever goods promiscuity and celibacy might achieve, they will likely not be achieved with perfection on earth—given that the reign of God is not yet fully present in time, space, religious practice, or sex.

IT'S COMPLICATED: HOLY PROMISCUITY

As a matter of definition, promiscuity simply refers to having sex with more than one person. But the term has also (and often) been wielded as a statement of moral indictment—an indication of sin, being dirty, potentially diseased, and in need of moral reform. Christianity's moral and historic campaign against promiscuity is largely grounded in theologies of marriage and monogamy. These have emphasized the reproductive utility of sexual relations and promoted the assertion that monogamy is the prerequisite for any kind of sexual morality to be achieved.

But in chapter 5 it was suggested that promiscuity might function well as a sexual metaphor for heaven. In fact, it was suggested that sexual promiscuity is emblematic of something already present in the Christian imagination about God and human relationships—whether in this life or the life to come. In particular, the expression of God's love is prodigal and indiscriminate. God's love is prodigal in that it is excessive and overflowing. It does not consider what is deserved. It gives eternally of itself and delights in doing so. What is more, God's love is indiscriminate insofar as it is impartial and dares to intermingle with all, through all, and in all.

Admittedly, there are Christians who believe that God's love is reserved for only a few: either for the "elect" whom God has predestined to salvation or for those few who believe the right thing about Jesus and make it to the altar call on time. Those theological perspectives are, indeed, ways to interpret God's love. But if so, then God's love is very conditional, arbitrarily partial, and uniquely limited in its scope. If this is true, then the God of Christianity must be in the family tree of that old deity Zeus: the god who loves those who please him; the god who offers selective mercy to a fortunate few, while tormenting those who have dared to transgress him (or wounded his ego). But just because such an image of God exists does not mean that it must be emphasized or advanced as the best theological ideal within Christianity. Whether in the New Testament texts themselves or in the work of theologians, the vision of a wholly loving God has also been present in the Christian religion. If we choose the more generous view of God as the definitive vision, then God's love is for all, not just for a few.

That prodigal and indiscriminate love of God for humanity is, arguably, one part of what Christ's earthly ministry sought to demonstrate. Recall the words of Christian ethicist Laurel Schneider: "The narratives of Jesus of Nazareth suggest that the divinity which his flesh reveals is radically open to consorting with anyone. It follows no rules of respectability or governing morality in its pursuit of connection with others, many others.... This kind of excess of intimacy and disregard for propriety is the definition of promiscuity in sexual terms."[2]

Indeed, Jesus consorted with people of various cultures, gender identities, religious traditions, and a spectrum of many other characteristics: outcasts, the righteous, sinners, women and men, prostitutes, soldiers, religious teachers, tax collectors, government leaders, condemned prisoners, the wealthy and the poor, the ritually clean and the ritually unclean, young and old, disabled, arrogant, loving, ruthless, and kind. These are only a few of those with whom Jesus entered into relationship—and not just by word, but also with his body. He used his hands, his saliva, his arms, and his bosom to heal and to hold people. With his tongue and his mouth he held the air of the world and released words of liberation, while questioning power and privilege. He showed vulnerability with his body, as when he willfully removed his clothing to clean his friends' feet. He warmly received the presence of John the beloved disciple as he reclined next to Christ at the last supper. He welcomed a cleansing massage from a woman who used her hands, her tears, and her hair to clean his feet and anoint his body. He transformed forced vulnerability into a declaration of forgiveness when soldiers stripped him of his clothes and crucified his naked body on a wooden post. He was willing to let the fingers of Thomas penetrate the wounds in his side, his hands, and his feet. He cooked, and he multiplied loaves of bread and the flesh of fish to feed the hunger of thousands. He made wine overflow to keep a wedding party going. He instituted the eating and drinking of his body, in a new and sensual Eucharistic feast. So yes, Schneider is correct to claim that this is the "definition of promiscuity in sexual terms."[3]

To say that sexual promiscuity is emblematic of the love of God and the ministry of Christ is not also to say that Christ was sexually promiscuous, nor that God has commanded such kind of sexual relating. Rather, it is to look for how sexual relations might mimic and embody the qualities of God's love, Christ's ministry, and the reign of God itself. One instantiation of that could be promiscuity. But neither the number of sexual partners nor the configurations that sexual relationships take (e.g., solo, monogamous, promiscuous, etc.) in any way guarantees the morality or perversity of sexual relations. What matters is *how* these are pursued qualitatively, and why. Thus, to say that sexual promiscuity can be emblematic of God's love in the fullness of heaven is only to advance a metaphor—it is not a complete moral argument. Promiscuity can only be seen as holy and good if the quality with which it is pursued reflects the qualitative goods of the reign of God.

To that end, if Christians look to the eschatological horizon and use sexual metaphors for heaven—including promiscuity—then the quality of that sexual promiscuity must be directly shaped by the context of participating in the reign of God. In chapter 5, it was suggested that the promiscuity of heaven is indeed a matter of consorting with many, but there it was depicted as a demonstration of divine prodigal love. This prodigal love of heaven is characterized by extravagant welcome, wholeness, fulfillment, and the enjoyment of an abundant life. Thus, the promiscuous sex of heaven is emblematic of sharing oneself with others as an expression of healing, vulnerability, mutual pleasure, grace, solidarity, and love of humanity. However, the question for the here and now is whether any of that holy promiscuity of heaven can be practiced on earth.

Some Problems with Promiscuity

The first admission that needs to be made here is an obvious one. The "already/not yet" dynamic of Christian eschatology means that here on earth, sexual promiscuity will be just as complicated as any other sexual relationship. That Christians might dare to name promiscuity as a meaningful reflection of heaven is not also a statement that "anything goes." There are complications that come with promiscuity. That said, people will likely disagree about what we should and should not be concerned with—ranging from traditional critiques of promiscuity to more radical postures of moral relativism that embrace it. But we can bracket the concerns of both traditionalists and radicals and seek to talk about promiscuity more pragmatically. Namely, we can return to the admission that even if sexual promiscuity might be a valid eschatological metaphor, promiscuity cannot be practiced on earth with any kind of spiritual or moral perfection. Heaven is not yet fully here. There will be problems, and our experiences of life indicate what some of these problems really are. In the next several pages, the reader is invited to consider some of these problems and their significance to sexual ethics.

Boundaries and Prejudice

For some people, problems with promiscuity will include how to articulate sexual boundaries that are just and good. Honest disclosures about one's personal boundaries are important. To have boundaries is not to be rigidly inflexible when it comes to trying new things. But it does mean that people have various levels of comfort and vulnerability, which need to be respected. Boundaries may change over time. That can include matters pertaining to particular sex acts or configurations of sexual partnerships. But when seeking sex with many people, it is important to remember that each person is unique. Only honest conversation will allow all parties to respect each other's boundaries.

But to have honest conversations about boundaries requires an examination of the personal and social influences that inform people's sense of sexuality overall. For example, sometimes the matter of sexual boundaries concerns the people with whom sex is desired. On the one hand, that can be as simple as stating one's sexual orientation in relation to one's physical sex and gender identity. On the other hand, one's discrimination of sexual partners can sometimes take prejudiced turns. Consider social media platforms like Grindr, Tinder, Whiplr, and Down (to name a few). There, people create profiles that not only indicate what they are there for (friendship, networking, sex, etc.), but also the kind of people they are seeking. This is precisely where an interrogation of prejudice and sexual boundaries is important. Namely, while there is nothing inherently wrong with seeking short-term sexual partners (whether for the enjoyment of pleasure, fantasy, recreation, or the like), how people choose their short-term playmates can be infected by bigoted prejudice. In particular, there are many cases in which people confuse racism, body shaming, and patriarchal norms as valid markers for personal boundaries. For example, it is frequently reported that social apps for gay males are littered with phrases like, "No fats, no fems, no Asians, no Blacks." In fact, the clothier *Marek + Richard*—a company that markets primarily to gay men—still sells (as of this writing) a tank top that reads, "No Fats No Fems."[4]

Some will argue that this statement of prejudice is merely a statement of personal preference or a matter of natural attraction. But that defense confuses what are actually our natural inclinations with prejudices that are influenced by social values. It is important to recognize the difference.

Let's consider this point in more detail. In particular, there is (in fact) significant research indicating human sexuality is not merely a social construct, but rather has grounding in our biological makeup.[5] That's not just a matter of sexual orientation or gender identity. It also includes matters of innate attraction according to bodily symmetry, biochemical synchronicity, and so forth.[6] That, however, does not explain all of human sexuality. Our innate sexuality is informed (and complicated) by our rational and social capacities—and these are much more malleable in terms of how we come to value certain aesthetics or why we value some groups of people more than others.

For example, consider something basic, like aesthetic fads within our own lifetime. We tend to look back on fashion trends of ten, fifteen, and twenty years ago and wonder, "What were we thinking?" Back then social forces made us feel that some expressions of fashion (and thus attraction) were more valuable than others. Now consider something far more important. Namely, social forces can (and do) shape our malleable ideas about who is valuable as a sexual partner. To the point, so long as a dominant demographic group in a given culture continues to dominate and market sexuality, we should not be surprised to see prejudice infect social sexual values. Rampant sexism, classism, able-ism, racism, and body shaming are but a few contemporary examples. From a Christian perspective, we should identify this as sin. Indeed, the eschatological metaphor of promiscuity should challenge every bit of bigotry and prejudice in sexual relationships (whether those relationships are long or short term). In heaven, promiscuous sex is shared as a form of healing love and a celebration of humanity. As a result, eschatological sex cannot be infected by things like racism or body-hating. Rather, eschatological promiscuity is an opportunity to delight in the humanity of another, as an expression of eternal welcome and inclusion. As it has been mentioned, eschatological promiscuity is hardly obligatory. But when it is pursued, it is pursued as a meaningful expression of prodigal love.

There is no question that such heavenly promiscuity will not be practiced perfectly on earth. But neither should Christians confuse gross prejudice with mere "personal preference." Christian eschatology calls all human beings to confront their prejudices as sin and work toward healing them with divine love. What that looks like in practice involves not only discerning and naming one's prejudices, but also overcoming them through better human relationships. To do so requires challenging oneself to test and see what really comes from our natural inclinations (such as sexual orientation or gender identity), what preferences are truly just personal matters of aesthetics, and what portion of our preferences are, in fact, bigoted prejudices.

Sexual Health: Emotional and Psychological Well-Being

As we learn to reform and heal our prejudices, another topic that requires honest conversation is sexual health. Sexual health is inclusive of mental, emotional, and physical concerns. Consider, first, emotional well-being. As noted in the previous chapter on monogamy, there are some people who turn to sex in order to mask or medicate emotional pain. When this happens, the habitual use of sex to avoid emotional turmoil can potentially lead to psychological and emotional disorders. To that end, while turning to sex in order to soothe the troubles of life can sometimes be a fine thing to do, it can also be misused as much as food, alcohol, and drugs are. When this happens, it can hinder people's emotional and psychological well-being.

The emotional and psychological dimensions of human sexuality should not be underestimated. As we respond to our desires and emotions, we have the capacity to habituate to both virtues and vices. Thomas Aquinas, Diana Cates, and Martha Nussbaum are but a few of the theologians and scholars of religion who have made important cases for the rational illumination of our desires.[7] In particular, when it comes to sexual relationships, prudence and temperance are the virtues that help people to apprehend *what* is good to pursue, *when* to pursue it, and with *whom*.[8] When prudence and temperance are not firmly in place, vices of excess and deficiency can result in any number of consequences—including the bad emotional habits that can develop from regularly indulging desires without the light of reason. While it is beyond the scope of this book to make any sort of psychological diagnoses, the field of ethics does concern itself with the emotional life. In particular, habituated choices (whether good or bad) can also lead to the habituation of emotional states (to the extent that our emotions are malleable). Thus, emotional well-being does matter to moral analyses. To that end, a Christian ethic should not deny that pursuing promiscuity without prudence and temperance could very well lead to both bad decision making and undisciplined emotional states. That said, sometimes we may discover that our emotional and psychological lives are complicated by factors that require more than just moral analysis. In particular, one's emotional complexities may need aid from specialists in the psychological and psychiatric sciences. Should sexual relations be complicated by such factors of mental health, it would be imprudent to advise the pursuit of promiscuity without considering that things like addiction, hypersexual disorder, and any other afflictive condition may need treatment first.

Sexual Health and Well-Being: Pregnancy

Sexual health includes matters of *physical* well-being too. For half of the world's population, this especially concerns pregnancy during the reproductive years. Women bear a unique role in human reproduction. While fertile men contribute to reproduction through the brief act of intercourse and ejaculation, women are faced with forty weeks of physical and biochemical change, as well as the often harrowing experience of delivery. Thus, to talk about promiscuity without being mindful of the ways in which women's bodies are uniquely affected by frequent sexual activities would be irresponsible.

Recall, then, that if Christians create sexual metaphors for heaven it is to recognize that human sexuality is capable of expressing a wide variety of goods such as affirmation, love, grace, and healing—without at the same time aiming at (or being open to) reproduction. But seeking to achieve these goods through sexual relations in the here and now requires us to fully respect and guarantee women's agency. In other words, it requires that we trust women to make choices about their own reproductive health and goals.

Unfortunately, in places where access to contraception and reproductive choice are forbidden or diminished, the heavenly metaphor of promiscuity becomes difficult for many women to fully realize on earth. Arguably, when women are held back from actualizing their potential for manifesting heavenly goods, it is a sin against all women (and likely the product of patriarchy). In truth, many patriarchal cultures have only added insult to injury when it comes to women's liberty. Men have been responsible for heinous sexual violence against women yet then turn to assign blame to women for their experiences of sexual assault (e.g., "she was asking for it"). Men have participated as the progenitors of unwanted pregnancies while simultaneously denying women the right to protect themselves from unwanted sperm or to terminate unwanted pregnancies. Men have done so by holding disproportionate representation in positions of power—the same positions of power (whether of government or religion) that have denied women access to equal rights, contraception, and abortion.

Admittedly, certain Christians will recoil at the suggestion that contraception or abortion should be recognized as valid options within a Christian ethic. Their feelings about such things are real, but their outrage certainly demands vigorous interrogation. As a matter of historical fact, it is only recently that certain Christian churches began assigning personhood to fertilized eggs and embryos. This has not always been the belief among Christians—even among those we might call traditional. For example, theologians like Anselm, Augustine, and Aquinas all agreed that *personhood* requires the presence of a rational soul. All three theologians agreed that the rational soul is not infused in the body until there is enough of a human body there to receive it. (They disagreed on when that occurred.) Likewise, the oldest monotheistic statement on personhood can be found in traditional Judaism. There we find that personhood is not assigned until birth, when born infants take their first breath. Indeed, even Exodus 21:22–25 treats an injured and miscarried fetus as the property of its biological father, not as a person deserving retaliation under the ancient code of *lex talionis*, which is defined as "an eye for an eye and a life for a life."

What is more, the anticontraception positions of various Christians (whether medieval Catholics, early Protestants, or the modern Catholic Church) each represent a reading of human sexuality that subverts all sexual functions to the primacy of reproduction. But even traditionalists have revisited that narrow reading. For example, it is noteworthy that the Catholic Church explored changing their position on contraception in the 1960s, during the Second Vatican Council, and beginning with the leadership of Pope John XXIII. It was then that a theological commission was to be appointed to study the issue of contraception.[9] But with the death of Pope John XXIII, it was left to Pope Paul VI to assemble the commission and review their recommendations. It is reported that the commission largely concurred that certain forms of contraception would be permissible as a matter of prudence for married couples. Upon reflection of the commission's report, Pope Paul VI nevertheless rejected contraception as a licit option.[10] Even so, Pope Benedict XVI declared in 2010 that the use of contraception would be a "lesser evil" if sexual partners risked infecting one another with life-altering diseases. This statement caused some controversy. Some took it as a new permissive attitude of the church on contraception. The Vatican was quick to clarify and articulate the narrow scope of the pope's comments.[11] Meanwhile, in the early part of the twentieth century, Protestants freed themselves from the contraceptive ban. What is more, even in conservative Protestant traditions like the Southern Baptist Convention, the right to abortion was affirmed in the 1970s "for a variety of reasons," including the belief that "the government should play a limited role in the matter"—which is something one does not hear as often among self-professed conservative Protestants today.[12] So when certain Christians claim that either abortion or contraception are absolute moral evils according to the resources of the Christian faith, they most certainly claim too much.

Women's health and well-being must be an equal part of the Christian vision for sexual ethics. An eschatological view can empower Christians to do better on women's rights. When women are restricted from realizing the heavenly goods that sexual relations can embody, the agency of that restriction should be challenged. Where women's bodies are transgressed by violence and their reproductive health is controlled by outside forces, Christians should resist and promote healing and just communities. Health and well-being are gifts to be treasured; they are not superfluous luxuries. In the same vein, Christians should be concerned for the sexual health of all people, and this includes matters of infection and disease.

Sexual Health and Well-Being: Disease

While no sexually transmitted infection or disease should ever be stigmatized, it is not unfair to say that some people would prefer not to deal with their complications. This is true for any number of valid reasons. Perhaps chief among them is the fact that infection and disease have the potential to limit human relations. For example, people living with a common virus like genital herpes (an estimated one in six people) must not only experience the physical symptoms of the virus, but they also need to avoid sexual contact with people during outbreaks, in an effort to prevent the spread of the virus—even though the virus can spread at other times as well.[13] Limiting human contact due to a viral or bacterial infection is something that many people find interruptive of human connection and expressions of affection. This is not only true with sexually transmitted infections and diseases, but with many other sorts of infections and diseases as well. For example, when our friends and lovers have strep throat, we avoid sharing plates, cups, and kisses. If the same people contract MRSA and are hospitalized, visitation (if allowed) requires one to gown up and literally put up barriers to prevent human touch. In the pandemic era of COVID-19, people were commanded to stay home and avoid human contact. So it is not that the presence of bacteria and viruses make people "bad," it is that they complicate our ability to touch one another and connect as we normally would.

One response to sexual health concerns is to knowingly accept the risk of infection. In one sense this is the choice that many (if not most) people make, in a world in which some infections (especially viral ones) may not show any symptoms for years.[14] Such risks in sexual relations are not all that different from many of the other risks people take in their day-to-day life. For example, people now ride in cars and airplanes knowing that significant, life-changing harm might come from them (and sometimes does). In the face of that knowledge, many people decide to accept the risk in the interest of the benefits. The same is true with sexual relations. Just as we put on our seatbelts and outfit our cars with airbags, so too many people have access to prophylactics, testing, and treatment in order to pursue relatively safer sexual activities. Moreover, part of establishing informed consent involves asking any sexual partner about their sexual health.

When certain diagnoses of viruses or bacteria are known, people must approach choices about sexual relations from that knowledge. Sometimes people choose to avoid sexual relationships where such communicable diseases are present. However, in other cases, people may choose to pursue sexual relationships as one part of a personal or theological orientation of loving and accepting others just as they are.[15] This is a choice that needs to be considered within the context of Christian ethics.

Touching people who live with disease is one part of the Christian story. In particular, as Jesus exposed his flesh to people who had infectious diseases, so too there are many Christians who choose to do the same. This can take many forms, including medical work, social work, education, and personal care. It can also include sexual partnerships. When a person chooses not to let a sexual infection or disease dissuade them from sexual activity with another, it can be a work of love. As Jesus refused to let anyone be untouchable—thus bridging the social gap that disease can create—so too there are those who seek to bridge the same gap where sexual disease is present. Sometimes this is done with the aid of prophylactics like condoms and dental dams or with stimulants like sex toys. In other cases it might be through mutual sexual activities that express eroticism and intimacy but without flesh-on-flesh contact. Exhibitionism, voyeurism, and forms of masturbation prove to be very satisfying sexual connections for some people (regardless of health diagnoses).

However, sometimes sexual relations are pursued in ways that are open to the transmission of infection and disease. In these cases, the intent is to demonstrate loving solidarity with other human beings, such that infection is a secondary concern to the primacy of human connection and communion.[16] For example, in his book *Queering Christ*, Robert E. Goss shares how he and his partner chose to navigate sexual relations, knowing that one of them was HIV-positive and the other was HIV-negative.[17] Goss's description is a poignant one, which, arguably, incarnates the love experienced in the eschatological life.

Sexual Health and Well-Being: Staying Healthy

The choices people make with respect to sexual health are important. An ethic of risk is always at play. That said, it is not wrong for people to protect their health by avoiding infection and disease where possible. Admittedly, some people do so with a scrupulous attitude of moral perfectionism. Health, like all other things, can become an idol—or a false indicator of righteousness. Therefore, to obsess over health is certainly wrong—but to be careless with it is surely a deficiency. Between these two extremes we can choose to tend to health as a matter of stewardship. In particular, stewarding our health can be appreciated as treasuring the life we have and treating it as a precious gift.

To that end, we need to be careful about how we talk about sexual health and sexually transmitted diseases within the context of sexual ethics. Some people may choose to share sexual relations with others whose bodies may transfer infection or disease. That is not in itself a bad choice. Such decisions can be made intentionally and with honest communication between sexual partners. The reasons for those decisions will likely be very personal, differing on a case-by-case basis. Such choices will need to be made carefully. That someone is willing to risk infection in order to connect with another is surely an act of loving solidarity. However, such a choice does not also mean that people who risk infection will be mindless about transferring an infection or disease to others. This matter requires prudence, wisdom, and compassion.

That said, it is not snobbish or anti-Christian to seek to steward one's health by choosing practices that make sex safer. For some this will include knowing how best to use condoms, dental dams, and other prophylactics, which aim to keep people free of infection or disease. Having to think about such things is certainly part of the already/not yet dynamic of Christian living. In heaven, such concerns about health and well-being will not exist. On earth, they must be treated mindfully—without prejudice. Namely, one must not adopt a prejudiced attitude toward those living with sexually transmitted infections and diseases; nor should one adopt a prejudiced attitude toward those who seek to steward their health on earth.

Jesus did indeed bridge the social gap that disease so often brings. He did so with his body, boldly and without protection. But the narratives of Jesus also show that he was able to manifest healing for those so afflicted. There is no narrative of Jesus contracting a disease and showing how to live well with it, in solidarity with others. Only in his torture and death is Jesus shown to embody such vulnerable solidarity with mortality. That said, what the New Testament texts do show is that Jesus sometimes defended himself from physical harm. For example, according to some texts, Jesus found ways to slip through the crowd when his bodily integrity was at stake. In a similar way, some people may choose not to engage in sexual activities (at certain times or with certain people) so as to maintain the integrity of their body and their health. Perhaps they will change their mind another day or with other people. But the choice to remain infection free (as that is possible) is not in itself a form of disregard for those who do live with disease. Indeed, many people with an illness encourage their friends, lovers, and families to avoid contracting it.[18] What is more, sex is not the only route by which the love of heaven can be made known on the earth. To that end, it would be absurd to say that a failure to be completely promiscuous is somehow a failure of showing the love of God.

Thus, while a vision of promiscuity in heaven can reveal the delights of consorting with many others (sexually), one's earthly location reveals the problems of practicing promiscuity in the here and now. But nonetheless, the problems of earth do not mean that promiscuity cannot be pursued and enjoyed, some way and somehow. Indeed, there are a number of practical possibilities of embodying heavenly promiscuity that can be imagined and prudentially pursued. A few options that will be explored, next, are sex with friends, polyamory, and the production and use of pornography.

Promiscuity as Sex with Friends

First, let's consider sex with friends. In my book, *Sexual Virtue: An Approach to Contemporary Christian Ethics*, I suggested that friends might be the best people with whom to enjoy recreational sex. There, I wrote, "Friends are people with whom we have cultivated the habit of exercising mutual regard for one another's total well-being. Indeed, if the designation of 'friendship' means anything, it is that friends are people who do not intend to exploit, hurt, or use one another (selfishly). Thus, friends that can negotiate sexual relating toward the 'end' of recreation can do so in ways that avoid the pitfalls of hooking up."[19] The theologian and ethicist Mary Hunt has said something similar. She writes, "Friendship becomes the bedrock of all love relationships. It is a good foundation. It is articulated in a range of ways, including a range of erotic expressions. There is no reason to single out a sexual partnership as somehow qualitatively different from other friendships. Rather than separating sex as something one engages in with a lover, it is far healthier and safer to see friendship as the basis on which one engages in sex."[20] Admittedly, these comments represent relatively new ways of conceiving friendships and sexual ethics within a Christian context. However, if friendships can both facilitate the practice of sexual virtue and function as the bedrock for all expressions of love relationships (broadly conceived), then friendships might also provide good locations where the promiscuous sex of heaven can be incarnated upon earth.

At issue is the question of whether friends are actually able to enjoy genital sexual experiences together without a romantic context. This is difficult for some people to comprehend. When sex is equated with romance, the whole proposition of "sex with friends" will likely seem absurd, or perhaps a stealth agenda to transform friendships into romance. Such need not be the case. It is possible for friends to enjoy sex together without a romantic agenda. That said, sex between friends might signal the presence of some kind of physical attraction. But physical attractions do not, at the same time, necessarily translate into a secret desire to form an exclusive romantic relationship. Too often physical attraction has been mistaken for, or blanketed with, romantic love. This is not to say that physical attraction and romantic love are not sometimes simultaneous. They certainly can be. However, a person's physical or sexual attraction to a friend might represent any number of general attractions to physique, some kind of sexual partialism, or a fetish; alternately, it may simply reflect that some friends see each other as people who would be "fun" in the proverbial bed.

Sex with Friends: Experimentation

However, where immediate physical attraction is not present, sex between friends may nevertheless still happen. If so, it could signal that some human beings are capable of enjoying the sensual pleasures that our bodies provide. This can happen in episodes of experimentation, exploration, play, or emotional and physical release. For example, a number of friends might share sexual experiences with one another as a way of figuring out everything from sexual identity to how certain acts of sex feel or work. This is not just the domain of adolescent activity. For example, according to one study conducted by the National Science Foundation through the General Social Survey, same-sex experimentation in America has more than doubled among adult women (3.6 to 8.7 percent) and nearly doubled among adult men (4.5 to 8.2 percent).[21] It is unclear if such reported experimentation represented the actualization of innate homosexual or bisexual desire or rather represented experimentation as a matter of *heteroflexibility* (itself a fluid and contested term).[22] According to another study, 12 percent of *heterosexual* American adults admitted to experimenting with same-sex acts—which suggests that sexual performances do not always reveal sexual orientation or identity.[23]

That sexual experimentation happens is a given. But if we turn and ask the moral question about where experimental sex might best take place, "within friendships" is one viable answer. The alternative is to seek out sexual experimentation with people who are not really known, with whom trust is neither established nor guaranteed. That said, some people would prefer experimentation with strangers in order to retain some anonymity concerning erotic matters (about which they do not yet have confidence). However, sex with strangers for the sake of experimentation may carry with it more risks than benefits. Heaven is not yet fully on earth, and some episodes of experimentation with strangers may end up doing more harm than good, whether physically, emotionally, sexually, or psychologically. Sometimes it's best to obey the old adage, "Don't accept candy from strangers." At issue, specifically, is whether promiscuous sex with strangers could truly realize the heavenly goods of extravagant welcome and healing love. If the strangers that one is consorting with do not share the same intentions, the experiences of promiscuous sex (whether for experimentation, or anything else) may prove quite disappointing. That said, one should be careful not to assume that all anonymous encounters will be exploitative or wrong—rather, it is that the ethics of risk greatly increases in such scenarios.

Sex with Friends: Domestic Heaven on Earth

Beyond experimentation, sex with friends may simply be one more enjoyable way of embodying heaven on earth. Recall the idea of a domestic heaven. It entertains the notion that we will delight in our loved ones for all eternity. In heaven there will cease to be distance and departures that rob us of our closeness and love for one another. Translated into sexual terms, promiscuity among friends would allow people one way to mimic and enjoy the closeness and ecstasy of heaven and to prefigure what the pleasures of heaven will be like. In particular, if heaven is eternal welcome, comfort, love, solidarity, and fulfillment, sex with our friends on earth is one way for us to realize a bit of those heavenly goods now. Not only foreshadowing the pleasures of heaven, sex with friends can be grounded in earthly goods, too. Recall, for example, that our ancient hunter-gatherer ancestors may have shared their bodies as a sign of social bonding.[24] So, too, (in the here and now) friends can share their bodies as declarations of welcome, comfort, love, solidarity, and fulfillment. Christians can do so by looking not only to humanity's ancestral past, but also to the eschatological horizon where promiscuous sex is emblematic of these goods—and not necessarily signs of romantic interest.

The risk of developing a romantic interest is what worries many people. There is a rather common assumption (or fear) that sex between friends will turn into a romantic relationship. However, according to one study presented at the 2014 meeting of the Society for the Scientific Study of Sexuality, that's not entirely true.[25] In that study, 191 people were followed who were involved in a "friends with benefits" relationship.[26] After one year, only 15 percent of the group had transitioned to a romantic relationship.[27] In fact, those who *wanted* to evolve into a romantic relationship were the least successful of all the other documented outcomes. These other outcomes included 26 percent of the participants still functioning as friends with benefits and 28 percent who had gone back to being just friends.[28] Moreover, 31 percent of the participants no longer had any relationship.[29] Thus, 54 percent of those who enjoyed sexual friendships either continued with that arrangement or were successfully able to transition out of it when it was no longer desired.

Imagine, then, a Christian moral curriculum that actually celebrates the idea of sex with friends as a manifestation of a variety of moral and religious goods. In such a curriculum, sex with friends may not be a path that everyone takes, but neither would it be regarded as innately sinful or immoral. To encourage friends to enjoy sexual encounters with one another is to accept that genital sexual expressions are capable of communicating both earthly goods and heavenly ones. It is to know that touching and being touched are good for human beings—without a romantic context. Indeed, this view frees sex from the isolation of relational exclusivity and allows sexual experiences to manifest between many persons as consensually desired, with mutuality, and in various ways—expressing joy, delight, affirmation, and sometimes even healing.

What is more, sexual promiscuity between friends may liberate sexual relations from the rigid categories of sexuality and gender that are known today. This too may be difficult for some people to imagine. Many people can only conceive of sexual relationships (with friends or otherwise) according to their innate sexual orientation. That is understandable. However, in other cases, sex with friends might require nothing more than a mutual commitment to play and to explore the delights of eroticism. In the same way that friends can give one another pleasurable body massages—regardless of physical sex, sexual orientation, or gender identity—perhaps it will also be possible for some people to trade the pleasures of sex as a simple yet profound act of sharing. This is not to say that these friends are "making love" in the way we might imagine in romantic relationships. Instead, they are enjoying the mutuality of sexual pleasure toward other good ends. Recreation is one of them.[30] But so, too, are the basic goods of human connection, creating safe spaces for pleasurable activities and allowing a shared exploration of sexuality. If people choose to do so, it will not be as a perversion of their innate inclinations, but rather as an extension of their ability to manifest joy, affirmation, and radical welcome. If people choose not to share sex in this way, they are not necessarily deficient. They may simply enjoy manifesting moral and heavenly goods in other ways (sexual or not).

If this sounds unrealistic, that assumption may not be altogether accurate. Consider again the aforementioned statistics of those who identify as heteroflexible (i.e., those who are heterosexual by orientation but who sometimes enjoy sexual experiences with the same sex for physical pleasure). Consider also that there is a growing population of people who identify as bisexual. For them, the ability to engage in sex with many different kinds of people is simply part of who they are. As a matter of fact, one study has revealed that nearly half of all young adults (age thirty and under) in the United Kingdom do not identify as "100% heterosexual."[31] In the United States, one out of three young adults also report being on the bisexual spectrum.[32] And when we consider those people who identify as *demisexual* (emphasizing emotional attraction over physical attraction), *queer, nonbinary*, and so forth, what we find is a far more dynamic and complex field of sexuality and gender identity than what previous generations ever assumed. Thus, for a wide variety of people, sex with friends might be a very real possibility because of their innate inclinations, intentional choices, and/or emotional connections. Some gay and straight people may not feel that they have the same kind of range. But perhaps as human beings learn that sexual orientation and gender identity need not necessarily limit the way we touch one another, sexual performances may transcend identity, functioning more as a sign of earthly friendship and heavenly goods.

Admittedly, the refrain that promiscuous sex with friends can realize certain qualities of heaven will likely be met with a healthy dose of skepticism, sarcasm, or both. The proposition that sex in heaven can manifest among friends on earth might sound like a mere excuse to "play around," without consideration or consequence. Such an interpretation would impose an intention upon this argument that is simply not present. The vision of sexual promiscuity in heaven draws upon a sexual metaphor to express what many Christians sincerely believe about the eschatological life, namely, that heaven is a state of being in which there is abundance, fulfillment of life, prodigal love, and the intermingling of the redeemed—forever. Heaven reveals the reign of God in its fullness, as it also erases the silos of exclusivity that keep people apart.

Embodying that vision of heaven on earth will be meaningful for some people. Even so, there are many callings and many vocations within the Christian path. Not everyone lives in the same way nor values certain priorities equally. For example, there are some Christians who hear the call to poverty, social services, education, parenthood, and ministry. They follow these paths when other Christians do not. Indeed, the lifestyles of those who choose extreme work for the sake of gospel might strike other Christians as peculiar choices. The middle-class Christian family who enjoys life in the suburbs may not fully understand the choices of those who take vows of poverty. Something similar might be true when it comes to a sexual ethic borne of an eschatological imagination. Some people will find the vision of sex in heaven a helpful one, and in turn they may find ways to manifest the goods of heavenly sex on earth. Others may stick with more conventional scripts for sexual morality. That's fine. But just because some might find an eschatological sexual ethic odd, it doesn't mean that anyone should take the proposition of that ethic—or those who engage with it—as less than serious. To that end, pursuing promiscuity as a matter of sex with friends may not become a characteristic path for all Christians, but it certainly might be an ethic explored by some.

Promiscuity as Polyamory

As we think about sex with friends, we may be thinking about people who are not attached to anyone else romantically. However, sometimes people who are in romantic relationships also wish to pursue sexual relations with others, in addition to their partner or spouse. When this is the case, the promiscuous sex of heaven might also be incarnated in polyamory. *Polyamory* is a term that refers to having many loves. That might mean having many romantic loves, or it might mean having a particular person for romantic love but also sharing the love of eroticism and sexuality with (many) others. It is one way in which people navigate romantic relationships without at the same time committing to sexual monogamy.

The idea of polyamory is not new. In fact (generally speaking) it is the traditional model of domestic love within the Hebrew Scriptures. There we find that most of the male biblical characters not only have more than one wife but also have extramarital lovers with whom they consort for pleasure, procreation, or both. Plural wives, concubines, prostitutes, and other sexual consorts are not uncommon in the pages that tell the stories of Abraham, Isaac, Jacob, Moses, David, Solomon, and many other prophets and kings. But in many of these cases the constellation of sexual relationships are also expressions of polygamy—and specifically, *polygyny*. By definition, polygyny demands that one man functions as the husband, lover, and ruler over all of the women in his harem. Contemporary readers should immediately recognize the significant imbalance of gender equality. In biblical polygamy, women were not allowed to take multiple husbands or other sexual consorts. Nor do the texts demonstrate any awareness (or much representation) of gender and sexual diversities to challenge the patriarchal model. Nevertheless, polyamorous and open relationships (albeit in patriarchal forms) are right there in biblical texts.

Thus, when polyamory or open relationships are mentioned today, there really shouldn't be all that much surprise among Christian communities. They exist in the pages of their scriptures, even if in imperfect ways. Pointing this out will not be a revelation to most Christians. "It happened," we might be told, "but polygamy was in the past."[33] This is coded language for the assumption that monogamy is the prerequisite for any kind of good relationship today and for the practice of sexual virtue. But again, that assumption is a moral assertion, and one that has already been critiqued by decades of scholarship. There may be very good reasons why certain couples choose monogamy as part of their relational boundaries or as one of their relational goals. However, that choice does not override the moral proposition that open relationships can also achieve moral goods.

At the heart of polyamory is an agreement that the sharing of hearts or bodies (with many others) is not antithetical to the cultivation of a real relationship between two (or more) people. It is an agreement to recognize that emotional and erotic loves are ample and present all around us. Polyamory looks to these relational possibilities as goods to be enjoyed. This is not to say that polyamory is a mere free-for-all of sexual activity or emotional courtships. Because polyamory is predicated upon an agreement between lovers, the agreement functions as a statement of boundaries. But what those boundaries are will be different depending on the people participating in the polyamorous relationships.

With respect to sexual relations, polyamory frees people to embody both the earthly pleasures of eroticism and also some of the goods of heaven. Recall from chapter 2 that this was precisely the intention of the nineteenth-century Oneida Community in Upstate New York. For them, Christ's eradication of marriage in the eschatological life meant that sexual relations needed to be negotiated through some other social arrangement. And so, rather than seeing one another as mutual friends, with whom sexual relations might be shared episodically, they understood themselves to be married to each other in one polyamorous unit. They did so believing that it was incumbent upon them to live on earth as it is in heaven.

Arguably, this kind of commitment to mutually belong to one another—without being sexually exclusive—manifests the reign of God in sexual and social terms. In other words, the reign of God is not a loose assembly of individuals doing their own thing. Rather, the reign of God that is proclaimed in the New Testament (and envisioned in Christian heaven) is one that advances the importance of collectivity—of belonging together in an extended communal family. Consider just a few examples. In the Gospel of Mark, the reader finds that Jesus identifies participants of the reign of God as one family. Mark 3:32–35 reads this way, "A crowd was sitting around him; and they said to him, 'Your mother and your brothers and sisters are outside, asking for you.' And he replied, 'Who are my mother and my brothers?' And looking at those who sat around him, he said, "Here are my mother and my brothers! Whoever does the will of God is my brother and sister and mother."[34] Likewise, in Matthew 25:40, the text reads, "And the king will answer them, 'Truly I tell you, just as you did it to one of the least of these who are members of my family, you did it to me.'"[35] Or consider one description of an early Christian community found in the Book of Acts, which reads,

"All who believed were together and had all things in common; they would sell their possessions and goods and distribute the proceeds to all, as any had need. Day by day, they spent much time in the temple, they broke bread at home and ate their food with glad and generous hearts, praising God and having the goodwill of all the people."[36] In each of these passages, those who belong to the reign of God are described as a communal whole. They are not individuals who simply believed something similar, but rather people who were bound or committed to each other (many others) through their common effort to realize the reign of God on earth. The same kind of dynamic community is projected into heaven. In the New Testament, we read that the redeemed are collectively the bride of Christ; it is a communion of saints who dwell in eternal happiness with God and one another for eternity.

To that end, polyamory is well poised to realize the reign of God in its own commitments to mutual belonging within loving constellations. These constellations represent people in dynamic relationships, where sexual relations are seen as renewable and sharable resources. In this realization, polyamorous people can be seen as expressing the prodigal love, mutual belonging, and radical welcome that heaven will bring.

Promiscuity as Pornography

As people negotiate polyamory and sex with friends, another possible expression of heavenly promiscuity might be found in pornography. That proposition is not something one might expect to find within an argument of Christian ethics. The word itself—pornography—is a compound word of two Greek terms, *porneia*, which means "sexual immorality," and *graphia*, which means to "write or depict." Thus, as a compound word, *pornography* means "a depiction of sexual immorality." If we take that term literally, then it would not be possible to see heaven in anything that is a depiction of actual immorality. But if we take the term in its current cultural usage, especially as it is used to mean the depiction of explicit sexual relations, then it might be possible to see some instances of pornography as iconography of heavenly sex. But that claim will require some explanation.

First, there is no question that much of what is called pornography today is very likely a depiction of sexual immorality. For example, the production and distribution of rape fantasies, child pornography, and bestiality all promote sexual encounters in which consent is either robbed of another person, grossly inadequate, or entirely not possible. While concepts of consent are more complex than the standard of "enthusiastic consent," as the queer theorist Joseph Fischel has argued, the pain that comes from its utter absence is well known by anyone who has suffered sexual assault, rape, or stalking.[37] To be concerned about consent is really a moral effort to promote equal regard and bodily integrity. Thus, to see the absence of consent scripted in media that is purposefully designed to sexually arouse its consumers is a serious moral matter. If people are sexually aroused by material that robs characters of their consent, there are good reasons to interrogate both their morality and the psychological mechanisms that allow them to enjoy such scenarios (and certainly there are critical questions to ask of those who produce such forms of pornography).

What is more, it has been argued by a number of feminist theorists that much of pornography that is produced and marketed for heterosexual men often distorts and diminishes the respectability of women and downplays their equality. Helen Longino provides commentary in this vein. Longino distinguishes between sexually explicit material that is pornography and sexually explicit material that is erotica. She writes:

> A representation of a sexual encounter which is not characterized by mutual respect, in which at least one of the parties is treated in a manner beneath her or his dignity as a human being, is no longer simple erotica. That a representation is of a degrading behavior does not in itself, however, make it pornographic. Whether or not it is pornographic is a function of contextual features. Books and films may contain descriptions or representations of rape in order to explore the consequences of such an assault upon its victim. What is being shown is abusive or degrading behavior which attempts to deny the humanity and dignity of the person assaulted, yet the context surrounding the representation, through its exploration of the consequences of the act, acknowledges and reaffirms her dignity. Such books and films, far from being pornographic, are (or can be) highly moral, and fall into the category of moral realism.
>
> What makes a work of pornography, then, is not simply its representation of degrading and abusive sexual encounters, but its implicit, if not explicit, approval and recommendation of sexual behavior that is immoral, i.e., that physically or psychologically violates the personhood of one of the participants. Pornography, then, is verbal or pictorial material which represents or describes sexual behavior that is degrading or abusive to one or more of the

participants in such a way as to endorse the degradation. The participants so treated in virtually all heterosexual pornography are women or children, so heterosexual pornography is, as a matter of fact, material which endorses sexual behavior that is degrading and/or abusive to women and children.[38]

By these comments Longino is not saying that all forms of sexually explicit material are immoral. Rather, she means only *pornographic* material, so defined. Any other kind of sexually explicit material (designed to arouse) is morally acceptable, and Longino categories it as *erotica*.

Thus, for Longino, the problem with pornography is not only in what it depicts, but also the skewed moral education it promotes. She writes, "Pornography, by its very nature, requires that women be subordinate to men and mere instruments for the fulfillment of male fantasies. To accomplish this, pornography must lie."[39] In particular, pornography (as so defined) lies about the inequality of women to men. It lies about women being objects for men's self-gratification. It lies about what the fulfillment of sexual desire looks like in relation to matters of mutuality and respect. For Longino, then (and many other feminist theorists as well), the sexism and misogyny present in pornographic material does nothing less than distort human sexuality in general, and women specifically.

That concern is an important one. However, it is also important not to read that concern as being sex-negative or prudish. Longino represents a point of view that more than accommodates the enjoyment of sexual material that is simultaneously explicit, arousing, and not degrading toward human beings (even if we have to recognize that "degrading" can be a slippery term). However, one small problem with her argument, it would seem, is a linguistic one. In many cultures, people are so accustomed to associating terms like "porn" and "pornography" with "sexually explicit" that it is easy to read comments like Longino's and suppose that she (and others) are condemning all sexually explicit material. That is simply not the case. Public discussions about sexually explicit material would certainly benefit from being as clear as Longino is in her separation of erotica and pornography. But so long as people might mistake the terminology, we will continue to draw on the word *pornography*, here, to mean sexually explicit material in general, with the recognition that there is much of it that is objectionable.

Indeed, still another concern with pornography has to do with how video production offices treat the performers themselves. Fair pay, sexual health screening, fulfilling contracts, performer willingness, and fair treatment are all issues that directly affect the real lives of those who enact sexual fantasies on screen. Consider just a few comments of those who have served in the industry and now have a negative view of it. For example, Vanessa Belmond has disclosed, "Like most porn performers, I perpetuated this lie. One of my favorite things to say when asked if I liked doing a particular scene was, 'I only do what I like! I wouldn't do it if I didn't like it!' (I would say this with a big fake smile and giggle.) What a total lie! I did what I had to do to get 'work' in porn. I did what I knew would help me gain 'fame' in the industry."[40] Another female performer reported, "It was the most degrading, embarrassing, horrible thing ever. I had to shoot an interactive DVD, which takes hours of shooting time, with a 104 degree fever! I was crying and wanted to leave but my agent wouldn't let me, he said he couldn't let me flake on it."[41] Still another reported, "The abuse and degradation was rough. I sweated and was in deep pain. On top of the horrifying experience, my whole body ached, and I was irritable the whole day. The director didn't really care how I felt; he only wanted to finish the video."[42]

Some male performers also report injustices behind the scenes. One said,

> I barely had money to feed myself and I wanted to stay in Los Angeles and look for a job. Then I was on Grindr, the gay networking app on phones, and a guy mentioned that he was a 'model scout' for porn. He talked me into coming over and taking pictures because he said I only had to do videos where I performed solo in front of the camera and there would be no one else. It seemed like the easy cash that I needed. Eventually, those videos moved into videos with other men.... The man who was my "model scout" began to require me to have sex with him in order to continue to get me more work. I felt like a sex slave![43]

Another reported, "Once, I was in a scene with a girl while three different guys had sex with her, and she vomited all over us. [The producers] still wanted us to keep going at it while she was limp and fainting. The director wanted the money shot or he would have to call us all back for another day. 'Do it or don't get paid.' That's the mentality of the porn industry.'"[44]

To say that these comments reflect the experience of every performer would be an overstatement. But there is no reason to deny that even if what is depicted on the screen passes the test of mutual regard and respect for one's personhood, it may be the case that injustices are taking place in its creation. Thus, the consumption of pornography not only requires a discerning eye toward the scenarios depicted, but the creation of the material itself. In a world in which we are increasingly concerned about the labor conditions of any number of industries, that we should include adult entertainment within our moral concern is hardly a repressive attitude to adopt.

What is more, it has been argued by some that the consumption of pornography can lead to sexual dysfunction. This is a concern that Patricia Beattie Jung articulates in her reflections on eschatology and sexual ethics. For her, the vision of heavenly sex is not represented in pornography. Indeed, Jung is concerned that those who consume pornography may be fostering an addiction that wounds their ability to participate in real-life sexual partnerships. Jung writes, "The central promise of porn is that it will spark sexual desire and in the end lead to sexual pleasure.... [But] those who develop a sex arousal addiction in response to their internet porn use—and this is a sizeable minority of viewers—will eventually experience a drop in their libido, followed by erectile dysfunction in men and a numbing of desire in women."[45]

There does appear to be some empirical information to back this claim. Jung cites the work of Joyce Ann Mercer, who explains, "When viewing internet pornography, 'dopamine rapidly and continually floods the brain,' effectively rewiring its reward circuit. Habituated to this flood of dopamine, porn use (this trigger) then becomes requisite for any experience of desire and its pleasures. For those who become addicted to internet porn, arousal requires an ever greater volume of, and constantly intensifying, sexually explicit imagery. No merely human sexual encounter can produce what technology has made requisite. Thus internet porn addicts frequently suffer [erectile dysfunction] and loss of desire."[46]

Jung is not only concerned with the physiological effects of porn addiction. She is also concerned that the narrative of pornography provides a false moral education about honest communication in sexual relations. She writes, "Pornographic fantasies do not eroticize the good communication about sex requisite for sharing pleasure. On the contrary they teach that there is no need for sexual partners to pay close attention to whether they are sharing pleasures with each other and/or to interrogate their sexual encounters. The message they send is that there is no need to communicate, that is, to speak about one's own and to attend to one's partner's sexual preferences."[47] Because of this, Jung believes that (in addition to addiction and loss of desire) the use of pornography in one's sex life will have an overall negative effect. Jung's parting comment on this issue is an important one, "People called to embody sex on earth as it might well be in heaven need to ask whether what they use to stimulate their sexual desire fosters both intimacy and respect for human dignity."[48]

Where porn addiction fosters a loss of libido and a breakdown of human relationships Christians have every reason to agree with Jung that pornography can be a problem. But just because a medium can be a problem doesn't mean that's always the case. Sex itself can become an addiction if not navigated mindfully. Yet the risk of sex addiction does not lead us to denounce sex itself. That much is obvious. Thus, if we allow the concern for addiction to arouse a moral panic about pornography as a whole, or to categorically reject it, then we might be indulging a legitimate concern to unsubstantiated ends.

For example, one reason why some people struggle with pornography is due to sexual shame inflicted by religious concerns. Psychologist David Ley notes, "Sexual shame is not solely a religious issue, but it is in the religious communities where we are now seeing this problem reach epidemic levels. Atheists who watch porn rarely report concerns or problems with it, while the strength of a person's religious beliefs and moral condemnation of porn, predicts that they will feel addicted to porn, regardless of how little they watch."[49]

Consider that claim closely. A person who experiences sexual shame for religious reasons is more likely to think that they have a problem with pornography because they enjoy it. If we were to confuse that kind of a person with someone who was actually addicted to pornography, we might be apt to think that pornography (i.e., sexually explicit material) should be wholly eradicated. But if it is really a scrupulous or sex-negative education that is causing many religious people to feel such shame about pornography, then we need to relearn how to view and enjoy sexually explicit material. If we do not, we may very well be contributing to (or sustaining) unneeded anxiety and suffering. Ley's insights on this bear repeating. "Sadly, when people within religious communities seek help for their sexual concerns, they are most often told to suppress or 'battle' their sexuality, or sent to pseudotreatments such as sex or porn addiction programs, where their desires are portrayed as a form of sickness. Shame creates a feedback loop of pain, fear, dysfunction, and self-hatred, which is the true root of most sexual problems."[50]

We need not deny that some pornography is indeed immoral. Shame might be the appropriate response to some sexually explicit depictions—such as rape scenes, and those that denigrate people through sexist, misogynistic, transphobic, and homophobic acts (and there are other examples). But if pornography is not all immoral, then we need some kind of criteria to know what of it is good—especially within a Christian sexual ethic. Here, the eschatological vision of promiscuity comes back into play. The metaphor of heavenly promiscuity means to communicate the radical welcome, prodigal love, and total fulfillment that the eschatological life will provide. Some forms of promiscuity on earth (e.g., sex with friends and polyamorous relationships) have the potential to mimic and embody aspects of these heavenly goods. Likewise, it may also be true that some forms of pornography could capture the vision of heavenly promiscuity. In other words, just as some Christian traditions believe that icons and iconography function as windows to heaven, so too some instances of pornography may do the same.

It would seem that such material already exists. For example, one erotic website that seeks to transcend some of the usual problems with pornography is Himeros.tv, a website that was created for gay men as an effort to help them connect with their sexuality. The website offers one telling description. "Most of us learn about gay sex from the porn we watch, but porn isn't created to teach you about pleasure, connection or the power of your sexuality."[51] The founder of the website speaks to this concern in more detail. Consider a few of his representative comments:

> We work on the videos with a team of sex coaches, tantric instructors and sex educators so that you take something from each and every video.
> As gay men, we're having a lot of sex. But how much of that sex is truly great? How much of it is connected? How much of it is ecstatic? If we're honest with ourselves, there is probably a lot of room for improvement....
> I don't think there's anything prudish about demanding consent and respect for your body.
> Porn is arousing. But Himeros.tv has a different intention. Instead of getting you off, it's about getting you in touch with your body, in touch with connection and intimacy, in touch with your desires and the expression thereof.
> ... I want [people] to see a reflection of themselves.... To accomplish that, we have been working with models of all ages, from 18 to 83. [For example] we were excited to find Norm, a sexually ecstatic 83-year-old who came out later in life, through one of our connections in Asheville, North Carolina. We were even more excited when he said YES, that he wanted to film with us. I don't think I've ever seen an 83-year-old in gay erotic content. And I definitely haven't seen 83-year-old men depicted as sexually alive, beautiful and empowered.[52]

When one considers the language with which the founder of Himeros.tv describes his pornographic website, it is with all of the moral (and spiritual) concerns that Longino, Jung, and others have expressed about the pitfalls of pornography. What this website offers, then, is a challenge to the claim that pornography is only about breaking down human connections, or the pursuit of selfish gratification. To the contrary, this website purports to offer a new kind of moral education about eroticism—one that attends to human connection, honest communication, and truth telling about the expressions of eroticism in an array of men's lives. In this, we might very well see iconography of sex in heaven.

This website is not an isolated case. For example, in recent years there has been a rise in pornography made for women by women. Consider the work of Anna Arrowsmith. She has been working on pornography as both a visual and intellectual endeavor. Arrowsmith holds a BA in fine art from Central St. Martins School of Art in London, and a PhD in the field of gender studies from Sussex University. Her bachelor's dissertation, *Towards a New Pornography*, "analyzed what a female perspective on porn would look like," while recognizing that pornography remained "a genre that was largely undeveloped and unexplored by female filmmakers."[53] While seeking to create better pornography for women, Arrowsmith is an ardent critic of censorship, who argues that "censorship only proves to change the direction of the censored thoughts, not eliminate them."[54] She further believes that "to sexually objectify, that is to fleetingly view a person's sexual attractiveness separately from their personality/person, is a natural human experience, not just a male one, as traditionally depicted."[55]

What concerns Arrowsmith about pornography is the sexist orientation that it can take. She writes, "The porn industry, I believe, is still largely sexist in that the male perspective (as in almost any other genre) is prioritized over the female. The female erotic gaze remains significantly underexplored."[56] However in one exchange of comments, Gail Dines criticized Arrowsmith, claiming, "Women who work in the sex industry and promote this in the name of feminism are the scabs of the feminist movement. I think you are an apologist, and selling women out."[57] Arrowsmith responded directly, arguing, "I'm not an apologist. I'm here because women want sexuality to be represented. If you hand over all sexual imagery to men, you hand over that power. I'm not saying all pornography is positive to women, but the only way you are going to change that is from working with the images themselves."[58]

Indeed, Arrowsmith not only seeks to change the way pornography is created and consumed, she has also worked to create safer work environments for adult performers. In 2011 she created the WeConsent.org website, which "promotes and campaigns on behalf of people who work in the erotic industries to enable them to have the same equal rights, security and acceptance that non erotic industry workers enjoy." Arrowsmith writes, "The erotic industries are not as scary as they are represented in the media, which is why the majority of people in them consent to and continue to work in them. We don't need saving, we need support."[59] The support Arrowsmith seeks is a change of both policy and attitudes about sex workers in order to keep them safe as they produce the on-screen fantasies that so many people consume.

Like Arrowsmith, Erika Lust has also sought to challenge the sexism in pornography. She reported to the *Guardian*, "We produce adult movies. We publish erotic books and magazines. Our works speak about sex, lust, and passion. We enjoy exciting you and exciting your mind. We make love, not porn. And we do all of this with a feminine, aesthetic and innovative approach."[60] What that means for Erika Lust (in part) is truth telling about women's sexuality, especially as it is depicted in video. She says, "Sex images make you hot, but pornography has been made by and for men. In mainstream porn everything is about male pleasure and women are objects. Oral sex for men can last forever, but when women's turn comes it last 10 seconds. Female orgasms are not an issue in most of the films. And women are shown mostly as prostitutes, which is sad."[61]

There is no question that what one sees in pornography "made by women for women" is quite diverse. At issue is not the sex that is had in these films, but the way it is depicted. Anna Arrowsmith and Erika Lust represent two of many female producers and directors who seek to make pornography better by robbing it of one of the chief vices that vexes so much of it: sexism itself, and the violent and degrading depictions that so often come from it. What Arrowsmith and Lust offer, interpreted from a Christian perspective, is a healing of sexism. They do so in order that the depiction of female eroticism can be fully enjoyed—with full concern for the moral well-being of women. From such a perspective, it is possible that some of their pornographic work might also function as iconography of promiscuity in heaven.

Of course, some people might ask why anyone would need iconography of sex in heaven. That is, indeed, a fair question. One answer is that some might not need it. However, others may find that visions of heaven do help them to live better lives on earth. This seems to be the same reason why some Christians cherish and venerate the iconography of the saints. To sit before an icon of a saint is to consider the grace of God that the saint manifests. It is also to reflect upon their earthly story, their heavenly bliss—and to be inspired to live likewise. Not all Christians draw upon iconography in this way, however. Indeed some Christians have expressed concern that the veneration of iconography can too easily become idolatry. To that end, if any kind of pornography is approached as iconography of heaven, one will have to be careful not to make an idol out of what is only a window into heaven. And to be clear, the best windows into heaven do not pull you away from this world, but rather inspire you to live in it as it could be, and not as it is. In this sense, the pornographic materials that might function like iconography would not merely arouse sexual desires, but would also motivate people to embody heavenly qualities on earth with other human beings, wherever those relationships are made possible. That some pornography depicts promiscuous sex really isn't a problem. When that promiscuity is also emblematic of the radical welcome, prodigal love, and eternal delights of heaven, such promiscuity can be understood to reveal real goods of the reign of God. Perhaps one project for Christian communities so convinced, would be to catalogue pornography that meets these criteria for the sake of moral and spiritual edification (and perhaps also those examples of pornography that do not).

CELIBACY: A REFRAIN FROM SEX FOR THE SAKE OF PRODIGAL LOVE

Finally, it is important to recognize that another metaphor for heaven is one that does not include genital sexual relations at all. In the last chapter it was suggested that celibacy is a third way to envision the eschatological life. A celibate heaven allows the Christian to see that the relationship between God and humanity need not draw on the metaphor of sexual relations in order to show God's powerful and prodigal love. A celibate heaven favors the vision of the human being caught in a transcendent state of love and union with God forever. This union is so exquisite and irreducible that to describe it through the metaphor of genital relations would be too narrow.

Whereas a celibate heaven celebrates the transcendent love of God in the fullness of glory, a celibate life on earth seeks to revel in that divine love by devoting oneself to worship, contemplation, and service to others. In fact, in something of an irony, the celibate person is positioned in a unique way to be promiscuous with the prodigal love of God, perhaps even more so than the person who seeks to embody the prodigal love of God through promiscuous sex. In particular, a celibate person can pursue being an expression of the prodigal love of God without needing to balance the special relationships of romance, sexual eroticism, or a private domestic life. In this sense, celibacy allows for as many embodied expressions of gospel and heavenly love as promiscuity might. But it does so in a way that is not limited to physical sexuality.

Indeed, examples of lived celibacy show that many celibate persons are very much prodigal in their consorting with humanity. If we read the New Testament texts without assigning Jesus a sexual partner, this was clearly his way of living: touching and being touched; loving indiscriminately, and consorting with anyone regardless of their social identity or status. Examples of such celibate prodigality certainly exist among religious persons to this day. Such people devote themselves to prodigal love through the practice of medicine, social work, education, and personal care.

For example, Sister Marilyn Lacey has devoted her entire life to the service of refugees. As she tells it in her book, *This Flowing toward Me*, Lacey's calling to refugee ministry helped her to learn a "new way to love." It first started by helping non-English-speaking refugees find their way from one concourse to another at the San Francisco International Airport. Then her love moved her to trek through war-torn countries in Africa and to live among and serve refugees throughout the world. Sister Lacey's life has become wholly devoted to making sure that "abundant life" and "human flourishing" are not just code words for affluence. This new way of loving that Lacey has discovered has been a process of coming to understand that she is a body through whom God works in the world (and further, that you the reader are another body able to do the same). For Sister Lacey, our bodies should be a sacramental presence of divine love to everyone we meet. And according to Sister Lacey, this is precisely what God desires of us, too.

That claim is a conviction that came to Sister Lacey through a vision. It came to her during a time in her life when she was angry at God for all the suffering in the world. She had seen, firsthand, human atrocities that a loving God would surely stop. One day, and while deep in thought, God finally responded. God revealed to Sister Lacey that where love is not present, God is only as powerful as a paraplegic. Where love is present, wholeness and healing (in many forms) still manifest themselves. From accusing God as a distant deity to seeing the divine presence in each person, Sister Lacey came to realize that the presence and empowering love of God requires willing (and many) bodies in which to dwell. Some of those bodies—like Sister Lacey's—channel the love of God through service to humanity. To do so does not require sexual relations. God can love humanity, prodigally, through the human flesh that celibate people provide. When celibate people open their flesh to God in such ways, it is as a gift and vocation.

To be clear, the best practice of celibacy should not be imagined as "giving up sex" as something bad to avoid. Rather, it is an embodied calling to so devote oneself to love, service, and contemplation that a sexual relationship is another gift that is simply not pursued. However, when people do take a vow of celibacy it is incredibly important that they discern in what ways sexual energies are present—and if so, how these are being channeled. Channeling the energy of desire is something that many people do. For example, stress and anxiety can be fuel for a good workout, and certain passions can be channeled as the energy to complete meaningful projects. However, in problematic cases (and especially with respect to sexuality), desire can be suppressed or hidden—as when sweeping something under the rug or hiding something in the proverbial closet. When channeling desire is practiced deficiently, that pent up energy is likely to express itself in other ways—not all of which are good or healthy.

For many Christians, the sexual abuse scandal in the Roman Catholic Church will come to mind. Christians have been horrified by an avalanche of certified reports revealing that thousands upon thousands of children experienced sexual abuse at the hands of Catholic priests and other religious celibates worldwide. Some people have highlighted the correlation of celibacy and sexual abuse, assuming that celibacy is the cause. That, however, is not wholly true. Consider one report by the Australian Royal Commission into Institutional Responses to Child Sexual Abuse. This commission found that "compulsory celibacy may . . . have contributed to various forms of psychosexual dysfunction, including psychosexual immaturity, which pose an ongoing risk to the safety of children."[62] Notice that it is the relationship between *compulsory* celibacy and psychosexual dysfunction that can contribute to sexual abuse. It is not celibacy itself.

To force celibacy onto a person who is not yet prepared to address the complexities of human sexuality (or to force it upon someone who assumes that a calling to ministry must also be a call to celibacy) can have terrible results. It is not difficult to imagine someone going into the seminary or a religious order with a calling to ministry, but without enough life experience or moral education to properly respond to sexual desires. Stunting that person's sexual development can lead to dysfunction, the painful effects of which have been endured by children and other parishioners. One solution, as analyst Father Thomas Reese has suggested, is to support voluntary celibacy over the current compulsory practice. That said, Father Reese also noted that the vast majority of clergy are not abusers, even under the rule of compulsory celibacy.[63] In fact, in the United States, available reports indicate that it is only 4 percent of Catholic priests who are sexual abusers.[64] That number may prove to be incorrect as more information comes to light, but this is the data that is currently available. If this is true, then it would not be fair to say that celibacy itself will predictably lead to child abuse. That said, as we interrogate the relationship between forced celibacy, psychosexual dysfunction, and sexual abuse, we dare not lose sight of the victims. Sexually abused children and parishioners have to live with that pain for the rest of their lives. Thus, when conversations turn toward the percentage of celibate religious persons engaged in abusive behavior, a "low" number should not be used as another blanket to cover up the thousands of people who have been traumatized. Rather, the low correlation between celibacy and sexual abuse only indicates that celibacy is not itself the cause of abuse. Thus, if we are to talk about celibacy and sexual abuse carefully, it should be with an effort at both accuracy and the avoidance of anti-Catholic rhetoric.[65] But where clergy sexual abuse has happened, nothing should censor our condemnation of such heinous transgressions.

What is more, it is important to distinguish between clergy sexual abusers who are celibate and celibate people who occasionally engage in mutual sexual relationships with other adults. Some Christians will certainly scoff at the idea that an avowed celibate person would ever indulge in an adult sexual relationships. But asking celibate people to be perfect in celibacy is as unrealistic as demanding people to be perfect in monogamy or promiscuity. The already/not yet realities of life on earth *also* mean that those who feel called to celibacy may find that their practice of celibacy is not wholly perfect. In short, heaven is not yet fully on earth.

For those pursuing celibacy, sexual fantasies, desires for certain people, and flirtations with physical relationships may occur. To say so is not to categorize sexual desire or activity as bad or afflictive to spiritual wholeness. Sometimes the passions of sexuality may so impress themselves upon a celibate person that the commitment to celibacy may feel like an episodic struggle. That said, if the struggle is consistent and problematic, one might wish to revisit whether celibacy is really their calling—whether for a lifetime or just a season. Indeed, seasonal celibacy may be of some benefit to Christians as a whole. Celibacy not only allows one to uniquely channel the love of God to others, but it also provides for one to engage in deep contemplation. To that end, seasonal celibacy may allow Christians to work through any number of issues—including those about sexual relationships. For example, after the end of a relationship (whether due to death, divorce, or separation), a time of celibacy may prove healing. Likewise, a season of celibacy may help people to mindfully probe the meaning of human sexuality without actualizing it in physical terms. In truth, it is sometimes good to hold back from sexual relationships in order to allow oneself to reflect on the meaning of sexual relationships for one's life, and, to give oneself ample time to engage in that reflection.

Thus, whether seasonal or for a lifetime, Christians can embrace celibacy as one good path of living life on earth. Indeed, Christians should be encouraged to see celibacy as a special way of living life for the sake of knowing and sharing the love of God. It is a kind of orientation that does not reject sex, but rather it incarnates a full-bodied love for humanity without sexual-genital expressions. By doing so, it provides another way in which God's prodigal love can be shared and heavenly goods can be realized upon the earth.

CONCLUSION

If there is one persistent theme within an eschatological sexual ethic, it is that the goods of heaven can indeed be realized on earth, even if imperfectly so. Indeed, such an ethic suggests that there is much more that can be said about sexual morality than what we are used to considering within Christian ethics that rely more conventionally on the Bible, church teaching, reason, and experience. This eschatological ethic invites Christians to reexamine traditional codes of morality about monogamy, marriage, promiscuity, and celibacy. It humbles any claim to moral perfection, especially in monogamy and celibacy. But it also restrains promiscuity from becoming unenlightened hedonism.

To say that this is a Christian ethic is not to claim that it is the sole ethic that all Christians should follow. It is to take seriously the claim that when sexual relations are used as metaphors to describe the goods of heaven, something other than monogamy or celibacy appears. And yet, such a vision of heaven does not eradicate monogamy or celibacy as good options. Rather, it takes seriously the argument that monogamy and celibacy should be treated as chosen vocations, and not absolute moral norms. What is more, this ethic takes seriously the assertion that promiscuity may be infused with heavenly goods, namely, that the experience of radical welcome, healing love, and fulfillment are not simply eschatological realities, but also goods that can be realized between lovers (whether long or short term, few or many). In short, this vision of heaven and the sexual ethics it produces takes seriously that Christian morality must be as radical and bold as the central character around which the Christian imagination orbits: Jesus of Nazareth, Christ the Word made flesh.

In fact, if there is one word that can be used to describe this eschatological ethic, it is *incarnation*. To incarnate is to embody something in the flesh, or in human form. One of the cardinal theological doctrines that many Christians affirm is that the Word and Wisdom of God became incarnate in the person of Jesus. In Christ, God is made known, not through the utterances of a conventional prophet who speaks human words on behalf of God, but as the Word made manifest in human flesh. Thus, when Christ spoke of prodigal love, he incarnated the essence of God. When Christ interrogated power and privilege, he incarnated God's solidarity with the oppressed. When Christ uttered forgiveness from the cross, he incarnated what God is really about—that God is the one who perpetually seeks out restoration in the face of alienation. In Christ, the letter of the law was subverted to the practice of love. Therefore, to follow in the way of Jesus is not something so simple as saying what one believes about God doctrinally or theologically. Rather, to follow Jesus is to incarnate the reign of God, as Christ's life declared and defined it. For Jesus, anywhere—and in anyone—that the goods of the reign of God were manifest (even imperfectly) was something to celebrate. Indeed, for Jesus it was something to bless and venerate.

Sex has too often been left behind when thinking about the incarnation of the reign of God. Arguably, neither Jesus nor apostles like Paul are to blame. Their texts, or texts written about them, have been interpreted to various ends. Indeed, as history shows, Christians struggled with the moral and theological status of sex. Christians struggled to embrace sexual desire as part of God's creation. They couldn't quite agree if marital sex was always a good thing. And Christians took a long time to realize that those theologians who saw sex as dirty and sinful weren't telling the whole truth about God's gifts for humanity.

In the two thousand years during which Christianity has endured, sex is only beginning to be appreciated as incarnation. Even so, global Christianity is now struggling through another period of embracing sexuality for all that it can be. Some Christians feel righteous by clinging to marital, monogamous, heterosexual, or procreative norms. If that brings them contentment—and they do no harm—so be it. But clinging to tradition does not wholly capture the daring, radical legacy of Christ. Christians are not called to merely catalogue and preserve doctrines that have helped them to make sense of the mystery of God. They are called to boldly incarnate and celebrate the reign of God—to live on earth, as it is in heaven. Where sexual relationships can do this, be they monogamous or promiscuous, Christians need not shy away from celebrating that the reign of God has truly drawn near. The suggestion here is that as we look to eschatology for visions of sex in heaven, then heaven becomes a bed under which we might sit and learn—and if we dare to be so faithful, to incarnate what we see in heaven in our lives on earth.

NOTES

INTRODUCTION

1. Justin Jaron Lewis, *Imaging Holiness: Classic Hasidic Tales in Modern Times* (Montreal: McGill-Queen's University Press, 2009), 120.

2. Lewis, 120.

3. Rachel Biale, "Sexuality and Marital Relations," in *Sexuality: A Reader*, ed. Karen Lebacqz, 46–59 (Cleveland, OH: Pilgrim Press, 2000).

4. It is not a caricature to say that some Christians have threatened the faithful with eternal hell for transgressions of sexual ethics. What has to be considered more carefully is what official church teaching of any denomination has to say on these matters, as well as what the laity construct and affirm as part of their faith formation. For example, the Catholic Church teaches that a wide variety of sexual sins are mortal sins; and by definition, the church teaches that God would be just to sentence a person to hell for violations of mortal sin. But what the church does not teach is that God will send all such violators to hell. The concept of absolute and certain eternal damnation is very often theological rhetoric deployed by individual Christians. So, too, some Protestant Christians have insisted that while humans are saved by grace alone, through proper faith in Christ; those who persist in certain sins (sexual ones included) might indicate a lack of true faith, and thus no sure hope of grace. These pronouncements of judgment are often central in Christian debates about sexual morality.

5. For example, a wide variety of *creation* theologies honor God as the ground of our being; as the source of all things seen and unseen. Such theologies have allowed many people of faith to affirm that the human body is part of God's artistry. From the perspective of creation, possessing a physical body is not an inherently bad thing, nor a problem to overcome. This suggests that a robust theology of creation can open the door to a meaningful celebration of sexuality as a divinely intended and approved part of embodied living—but to what end is highly disputed. Some

Christians see God's intention for human sexuality only in heterosexuality; others see diverse sexual orientations and identities as another beautiful reflection of God's handiwork, no less so than the diversity of stars, trees, animals, and human beings. So, too, a person need not reduce theologies of creation to inaccurate, fundamentalist claims about the book of Genesis as a science text. Arguably, a more meaningful theology of creation intends to communicate—within the finitudes of human language—the spiritual relationship between the natural order and the one we call God. A *theology* of creation need not seek to hijack and replace modern science. As science helps us to understand the natural order empirically, a theology of creation portrays the cosmos as part of the divine story. To tell this story, the scriptures rely on poetry, myth, and song. Only qualitative works of narration can begin to connect the knowable world with the ineffable mystery of God. In turn, systematic theologians spill much ink explaining why this is believable.

6. Christian doctrines of sin have long declared that not one part of creation is untouched by its ruining powers. According to traditional Christian theology, humans introduced sin—not God. With respect to sexual ethics, the theological problem of sin requires Christians to account for what kind of injury sin brings to the sexual self and to our sexual relationships (inclusive of what we desire, what activities we engage in, with whom, and why).

7. The redemption of sexuality tends to be controlled by moral theologies of chastity; recognizing sex as a temporal good (at best), and not something to which one should be attached when thinking about the redemption of our bodies in the eschatological life. For example, Augustine's *City of God*, the *Catechism of the Catholic Church*, and even John Calvin's *Institutes* all seem to agree that the continuation of sex in the life of the redeemed is not something we should hope for. These texts will be addressed in later chapters.

8. For example, St. Gregory of Nyssa believed that biological sex was a consequence of the fall of humanity into sin—a necessary means for reproduction that fallen human beings would have to rely on in a (now) mortal, imperfect world. As someone who believed in the resurrection of the dead, Gregory of Nyssa also asserted that this temporal necessity of genitals would not continue with us into the life of the world to come. For Gregory of Nyssa, the lasting identity of a person is their redemption in Christ, not their physical sex. Other theologians, like St. Augustine, could imagine physical sex as part of God's intention for humanity—but the theologian also relegated sexual activity to marriage, and only for the sake of reproduction. In fact, it wasn't until the twentieth century that Protestant Christians began authorizing the use of contraception. Advances in artificial contraception opened the door for these Christians (and others) to consider why people might draw on contraceptives for good reasons, both moral and religious. Many of these Christians have concluded that reproduction need not be the intent of sex when other relational goals might be achieved. This was an insight first articulated by heterosexual married couples in light of reproductive health concerns, family

planning, and so forth. What is more, with the rise of studies in gender and sexual diversities, contemporary Christian churches are divided about what to do with lesbian, gay, bisexual, transgender, and queer (LGBTQ) people. Some churches have become remarkably affirming, while others (quite painfully) have chosen to pronounce condemnations and to exile their LGBTQ members. For more information on Gregory of Nyssa, see Peter Brown's analysis of St. Gregory of Nyssa's teachings on humanity before the fall into sin, *The Body and Society: Men, Women, and Sexual Renunciation in Early Christianity (Twentieth Anniversary Edition)* (New York: Columbia University Press, 2008), 293-296. For another perspective, see the commentary of David J. Dunn, "Gregory of Nyssa on Sin and Sex," December 14, 2013, https://www.davidjdunn.com/2013/12/14/gregory-of-nyssa-on-sin-and-sex/#_ftn8.

9. For example, we will explore the website *Himeros.tv* in chapter 6.

10. *Summa Theologica* (*ST*) II–II.154.11.

11. *ST* II–II.154.1.

12. See Pope John Paul, *Catechism of the Catholic Church* (1992), "Part Three: Life in Christ, Section Two: The Ten Commandments, Chapter Two: 'You Shall Love Your Neighbor as Yourself,' Article 6: The Sixth Commandment," para. 2331–2440.

13. Joshua J. McElwee, "Francis Explains 'Who Am I to Judge?,'" *National Catholic Reporter*, January 10, 2016, https://www.ncronline.org/news/vatican/francis-explains-who-am-i-judge.

14. McElwee.

15. See Father George Plathottam, "Pope Francis and Homosexual People: A Time to Speak and a Time to Be Silent," *Light for the Voiceless*, October 24, 2020, https://www.licas.news/2020/10/24/pope-francis-and-homosexual-people-a-time-to-speak-and-a-time-to-be-silent/.

16. Margaret Farley, "Sexual Ethics," in *Sexuality and the Sacred*, ed. James Nelson and Sandra Longfellow (Louisville: Westminster John Knox Press, 1994), 65–66.

17. Ed Wheat and Gaye Wheat, *Intended for Pleasure: Sex Technique and Sexual Fulfillment in Christian Marriage*, 4th ed. (Grand Rapids, MI: Revell, 2010).

18. Wheat and Wheat, 80.

19. For example, see the Evangelical Lutheran Church in America (ELCA), "A Social Statement on Human Sexuality: Gift and Trust," Minneapolis, MN, August 19, 2009.

20. See, for example, the United Church of Christ or the Presbyterian Church (USA).

21. John 20:19–20.

22. Luke 24:42–43 and Luke 24:50–51.

23. See, for example, Luca Signorelli, *The Resurrection of the Flesh* (c. 1500).

24. Theologians have different ways of describing the eschatological life. I draw on the language of theocentric and domestic versions of heaven from the academic

work of Samuel Morris Brown in *In Heaven as It Is on Earth: Joseph Smith and the Early Mormon Conquest of Death* (Oxford: Oxford University Press, 2012).

25. Samuel Morris Brown.

26. I am indebted to Diana Cates for her conception of ethics, as found in *Aquinas and the Emotions* (Washington, DC: Georgetown University Press, 2009).

CHAPTER 1

1. For example, the Catholic theologian Thomas Aquinas drew on the virtue ethics of the Greek philosopher Aristotle in order to settle a great number of moral questions. Because Aquinas's reflections on virtue were situated within a medieval Christian context, his theological reasoning greatly influenced his application of Aristotle's theory. But if we put Aristotelian virtue ethics within a different Christian mindset—for example, a broadly ecumenical or Protestant mindset, or one that draws upon contemporary insights of science and rational social inquiry—the conclusions we reach will very likely be different than those of Aquinas.

2. See, for examples, Lisa Sowle Cahill, *Sex, Gender, and Christian Ethics* (Cambridge: Cambridge University Press, 1996), 46. See also Richard W. McCarty, *Sexual Virtue: A Contemporary Approach to Christian Ethics* (Albany: State University of New York Press, 2015), 41–45, 53–58.

3. See Martha Nussbuam, *Sex and Social Justice* (Oxford: Oxford University Press, 1995), 30.

4. John Sporger, "In Interview, Mother Details Delusions That Spurred Her to Kill Sons," *CNN.com*, April 1, 2004, Law Center, http://www.cnn.com/2004/LAW/04/01/laney/.

5. Sporger.

6. Ibid.

7. Genesis 22:2. *New Revised Standard Version* (NRSV).

8. Anthony Colarossi, "Man Gets 90 Years in Arson, Murder Attempts on Family," *Orlando Sentinel*, April 25, 2006, http://articles.orlandosentinel.com/2006-04-25/news/GASATTACK25_1_gasoline-kest-hans.

9. The Bible is also a collection of texts that describe genocide, slavery, war booty, and other violent actions that Christians tend to think of as immoral.

10. See, for example, Leviticus 18:21 and the reference to child sacrifice to Molek.

11. See Lawrence Kohlberg's stages of moral development (*The Philosophy of Moral Development* [New York: Harper and Row, 1981]).

12. *Summa Theologica* (*ST*) I–II.62.

13. Anthony Ramirez, "Seminary Votes Out Leader over Daughter's Gay Wedding," *New York Times*, February 12, 2005, New York Region, http://www.nytimes.com/2005/02/12/nyregion/seminary-votes-out-leader-over-daughters-gay-wedding.html.

14. Anthony Ramirez, "Minister Faces Church Trial for Performing Gay Wedding," *New York Times*. June 17, 2005, New York Region, http://www.nytimes.com/2005/06/17/nyregion/minister-faces-church-trial-for-performing-gay-wedding.html.

15. Heather Hahn, "Gay Clergywoman's Case Heads to Top Court," *United Methodist News*, July 7, 2017, http://www.umc.org/news-and-media/gay-clergywomans-case-heads-to-top-court#.WV-3rucQkSA.facebook.

16. Anna Blaedel, "An Open Letter to the UMC," May 1, 2018, https://www.facebook.com/anna.blaedel.

17. Pope John Paul, *Catechism of the Catholic Church* (1992), para. 2032.

18. For example, see the Left Behind series and the premillennial theology that supports it.

19. 1 Corinthians 7:25–35, *New Revised Standard Version (NRSV)*.

20. 1 Corinthians 7:25–35, v. 31.

21. See, for example, Sarah Harding, *Paul's Eschatological Anthropology: The Dynamics of Human Transformation* (Minneapolis, MN: Augsburg Fortress Press, 2015).

22. For example, Christopher Rowland suggests that Paul's certainty about the end of time is not based in narrowly predictive notions of *when* it will come, but rather, in faithful certainty that the end of this present world *is* coming because of what Christ has accomplished. But also, it is a certainty that until Christ returns (whenever that may be), Christians are to live according to a new paradigm of spiritual autonomy and morality. Rowland writes, "For Paul, Christ had initiated the age of the Spirit, marked by prophecy, and, distinctively in the New Testament in the Pauline letters, the power for moral change and the ethical life. Romans 8:1–11 and 1 Corinthians 2:10–16 seem to commend the autonomous life of those guided by the eschatological Spirit, which places them above the obligations of the law code." This is not to say that Rowland thinks that Paul had a long-delayed eschatology. Rather, Rowland's suggestion reads Paul as encouraging Christians to live on earth in light of eschatological expectations instead of reading Paul as someone narrowly predicting judgment day. Rowland comments of Paul's eschatology, "It is only when all things are subjected to the Messiah that the Son will himself be subject to the Father and God will be all in all (1 Corinthians 15:28). Later in the chapter, Paul tells his readers of the mystery of the resurrection of the elect: not all will die but will be changed in the twinkling of an eye at the last trumpet (cf. 1 Thessalonians 4:16–17 and Matthew 24:31). It is not clear whether this passage contradicts the earlier hint of a period of a messianic kingdom on earth at some point during the lordship of the Messiah." Rowland also notes of Pauline eschatology, "A more specific problem emerges in 2 Thessalonians. It seems that some of the Christians decided that, with the imminence of the coming of Christ, there was no need to live a normal life in the world (3:6–13). Such people are rebuked by the apostle. In order to dampen

eschatological enthusiasm, which had emerged in the community, Paul sets out an eschatological program which is intended to diminish the intensity of expectation (2:3–12). Certain things have to take place before Christ will return. Until they do, there is no point in idleness; Christians should carry on with their normal lives and not be carried away with their enthusiasm." See Christopher Rowland, "The Eschatology of the New Testament Church," in *The Oxford Handbook of Eschatology*, ed. Jerry L. Walls, 62–63; 66 (Oxford: Oxford University Press, 2008).

23. Rex Butler, *The New Prophecy and "New Visions"* (Washington, DC: Catholic University of America Press, 2006), 21.

24. Scholar of religion Rex Butler has described the New Prophecy movement as "an effort to mold the whole life of the church in conformity to the expectation of the immediate, impending return of Christ, [in order] to define the essence of Christianity from this point of view, and to oppose everything by which ecclesiastical conditions should acquire a more permanent structure for the purpose of entering into a longer, historical generation" (Butler, 21).

25. Butler, 35.

26. For more details on Harold Camping's eschatology, see his book *Time Has an End: A Biblical History of the World 11,013 B.C.–2011 A.D.* (Alameda, CA: Family Stations, 2005).

27. Stevens, Sharifa. "Harold Camping STOLE my parents," *Manna Express*, accessed June 19, 2017, http://www.mannaexpressonline.com/harold-camping-stole-my-parents/.

CHAPTER 2

1. Eben Alexander, *Proof of Heaven: A Neurosurgeon's Journey into the Afterlife* (New York: Simon & Schuster, 2012), 71.

2. Rose Surnow, "I Gave a Handjob at Jew Camp," *Vice.com*, May 9, 2012, Travel, https://www.vice.com/sv/article/i-gave-a-handy-at-jew-camp.

3. Leviticus 18:22, 20:13.

4. Exodus 21:2–11, Genesis 22:24.

5. Exodus 21:2–11.

6. Deuteronomy 22:20–28.

7. Leviticus 18:6–18.

8. Genesis 38:1–11.

9. Deuteronomy 7:1–6.

10. Deuteronomy 23:12–14.

11. Leviticus 15:19–33.

12. Lynne Meredith Schreiber, "I'm an Orthodox Jew—Here's Why We Have Smokin' Hot Sex Lives," *Yourtango.com*, June 6, 2017, Self, Sex, http://www.yourtango.com/200623/forbidden-desires.

13. Song of Solomon 4:1–8, 7:1–9.

14. Song of Solomon 5:10–16.

15. Song of Solomon 4:16.

16. Song of Solomon 5:4–5.

17. As Danna Fewell notes, to read the Song of Solomon critically and contextually, we must recognize "the rather oppressive social structure that provides the backdrop for the scenario.... Hence, the poetic garden of equity, intimacy, and mutuality is not without its thorns." In Alice Ogden Bellis. *Helpmates, Harlots, and Heroes: Women's Stories in the Hebrew Bible* (Louisville, KY: Westminster John Knox Press, 2007), 179.

18. For example, in the late first century, Rabbi Akiba is remembered as saying that the Song of Solomon was "sung in taverns," suggesting that the text may not be worthy of its canonical location. Indeed, many contemporary biblical scholars have suggested that the "book is originally secular, a conclusion supported by the absence of any reference in it to God." What is more, a number of traditions both Jewish and Christian have preferred an allegorical reading of the book as a metaphor for the relationship between God and Israel, or God and the "Church." And yet, to the chagrin of those who would denounce the text as some form of pornography (i.e., a depiction of sexual vulgarity or immorality), the Song of Solomon has endured as a text that cannot be read allegorically without first understanding its physical and sexual dimensions. Thanks to those rabbis who included the Song of Solomon in the biblical canon, we can now say that the text reveals "the word of the Lord." And to turn a liturgical phrase, we might say, "Thanks be to God." Michael Coogan, *The Old Testament: A Historical and Literary Introduction to the Hebrew Scriptures* (New York: Oxford University Press, 2006), 496; see also Bellis, 178.

19. Bellis, 179.

20. George Robinson, *Essential Judaism* (New York: Pocket Books, 2000), 84–85.

21. Robinson, 244.

22. Robinson, 244.

23. Yoel Kahn, "Making Love as Making Justice," in *Sexuality: A Reader*, ed. Karen Lebacqz and David Somacore-Guinn, 581–589 (Cleveland, OH: Pilgrim Press, 2000).

24. For example, Genesis 44:29, 1 Samuel 2:6, 2 Samuel 22:6, Job 11:8, and Psalm 6:5.

25. 1 Samuel 28:3–19

26. Novak, David. "Jewish Eschatology." In *The Oxford Handbook of Eschatology*, ed. Jerry L. Walls, 119 (New York: Oxford University Press, 2008).

27. Ecclesiastes 3:19–22.

28. Ecclesiastes 3:19–22, *New Revised Standard Version (NRSV)*.

29. Robinson, 192.

30. Robinson, 192.

31. Novak, 123.

32. Rifat Sonsino, *Did Moses Really Have Horns? and Other Myths about Jews and Judaism* (New York: URJ Press, 2009), 184.

33. Jewish notions of resurrection, however, are complex. Maimonides accepted the possibility that even resurrected people will die a second time in order to allow the righteous to continue a purely spiritual life in the presence of God. See http://www.myjewishlearning.com/article/life-after-death/.

34. Novak, 126–128.

35. Robert Spencer, "72 Virgins Are Waiting for Me in Heaven—So Why I Should Prefer Only One Here?" *Jihad Watch*, August 3, 2015, https://www.jihadwatch.org/2015/08/72-virgins-are-waiting-for-me-in-heaven-so-why-i-should-prefer-only-one-here.

36. Qur'an 2:187, 2:223. Unless otherwise noted, all Qur'anic verses are taken from *Al-Qur'an, A Contemporary Translation*, trans. Ahmed Ali (Princeton, NJ: Princeton University Press, 1993).

37. Qur'an 4:15–16.

38. Indrani Mitra, "'There Is No Sin in Our Love': Homoerotic Desire in the Stories of Two Muslim Women Writers," *Tulsa Studies in Women's Literature* 29, no. 2 (2010): 311–329.

39. Mitra.

40. Ghazala Anwar, "Elements of a Samadiyyah Sharia," in *Heterosexism in Contemporary World Religion: Problem and Prospect*, ed. Marvin Ellison and Judith Plaskow (Cleveland, OH: Pilgrim Press, 2007), 85.

41. Anwar.

42. Qur'an 75:1–12.

43. One scholar of Islam describes Muslim conceptions of the postmortem life (before the resurrection) this way: "God himself takes the soul at death, though Koranic verses also say that he sends the Angel of Death or 'his angels' to perform the task. After her first night in the grave, the soul is confronted by Nakīr and Munakr, two angels who question it about its God, its prophet, and its scripture. If the soul gives the right answers, it is taken up through the heavens into the presence of God, but if it gives the wrong answers, it is prevented from entering the higher realms. In either case, it is then resettled in the grave, where it experiences foretastes of its situation after the resurrection. For the blessed, the time passes quickly and pleasurably; for the damned slowly and painfully." See William C. Chittck, "Muslim Eschatology," in *The Oxford Handbook of Eschatology*, ed. Jerry L. Walls, 133 (New York: Oxford University Press, 2008).

44. Qur'an 23:99–100.

45. Stephen Murray and Will Roscoe, *Islamic Homosexualities* (New York: New York University Press, 1997), 90.

46. Qur'an 44:51–44.

47. Qur'an 52:17–20.

48. Qur'an 4:124.

49. Qur'an 56:34–36.

50. John Portmann, *Sex and Heaven: Catholics in Bed and at Prayer* (New York: Palgrave Macmillan, 2003), 17, 18.

51. Murray and Roscoe, 90.

52. Qur'an 56:17–18.

53. Murray and Roscoe, 90.

54. Caroline Humphrey, "Sex in the City—The New Polygamy," *Cambridge Journal of Anthropology* 29, no. 2 (2009): 21–25.

55. Chris Perez, "These Christians Swingers Like Sharing Bible Verses, Sex Partners," *New York Post*, September 25, 2014, Living, http://nypost.com/2014/09/25/these-christian-swingers-like-sharing-bible-verses-sex-partners/.

56. See http://www.fitnessswingers.com.

57. Christy Anderson, "A Case for Christian Swinging,." *Swingers-in-Love*. Accessed June 27, 2017, http://swingers-in-love.blogspot.com/p/case-for-christian-swinging.html.

58. William Kephart, "Experimental Family Organization: An Historico-Cultural Report on the Oneida Community," *Marriage and Family Living* 25, no. 3 (August 1963): 264.

59. Ernest R. Sandeen, "John Humphrey Noyes as the New Adam," *Church History* 40 (1971): 83.

60. William Kephart, "Experimental Family Organization: An Historico-Cultural Report on the Oneida Community," *Marriage and Family Living* 25, no. 3 (August 1963): 264.

61. Kephart, 265.

62. Kephart, 267.

63. David White, "John Humphrey Noyes: Philosopher of Bible Communism," *Philosophy Now* 70 (November–December 2008), https://philosophynow.org/issues/70/John_Humphrey_Noyes_Philosopher_of_Bible_Communism.

64. Matthew 22:23–30, *NRSV*.

65. White.

66. Acts 2:44–45.

67. Lawrence Foster, "The Psychology of Free Love in the Oneida Community," *Australasian Journal of American Studies*, 5, no. 2 (December 1986): 17.

68. Foster, 19.

69. Foster, 19.

70. Kephart, 264–265.

71. David J. Whittaker, "Early Mormon Polygamy Defenses." *Journal of Mormon History* 11 (1984): 43–63.

72. Matthew 22:23–30, Luke 20:27–40.

73. Samuel Morris Brown, *In Heaven As It Is on Earth: Joseph Smith and the Early Mormon Conquest of Death* (Oxford: Oxford University Press, 2012), 205.

74. Charles R. Harrell, "The Development of the Doctrine of Preexistence, 1830–1844," *Brigham Young University Studies* 28, no. 2 (1988): 75–96.

75. Harrell.

76. Harrell, 208.

77. Harrell, 262.

78. "Is President Lorenzo Snow's Oft-Repeated Statement—'As Man Now Is, God Once Was; as God Now Is, Man May Be'—Accepted as Official Doctrine by the Church?" *The Church of Jesus Christ of Latter-Day Saints*, accessed March 25, 2021, https://www.churchofjesuschrist.org/study/ensign/1982/02/i-have-a-question/is-president-snows-statement-as-man-now-is-god-once-was-as-god-now-is-man-may-be-accepted-as-official-doctrine?lang=eng.

79. Brown, 274.

80. Brown, 277.

81. See chapter 3.

CHAPTER 3

1. See, for example, Nelson Electronic Publishing, *The Y2K Personal Survival Kit: How to Quickly Prepare for Any Man-Made or Natural Disaster* (Nashville, TN: Thomas Nelson, 1999). As a special note, Thomas Nelson is a publisher of Christian material, which is often oriented toward Protestant and evangelical perspectives.

2. See, for example, Teresa Watanabe, "The Year of Believing in Prophecies," *Los Angeles Times*, March 31, 1999, http://articles.latimes.com/1999/mar/31/news/mn-22793.

3. Watanabe.

4. Watanabe.

5. "Belief in the impending return of Christ and an ensuing period of divine punishment, tribulation, and judgment continues to influence responses to ongoing events, occasionally in ways decidedly contrary to the mainstream. In early responses to the terrorist attacks of September 11, 2001, some premillennial dispensationalists suggested they were a sign of God's retribution on a sinful nation—a view that was met with widespread outrage. That interpretation, however, was a logical conclusion drawn from premillennial thought. Just as premillennialists viewed the horror of the battle of Gettysburg in 1863 as a divine act aimed at chastising American for its sin, some saw the carnage of September 11 in the same light. Some fundamentalists and premillennialists take this interpretation further, seeing these horrific events as indications that Christ's return is imminent." Jeanne Halgren Kilde, "A Historical Look at Millenarian Thought," *Rapture, Revelation, and the End Times: Exploring the Left Behind Series*, ed. Bruce Forbes and Jeanne Halgren Kilde, 33–70 (New York: Palgrave Macmillan, 2004), 65.

6. See, for example, Terry James, "Iraq in Bible Prophecy," July 19, 2016, http://www.raptureready.com/2016/07/19/iraq-in-bible-prophecy/.

7. See, for example, Jennifer LeClaire, "Why So Many People Think Obama Is the Antichrist," August 7, 2015, https://www.charismanews.com/opinion/watchman-on-the-wall/50914-why-so-many-people-think-obama-is-the-antichrist.

8. See, for example: WND Staff, "End Times Harbinger: Nations Gang Up on Israel," January 14, 2017, http://www.wnd.com/2017/01/end-times-harbinger-nations-gang-up-on-israel/.

9. See, for example, the Left Behind series—which, although fiction, follows the premillennial dispensational theology of Tim LeHaye.

10. Some useful resources are Jerry L. Walls, ed., *The Oxford Handbook of Eschatology* (Oxford: Oxford University Press, 2008); Patricia Beattie Jung, *Sex on Earth as It Is in Heaven: A Christian Eschatology of Desire* (Albany: State University of New York Press, 2017); and Margaret D. Kamitsuka, ed., *The Embrace of Eros: Bodies, Desires, and Sexuality in Christianity* (Minneapolis, MN: Fortress Press, 2010).

11. Rosemary Radford Ruether, *Christianity and the Making of the Modern Family* (Boston, MA: Beacon Press, 2000), especially 36–50.

12. Elaine Pages, *The Origin of Satan* (New York: Vintage Books, 1996), 35–88.

13. Matthew 25:31–46, *New Revised Standard Version (NRSV)*.

14. As a Christian theologian writing about eschatology confessionally, Andrew Kuyvenhoven writes of the interim this way: "By choosing twelve apostles, Jesus began to gather the remnant of the twelve tribes of Israel. He trained his followers to be a new community that would practice the love of our Father in Heaven (Matt. 43–48), oppose worldly values, honor children, and prize servanthood (Matt. 20:25–27).... During the interim period between the resurrection and the return of their Master, the people of the Messiah will have to fulfill a mission for the kingdom of God." This mission includes, Kuyvenhoven notes, ways of being in the world that concern what Christians value and consider praiseworthy. Kuyvenhoven, *The Day of Christ's Return* (Grand Rapids, MI: CRC Publications, 1999), 33.

15. Jung, 38.

16. Romans 5:18, *NRSV*.

17. 1 Corinthians 15:22, *NRSV*.

18. 1 Corinthians 3:11–15, *NRSV*.

19. Rob Bell, *Love Wins* (New York: HarperOne, 2011), 48–52.

20. *Mathew Henry's Concise Commentary* notes, "Christ is a firm, abiding, and immovable Rock of ages, every way able to bear all the weight that God himself or the sinner can lay upon him; neither is there salvation in any other. Leave out the doctrine of his atonement, and there is no foundation for our hopes. But for those who rest on this foundation, there are two sorts. Some hold nothing but the truth as it is in Jesus, and preach nothing else. Others build on the good foundation what will not abide the test, when the day of trial comes.... Those who spread true and pure religion in all its branches, and whose work will abide in the great day, shall receive a reward." Accessed October 25, 2017, http://biblehub.com/commentaries/1_corinthians/3-11.htm.

21. Jan Bonda, *The One Purpose of God: An Answer to the Doctrine of Eternal Punishment* (Grand Rapids, MI: Eerdmans, 1998), 197.

22. 2 Peter 2:4–5, 9–10, *NRSV*.

23. See, for example, Luke 23:43 and 2 Corinthians 5:8.

24. See, for example, John 11:25–26, Romans 6:5, and 1 Thessalonians 4:16, among others.

25. Elna Mouton, "The Reorienting Potential of Biblical Narrative," in *Character Ethics and the New Testament: Moral Dimensions of Scripture*, ed. Robert L. Brawley, 36–96 (Louisville, KY: Westminster John Knox Press, 2007), 37.

26. Ilaria L. E. Ramelli, "Origen, Bardaisan, and the Origin of Universal Salvation," *Harvard Theological Review* 102, no. 2 (April 2009): 135–168.

27. In truth, it could be argued that the judgment passages in the New Testament were purposefully written to confront and destabilize the (pre)dispositions of the hearer or reader of the Christian scriptures for any number of reasons. When approached in this way, eschatological texts may not have been written to be received literally or simplistically, nor to be read so as to promote absolute doctrines of eternal damnation. That may sound like wishful thinking or an overly charitable reading of New Testament eschatology. Without question, it is not certain that any of the New Testament writers had such a charitable heart behind the harsh strokes of their pen. As Elaine Pagels has noted, many of the eschatological judgment passages in the New Testament likely functioned to create and maintain the social identities of true believers, orthodox leaders, and faithful communities—distinguishing them from those deemed heretical (*The Origin of Satan* [New York: Vintage Books, 1996], 149–178). If Pagels is correct, then the judgment passages were originally deployed, in part, to critique particular religious leaders and faith communities whose theologies (and practices) were seen as illegitimate. In other words, passages of condemnation in the New Testament scriptures may very well have functioned to create emerging categories of "us" (the righteous) and "them" (the condemned). Even so, more hopeful readings of New Testament passages on eschatology are not altogether weak (even if theorists like Pagels are, in part, also correct). After all, one of the repeated teachings of the New Testament texts is a call to repentance and transformation. That presence of a proselytizing agenda opens hopeful possibilities, even if the deployment of such an agenda is wrapped in the rhetoric of condemnation. Namely, when eschatological narratives of judgment are delivered to inspire repentance, such an effort must operate with some hope that the proclamation of judgment day might have as its most successful outcome the universal reconciliation of all people with God. Thus, even in the harshest of eschatological warnings one can find a seed of hope. That is not to ignore that there are different rhetorical efforts deployed by individuals using the New Testament texts in order to motivate people to seek communion with God. One rhetorical strategy seems to have been an effort to threaten people by drawing on the language of eternal hell and condemnation. Another rhetorical strategy to motivate faith in Christ has been to emphasize God's eternal love and grace. By entrusting salvation to the certain grace of God, it becomes possible to assert that "our free choices do not determine our eternal destiny," as Thomas Talbott has argued, "[but that] instead, they determine the lessons

we still need to learn in the present as we travel our own unique path in life" ("Universalism," in Jerry L. Walls, ed., *The Oxford Handbook of Eschatology*, 446–461 [Oxford: Oxford University Press, 2008], 457). Those life lessons, generally conceived, have been imagined (by some Christian theologians of antiquity and today) as causing all of creation to arc toward reconciliation with God. That said, Christians disagree about what reconciliation with God looks like. For some it means believing and confessing the right thing about Jesus. For others it means doing the right thing, whether in terms of ritual (such as baptism), personal morality, or social justice. For still others, the transformation that God seeks to bring upon human beings is something happening to all people, as a work of universal grace—a grace with which humans might learn to consciously cooperate. On this matter, Christian theologians speculate and argue.

28. Philip Schaff, *Creeds of Christendom*, rev. ed. (Ada, MI: Baker Books, 1984).
29. 1 Corinthians 7:29–31, *NRSV*.
30. 2 Peter 3:8–10, *NRSV*.
31. Matthew 24:36–44, *NRSV*.
32. For more on the already/not yet dynamic, see chapter 6.
33. Jarslov Pelikan, *The Christian Tradition: The Emergence of the Catholic Tradition (100–600)* (Chicago: University of Chicago Press, 1971), 124.
34. Jarslov, 355.
35. Jarslov, 355.
36. Mathew Keufler, "Desire and the Body in the Patristic Period," in *The Oxford Handbook of Theology, Sexuality, and Gender*, ed. Adrian Thatcher, 241–254 (Oxford: Oxford University Press, 2014), 246–247.
37. Matthew 19:12, *NRSV*.
38. See Ruether.
39. See Reuther, especially her chapter on the sexual ascetics.
40. Uta Ranke-Heinemann, *Eunuchs for the Kingdom of Heaven: Women, Sexuality, and the Catholic Church*, trans. Peter Heinegg (New York: Doubleday, 1990), 46–63.
41. Richard W. McCarty, *Sexual Virtue: An Approach to Contemporary Christian Ethics* (Albany: State University of New York Press, 2015), 21.
42. Ranke-Heinemann, 47.
43. Ranke-Heinemann, 47.
44. *Catechism of the Catholic Church*, para. 1008, English trans. (Liguori, MO: Liguori Publications, 1994), 263.
45. *Institutes of the Christian Religion*, 2.VIII.49. trans. and ed. John T. McNeill (Philadelphia, PA: Westminster Press, 1960), 422, 423.
46. See, for example, Anthony Petro's *After the Wrath of God* (New York: Oxford University Press, 2015).
47. Hans Schwarz, *Eschatology* (Grand Rapids, MI: Eerdmans, 2000), 259.
48. Schwarz, 259.

49. Schwarz, 259.

50. Schwarz, 259.

51. Richard W. McCarty, *Sexual Virtue: An Approach to Contemporary Christian Ethics* (Albany: SUNY Press, 2015), 98.

52. McCarty, *Sexual Virtue*, 99.

53. McCarty, *Sexual Virtue*, 101.

54. McCarty, *Sexual Virtue*, 101.

55. See Augustine, *On the Good of Marriage*, 401.

56. Augustine, *On the Good of Marriage*.

57. Augustine, *On the Good of Marriage*.

58. Augustine, *City of God*, trans. Henry Bettenson (London: Penguin Books, 1972), Book XIV.23, 26.

59. Augustine, *City of God*, Book XIV.23, 26.

60. Augustine, *City of God*, Book XXII.19.

61. Augustine, *City of God*, Books XIV.22, XXII.24; Peter Brown, *The Body and Society: Men, Women, and Sexual Renunciation in Early Christianity (Twentieth Anniversary Edition)* (New York: Columbia University Press, 2008), 294–295; Ruether,

62. Margaret Miles, "Sex and the City (of God): Is Sex Forfeited or Fulfilled in Augustine's Resurrection of the Body?" *Journal of the American Academy of Religion* 73, no. 2 (June 2005): 321–235.

63. Augustine, *City of God*, XXII.24.

64. Augustine, *City of God* XX–XXII.

65. See Augustine, "On Free Will," Book 1.1: "Evil deeds are punished by the justice of God. They would not be justly punished unless they were done voluntarily." In J. H. Burleigh, ed., *Augustine: Earlier Writings* (Philadelphia, PA: Westminster Press, 1953), 113.

66. Pope John Paul, *Catechism of the Catholic Church*, 1992, para. 997, 206.

67. Pope John Paul II, *Theology of the Body*, "The Resurrection and Theological Anthropology," 66, accessed September 15, 2017, http://www.catholicnewsagency.com/document/66-the-resurrection-and-theological-anthropology-877/.

68. David Jensen, *God, Desire, and a Theology of Human Sexuality* (Louisville, KY: Westminster John Knox Press, 2013), 67.

69. Calvin, 3.XXV.11.

70. Calvin, 3.XXV.11.

71. Stanley Grenz, *Sexual Ethics: An Evangelical Perspective* (Louisville, KY: Westminster John Knox Press, 1997), 26.

CHAPTER 4

1. Patricia Beattie Jung, *Sex on Earth as It Is in Heaven: A Christian Eschatology of Desire* (Albany: State University of New York Press, 2017), 97.

2. Revelation 4:1, *New Revised Standard Version (NRSV)*.

3. See, for example, Samuel Morris Brown, *In Heaven as It Is on Earth: Joseph Smith and the Early Mormon Conquest of Death* (Oxford: Oxford University Press, 2012), 145, 205–206, 208, 225, 230, 256. Paul J. Griffiths also considers possible theocentric varieties, including "simple stasis" and "repetitive statis." See Griffiths, *Decreation: The Last Things of All Creatures* (Waco, TX: Baylor University Press, 2014), 19–23.

4. I draw on the language of theocentric and domestic heaven as first articulated by Samuel Morris Brown in *In Heaven as It Is on Earth: Joseph Smith and the Early Mormon Conquest of Death*. Christian theologians may have other ways of describing heaven, for example: the exclusive gaze of God forever or the inclusive communion of saints.

5. David Jensen, *God, Desire, and a Theology of Human Sexuality* (Louisville, KY: Westminster John Knox Press, 2013). See chapter 4, "Eschatology and Sex—Making All Things New," 55–72.

6. Jensen, 68.
7. Jensen, 63.
8. Jensen, 63.
9. Jensen, 63.
10. Jensen, 64.
11. Jensen, 64.
12. Jensen, 64.
13. Jensen, 56.

14. For readers not yet familiar with this terminology, to be cisgender is to have a gender identity that conforms with one's physical sex: for example, a physical male who identifies as a man. This is in contrast with a transgender identity, in which a person's gender identity does not conform with their physical sex assigned at birth: for example, someone who identifies as a woman but who was born with genetic XY physical traits. Current MRI studies point toward the structure of the brain as potentially informing gender identity. When considering diverse instantiations of physical sex and/or gender identity (e.g., intersex, gender-queer, nonbinary, etc.) the reader is encouraged to consider insights from the biomedical sciences as well as critical gender/social theory.

15. Jensen, 56.
16. Jensen, 57.
17. Jensen, 57–58.
18. Jensen, 58.
19. Jensen, 60.
20. Patrick S. Cheng, *Radical Love: An Introduction to Queer Theology* (New York: Seabury Books, 2011), 121.
21. Cheng, 131–136.
22. Jensen, 66–67.
23. Jensen, 67. In particular, Jensen cites the Gospel of Mark, in which Sadducees ask Jesus questions about marriage in the resurrection of the dead (a trap in the

form of a riddle, given that the historic Sadducees did not believe in the resurrection as the Pharisees did).

24. Jensen, 59.

25. I have made a similar claim about recreation as a proper end of sexual virtue. See Richard McCarty, *Sexual Virtue: An Approach to Contemporary Christian Ethics* (Albany: State University of New York Press, 2015).

26. Jensen, 67.

27. Jensen, 68.

28. John 21.

29. John 20:24–29.

30. John 20:19–20.

31. Luke 24:13–35.

32. Luke 24:13–35, John 20:11–18.

33. Luke 24:50-53 and Acts 1:6-11.

34. Hebrews 12:2, *NRSV*.

35. Margaret Kamitsuka, "Sex in Heaven?" In *The Embrace of Eros: Bodies, Desires, an Sexuality in Christianity*, ed. Margaret D. Kamitsuka, 261–276 (Minneapolis, MN: Fortress Press, 2010), 263, my emphasis.

36. Kamitsuka, 263.

37. Kamitsuka, 264.

38. Kamitsuka, 264.

39. Kamitsuka, 265.

40. Kamitsuka, 265.

41. Kamitsuka, 268.

42. Kamitsuka, 268.

43. Kamitsuka, 268.

44. Kamitsuka, 270.

45. Kamitsuka, 270.

46. Kamitsuka, 271.

47. Kamitsuka, 271.

48. Kamitsuka, 271.

49. Kamitsuka, 272.

50. Kamitsuka, 272.

51. Kamitsuka, 272.

52. Kamitsuka, 274.

53. Kamitsuka, 274.

54. Kamitsuka, 274.

55. Kamitsuka, 275.

56. Kamitsuka, 275.

57. See, for example, Richard W. McCarty, "Objects of the Inquisition, or the Trials of Religion Scholars at Catholic Institutions Who Engage with Sexuality Studies," *Academe*, January–February 2014, 24–29.

58. Mark 12:18-27, *NRSV*.
59. Jung, 53.
60. Jung, 55.
61. Jung, 57.
62. See, for example, John 8 and Matthew 5:27-28.
63. Matthew 19:12, *NRSV*.
64. Matthew 19:3-9.
65. Matthew 19:10, *NRSV*.
66. Jung, 62.
67. Jung, 64; my emphasis.
68. Jung, 80.
69. Jung, 73-74.
70. Jung, 76.
71. Jung, 77.
72. Jung, 78.
73. Jung, 79.
74. Jung, 89.
75. Jung, 89.
76. Jung, 93.

77. That Augustine did not consider these possibilities is likely owed to the story of how he came of age and how he eventually came to faith. Augustine had been a sexual hedonist in his early adulthood. By his own admission, he was an indiscriminate pursuer of sexual pleasure. But he eventually exchanged the pleasures of sex for the pleasures of contemplation, finding his way through a number of religious and philosophical schools of thought. First it was Manichaeism, a dualistic religion that denigrated corporeal life. Next it was Neoplatonism, a mystical philosophy that was, in part, ordered toward transcending the physical plane. Augustine found that each of these systems of thought had something to say about the status of sexual relationships. Manichaeism taught that the physical world was a world of evil and darkness. Thus, sex was itself was to be eschewed. Neoplatonism taught that it is the goal of human beings to free their spirits in order to return to "the One," the intelligent source of all things. In this view, sex was not seen as inherently bad, but it certainly needed to be well ordered as a matter of moral philosophy. Thus, by the time he became a bishop in the Christian tradition, Augustine's reflections on creation, sin, sex, marriage, love, procreation, redemption, and eschatology were all inextricably informed by the life he had lived and the philosophies he had studied. These surely—in some way (whether conscious or not)—contoured the Christian faith that he eventually professed.

78. Jung, 96.
79. Jung, 112-113.
80. Jung, 113.

81. Jung highlights the work of Edward Vacek in his book, *Love, Human and Divine: The Heart of Christian Ethics* (Washington, DC: Georgetown University

Press, 1994). I too have made the argument to separate notions of sexual morality from a marital or procreative end in *Sexual Virtue*. See also Margaret A. Farley's book, *Just Love: A Framework for Christian Sexual Ethics* (New York: Continuum International Publishing, 2006).

82. Jung, 115.
83. Jung, 115.
84. Jung, 117.
85. Jung, 116.
86. Jung, 107.
87. Jung, 107.
88. Jung, 107.

89. On the one hand, we are sensory and bodily beings that experience a range of basic inclinations because of our biological and genetic makeup. Hunger, thirst, sex, fight, flight; these aren't just intellectual experiences. As physical sensory beings we incline toward, or shy away from, various stimuli (in part) because we possess bodies that are capable of apprehending certain objects as delectable or undesirable. This is part of our animal nature. We share it in common with our pets. For example, one's friendly dog might smell peanut butter as the jar is being opened. His nose starts sniffing, his tail starts wagging, and very soon that canine is yearning for a creamy treat. Human beings, too, experience such sensory, bodily inclinations; but they are never independent from intellectual inclinations.

This is an insight that the theologian Thomas Aquinas and scholar of religion Diana Fritz Cates have argued quite well. According to both Aquinas and Cates, that humans experience both sensory and intellectual inclinations is simply a matter of being the kind of creatures that we are. However, what distinguishes us as human is not our sensory inclinations (as these are shared by other animal lifeforms). Rather, we are distinguished by our rational capacity. Thus, as rational embodied beings, following our sensory inclinations may be *natural* to us, but it may not always be *good* for us. As Aquinas and Cates both say, the pursuit of the good and the enjoyment of human happiness require the light of reason. Such an insight is important to how we reflect on sexual ethics. Jung agrees. Namely, at the same time that we experience a sensory inclination toward something or someone, we intellectually apprehend those same objects or people. The human intellectual capacity (generally conceived) apprehends those objects as good, or beautiful, or suitable to us, in qualitative terms. We do so, because as rational creatures we are meaning-making creatures; we assign value to things. It is natural to us. Admittedly, arguments are ongoing as to whether the intellect first produces emotions that become sensory feelings (which would allow for rational therapy to transform desire) or if the intellect is *responding* to sensory inclinations (which would allow reason to reflect on emotions, but not necessarily transform all sensory feelings).

90. Jung, 134–135.

91. Jung, 137.
92. See McCarty, *Sexual Virtue*, Chapter 4.
93. McCarty, *Sexual Virtue*, 160.

CHAPTER 5

1. Ecclesiastes 8:15, *NRSV*.
2. 1 Corinthians 13:12, *NRSV*.
3. Hans Schwarz, *Eschatology* (Grand Rapids, MI: Eerdmans Publishing, 2000), 161.
4. Jaroslav Pelikan, *The Growth of the Medieval Theology (600–1300)* (Chicago: University of Chicago Press, 1978), 20, 101–102.
5. "Pseudo-Dionysus," in *Light from Light: An Anthology of Christian Mysticism*, ed. Louis Dupre and James Wiseman, 79–94 (New York: Paulist Press, 1988), 87.
6. Patrick Cheng, *Radical Love: An Introduction to Queer Theology* (New York: Seabury Books, 2001), 131.
7. For example, in paragraph 2709 of the *Catechism of the Catholic Church*, church teachers cite the Song of Solomon in one explanation of contemplative prayer and union with God. See *Catechism of the Catholic Church* (Liguori, MO: Liguori Publications, 1994), 650.
8. James Nelson, *Embodiment* (Minneapolis, MN: Augsburg, 1978), 15.
9. Luke 20:34–36, *NRSV*.
10. Rachel Biale, "Sexuality and Marital Relations," in *Sexuality*, ed. Karen Lebacqz and David Sinacore Guinn, 46–59 (Cleveland, OH: Pilgrim Press, 1999).
11. Luke 20:35–36, *NRSV*.
12. David Jensen, *God, Desire, and a Theology of Human Sexuality* (Louisville, KY: Westminster John Knox Press, 2013), 67.
13. Raymond Lawrence, *Sexual Liberation* (Westport, CT: Praeger, 2007), 5, 6, 12, 13, 31.
14. Laurel C. Schneider, "Promiscuous Incarnation," *The Embrace of Eros: Bodies, Desires, and Sexuality in Christianity*, ed. Margaret Kamitsuka, 231–246 (Minneapolis, MN: Fortress Press, 2010), 244.
15. David J. Ley, "Overcoming Religious Sexual Shame," *Psychology Today*, August 23, 2017, https://www.psychologytoday.com/us/blog/women-who-stray/201708/overcoming-religious-sexual-shame.
16. Ley.
17. Ley.
18. See, for example, https://www.livescience.com/11387-10-surprising-sex-statistics.html.
19. See Christopher Ryan and Cacilda Jetha, *Sex at Dawn: The Prehistoric Origins of Modern Sexuality* (New York: Harper Collins, 2010).

20. See 1 Samuel 13:14. Biblical scholars and theologians debate how this phrase should be interpreted. One thing seems certain: God had chosen David to be king in order to replace King Saul. David's nonmonogamous sex life did not seem to matter much in God's determination.

21. See William Countryman, *Dirt, Greed, and Sex*, rev. ed. Minneapolis, MN: Fortress Press, 2007).

22. 1 Timothy 3:2.

23. Psalm 19.

24. Luke 19:40, *NRSV*.

25. Patricia Beattie Jung, *Sex on Earth as It Is in Heaven: A Christian Eschatology of Desire* (Albany: SUNY Press, 2017), 64.

26. Emmanuel Swedenborg, *Love in Marriage: A Translation of Emanuel Swedenborg's The Sensible Joy in Married Love and the Foolish Pleasures of Illicit Love*, trans. David F. Gladish, 56 (West Chester, PA: Swedenborg Foundation, 2015).

27. Revelation 19:6–9, *NRSV*.

28. Revelation 21:9–10, *NRSV*.

29. Contemporary television series have explored these possibilities. See, for example, *Sister Wives* and *Big Love*.

30. Tim Keller, "Don't Be Gay for Jesus: Understand Why the 'Bride-Groom' Metaphor Doesn't Work for Individuals," *Pulpit & Pen*, April 21, 2018, https://pulpitandpen.org/2018/04/21/jesus-not-groom-ladies-men-not-jesus-bride/.

31. Keller.

32. Keller.

33. Keller.

34. *NRSV*.

35. *NRSV*.

36. *NRSV*.

37. Carol Bernice, "How Queer Is Celibacy?" in *Queer Christianities: Lived Religion in Transgressive Forms*, ed. Kathleen Talvachia, Michael Pettinger, and Mark Larrimore, 48–52 (New York: NYU Press, 2015), 51.

38. Bernice, 51.

39. Bernice, 51–52.

40. Bernice, 51–52.

CHAPTER 6

1. Hans Schwarz, *Eschatology* (Grand Rapids, MI: Eerdmans, 2000), 161.

2. Patricia Beattie Jung, *Sex on Earth as It Is in Heaven: A Christian Eschatology of Desire* (Albany: State University of New York Press, 2017), 117–118.

3. *Catechism of the Catholic Church*, Paragraphs 2331–2391 (Liguori, MO: Liguori Publications, 1994), 560–576.

4. Richard McCarty, *Sexual Virtue: An Approach to Contemporary Christian Ethics* (Albany: State University of New York Press, 2015), 233–236.

5. For example, Exodus 20:5, 34:14; Deuteronomy 4:24, 32:16; Joshua 24:19; and so on.

6. Noam Shpancer, "The Causes of Infidelity: Players Gonna Play?" *Psychology Today*, July 1, 2015, https://www.psychologytoday.com/us/blog/insight-therapy/201507/the-causes-infidelity-players-gonna-play.

7. Matthew 13:24–30.

8. *Catechism of the Catholic Church*, Paragraph 2351.

9. John 8:11. Biblical scholars note, however, that older manuscripts of the Gospel of John lack 7:53–8:11. Even if not original to the Gospel of John, it does suggest that early Christians were interested in applying concepts of mercy and restoration even to Torah capital offenses like adultery (as it was defined in those days).

10. Susan Krauss Whitbourne, "Why Sexual Narcissists Make Unfaithful Partners: New Research into Why Some Partners Are Prone to Stray," *Psychology Today*, December 27, 2014, https://www.psychologytoday.com/us/blog/fulfillment-any-age/201412/why-sexual-narcissists-make-unfaithful-partners.

11. Whitbourne.

12. Whitbourne.

13. See Christopher Ryan and Cacilda Jetha, *Sex at Dawn: The Prehistoric Origins of Modern Sexuality* (New York: HarperCollins, 2010).

14. Ryan and Jetha.

15. John Portmann, *The Ethics of Sex and Alzheimer's* (New York: Routledge, 2014).

16. "Hypersexuality (Sex Addiction)," *Psychology Today*, accessed July 9, 2018, https://www.psychologytoday.com/us/conditions/hypersexuality-sex-addiction. The article references include S. Adelson, R. Bell, D. Goldenberg, E. Haase, J. L. Downey, and R. C. Friedman, Toward a Definition of "Hypersexuality" in Children and Adolescents," *Psychodynamic Psychiatry* 40, no. 3 (2012): 481–503; American Psychiatric Association, *Diagnostic and Statistical Manual, Fifth Edition* (Washington, DC: APA, 2013); M. P. Kafka, "Hypersexual Disorder: A Proposed Diagnosis for DSM-V," *Archives of Sexual Behavior* 39, no. 2 (2010): 377–400; R. C. Reid, B. N. Carpenter, J. N. Hook, S. Garos, J. C. Manning, R. Gilliland, and T. Fong, "Report of Findings in a DSM-5 Field Trial for Hypersexual Disorder," *Journal of Sexual Medicine* 9, no. 11 (2013): 2868–2877.

17. "Hypersexuality (Sex Addiction)."

18. "Hypersexuality (Sex Addiction)."

19. "Hypersexuality (Sex Addition)."

20. Michael Patrick King, dir., *Sex and the City: The Movie* (New Line Cinema, Home Box Office [HBO], and Darren Star Productions, 2008); dialogue transcribed July 10, 2020.

21. Irina Baechle, "Lessons from a Couples Therapist: Marriage Is Destroyed by Emotional Distance, Not Conflict," *PsychCentral*, January 12, 2019, https://psychcentral.com/blog/lessons-from-a-couples-therapist-marriage-is-destroyed-by-emotional-distance-not-conflict/.

CHAPTER 7

1. See, for example, Ian Lecklitner, "Life as a Mega-Virgin: The People Who Save Kissing for Marriage," *Mel Magazine*, 2018, https://melmagazine.com/en-us/story/life-as-a-mega-virgin-the-people-who-save-kissing-for-marriage.

2. Laurel C. Schneider, "Promiscuous Incarnation," in *The Embrace of Eros: Bodies, Desires, and Sexuality in Christianity*, ed. Margaret Kamitsuka, 231–246 (Minneapolis, MN: Fortress Press, 2010), 244.

3. Schneider, 244.

4. *Marek + Richards*, accessed July 10, 2018, https://marekrichard.com/products/no-fats-no-fems-low-arm-tank-pink-sparkle?variant=19748675843.

5. See, for example, C.J. Wysocki and Y. Martins et al., "Preference for Human Body Odors Is Influenced by Gender and Sexual Orientation," *Psychological Science* 16, no. 9 (2005): 694–701.

6. Rowland Miller, *Intimate Relationships*, 6th ed. (New York: McGraw-Hill, 2012), 70–71, 77–84.

7. See Thomas Aquinas, *Summa Theologica*, on Temperance; Diana Cates, *Aquinas on the Emotions* (Washington, DC: Georgetown University Press, 2009); and Martha Nussbaum, *The Therapy of Desire* (reprint, Princeton, NJ: Princeton University Press, 1996).

8. See Richard W. McCarty, *Sexual Virtue: An Approach to Contemporary Christian Ethics* (Albany: State University of New York Press, 2015).

9. For one contemporary journalistic take, see Elaine Tyler May, "How the Catholic Church Almost Came to Accept Birth Control—In the 1960s," *Washington Post*, February 24, 2012, https://www.washingtonpost.com/opinions/how-the-catholic-church-almost-came-to-accept-birth-control/2012/02/21/gIQAdy1JYR_story.html. One can also examine the critical comments of Pope Paul VI on contraception (and the Catholic argument for it) in his *Humanae Vitae* (1968).

10. Elaine Tyler May.

11. See "Note on the Banalization of Sexuality Regarding Certain Interpretations of 'Light of the World,'" Congregation for the Doctrine of the Faith, the Vatican, 2010, http://www.vatican.va/roman_curia/congregations/cfaith/documents/rc_con_cfaith_doc_20101221_luce-del-mondo_en.html.

12. For a particularly helpful narrative on Protestant attitudes about abortion, consider the NPR interview, Rund Abdelfatah, interviewed by Noel King, "'Throughline' Traces Evangelicals' History on the Abortion Issue," *Morning Edition*, NPR, June 20,

2019, https://www.npr.org/2019/06/20/734303135/throughline-traces-evangelicals-history-on-the-abortion-issue.

13. Centers for Disease Control and Prevention, "Genital Herpes—CDC Fact Sheet," August 28, 2017, https://www.cdc.gov/std/herpes/stdfact-herpes.htm.

14. For example, in some people the HIV virus will not cause any symptoms for as long as ten years. See HIV.gov, accessed July 10, 2018, https://www.hiv.gov/hiv-basics/overview/about-hiv-and-aids/symptoms-of-hiv.

15. See, for example, Robert E. Goss, *Queering Christ: Beyond JESUS ACTED UP*, "Is There Sex in Heaven?," pp. 72–87. In this chapter, Goss recounts how he and his partner chose to navigate sexual relations with the knowledge that one of them was HIV-positive and the other was HIV-negative.

16. Goss, 72–87.

17. Goss, 72–87.

18. See, for example, Malia Jacobson, "Would You *Bleep* Someone with an STD?," *Women's Health*, June 13, 2012, https://www.womenshealthmag.com/relationships/a19923537/std-sex/.

19. McCarty, *Sexual Virtue*, 224.

20. Mary Hunt, "Love Your Friends," in *Queer Christianities: Lived Religion in Transgressive Forms*, ed. Kathleen T. Talvacchia, Michael F. Pettinger, and Mark Larrimore, 137–147 (New York: New York University Press, 2015, 140.

21. See Jess Singal, "Americans Are Sexually Experimenting Way More Than They Used To," June 1, 2016, https://www.thecut.com/2016/06/americans-are-sexually-experimenting-more.html.

22. For a short exploration of heteroflexibility, see Sian Ferguson, "What Does It Mean to Be Heteroflexible," *Healthline*, November 20, 2019, https://www.healthline.com/health/heteroflexible#underlying-contention.

23. Eliel Cruz, "Study: 1 in 3 American Young Adults Identify on Bisexual Spectrum," *Advocate*, August 20, 2015, https://www.advocate.com/bisexuality/2015/08/20/study-1-3-american-young-adults-identify-bisexual-spectrum.

24. See chapter 5

25. M. Loerger, J. J. Lehmiller, and L. E. VanderDrift, "Can Friends Who Have Sex Stay Friends?: A Longitudinal Study of 'Friends with Benefits,'" paper presented at the Society for the Scientific Study of Sexual Conference, Omaha, NE, November 2014, https://www.lehmiller.com/blog/2014/11/24/can-friends-with-benefits-stay-friends.

26. Koerger, Lehmiller, and VanderDrift.

27. Koerger, Lehmiller, and VanderDrift.

28. Koerger, Lehmiller, and VanderDrift.

29. Koerger, Lehmiller, and VanderDrift.

30. See McCarty, *Sexual Virtue*.

31. Cruz.

32. Cruz.

33. More strictly speaking, polygyny was practiced in the scriptures: one man with many wives; recognizing that polygamy may be conceived of as multiple husbands or wives in such gendered terms.

34. Mark 3:32–35, *NRSV*.

35. Matthew 25:40, *NRSV*.

36. Acts 2:44–47, NRSV.

37. Joseph Fischel, *Sex and Harm in the Age of Consent* (Minneapolis: University of Minnesota Press, 2016), 4.

38. Helen Longino, "Pornography, Oppression, and Freedom: A Closer Look," in *Representing Women*, ed. Linda Nochlin (New York: Thames and Hudson, 2019), 155.

39. Longino, 156.

40. "10 Popular Ex-Porn Performers Reveal the Brutal Truth behind Their Most Famous Scenes," *Fight the New Drug*, October 26, 2017, https://fightthenewdrug.org/10-porn-stars-speak-openly-about-their-most-popular-scenes/.

41. "10 Popular Ex-Porn Performers," "Jessie"

42. "10 Popular Ex-Porn Performers," "Genevieve."

43. "5-Ex Male Porn Performers Share Their Real Experiences Doing Porn," *Fight the New Drug*, September 29, 2017, https://fightthenewdrug.org/3-male-porn-stars-share-their-most-disturbing-experiences-doing-porn/ on July 13, 2018, "Aaron."

44. "5-Ex Male Porn Performers," "Trent."

45. Patricia Beattie Jung, *Sex on Earth as It Is in Heaven: A Christian Eschatology of Desire* (Albany: State University of New York Press, 2017), 178.

46. Jung, 178, 179.

47. Jung, 180.

48. Jung, 182.

49. Ley, David. "Overcoming Religious Shame," *Psychology Today*. August 23, 2017, https://www.psychologytoday.com/us/blog/women-who-stray/201708/overcoming-religious-sexual-shame.

50. Ley.

51. "About Himeros TV," accessed July 13, 2018, https://www.himeros.tv/tour/about/.

52. "Davey Wavey Wants You to Get Off—And Get In—With Himeros.tv," *Boy Culture*, February 12, 2018, http://www.boyculture.com/boy_culture/2018/02/davey-wavey.html.

53. "About Anna," *Dr. Anna Arrowsmith*, accessed July 13, 2018, https://annaarrowsmith.com/about-anna/.

54. "About Anna."

55. "About Anna."

56. Anna Arrowsmith, "My Pornographic Development," in *Pornographic Art and the Aesthetics of Pornography*, ed. H. Maes, 287–298 (London: Palgrave Macmillan, 2013), 287.

57. Emine Saner, "Can Sex Films Empower Women?" *Guardian*, March 5, 2011, https://www.theguardian.com/commentisfree/2011/mar/05/conversation-gail-dines-anna-arrowsmith?INTCMP=SRCH.

58. Saner.

59. "About We Consent," *Dr. Anna Arrowsmith*, accessed July 13, 2018, https://annaarrowsmith.com/about-weconsent-2/.

60. Catalina May, "Porn Made for Women, by Women," *Guardian*, March 22, 2011, https://www.theguardian.com/lifeandstyle/2011/mar/22/porn-women.

61. Catalina May.

62. Government of Australia, Royal Commission into Institutional Responses to Child Sexual Abuse, "Final Report," December 2017, https://www.childabuseroyalcommission.gov.au/final-report.

63. Thomas Reese, "Abandoning Celibacy Won't Stop Sexual Abuse by Priests," *Religion News*, December 19, 2017, https://religionnews.com/2017/12/19/abandoning-celibacy-wont-stop-sexual-abuse-by-priests/.

64. Thomas Plante, Thomas. "Six Myths about Clergy Sexual Abuse in the Catholic Church," *Psychology Today*. March 24, 2010. Accessed from https://www.psychologytoday.com/us/blog/do-the-right-thing/201003/six-myths-about-clergy-sexual-abuse-in-the-catholic-church.

65. See, for example, the editorial, "Priests & Pedophilia": "There is easy talk about how a celibate priesthood, the church's 'retrograde' sexual teachings, and its hierarchical structure conspire to produce [sexual] crimes. . . . Certainly the church is in need of rethinking and reform in these and many other areas. But linking them to pedophilia should be viewed for what it is: mere speculation and often highly partisan speculation at that. Just as priesthood is no excuse for sexual crime, so it is no explanation." *Commonweal*, June 16, 2004, https://www.commonwealmagazine.org/priests-pedophilia.

SELECTED BIBLIOGRAPHY

"About Anna." *Dr. Anna Arrowsmith*. Accessed July 13, 2018, https://annaarrowsmith.com/about-anna/.

"About We Consent." *Dr. Anna Arrowsmith*. Accessed July 13, 2018. https://annaarrowsmith.com/about-weconsent-2/.

Adelson, S., Bell, R., Goldenberg, D., Haase, E., Downey, J. I., and Friedman, R. C. "Toward a Definition of 'Hypersexuality' in Children and Adolescents." *Psychodynamic Psychiatry*, 40, no. 3 (2012): 481–503.

Al-Qur'an: A Contemporary Translation. Trans. Ahmed Ali. Princeton, NJ: Princeton University Press, 1993.

American Psychiatric Association. *Diagnostic and Statistical Manual*. 4th ed., rev. Washington, DC: APA, 1994.

Anderson, Christy. "A Case for Christian Swinging." *Swingers-in-Love*. Accessed June 27, 2017. http://swingers-in-love.blogspot.com/p/case-for-christian-swinging.html.

Anwar, Ghazala. "Elements of a Samadiyyah Sharia." In *Heterosexism in Contemporary World Religion: Problem and Prospect*, ed. Marvin Ellison and Judith Plaskow. 85-86. Cleveland, OH: Pilgrim Press, 2007.

Aquinas, Thomas. *Summa Theologica* (ST) I–II.62; II–II.154.1, 11.

Archer, Clint. "SCOTUS and Premillennialism." *The Cripplegate*, June 29, 2014. http://thecripplegate.com/scotus-and-premillennialism/.

Arrowsmith, Anna. "My Pornographic Development." In *Pornographic Art and the Aesthetics of Pornography*, ed. H. Maes, 287–298. London: Palgrave Macmillan, 2013.

Augustine. *City of God*. Trans. Henry Bettenson. London: Penguin Books, 1972.

———. *On the Good of Marriage*. Trans. C. L. Cornish. *Nicene and Post-Nicene Fathers, First Series*, ed. Philipp Schaff. Buffalo, NY: Christian Literature Publishing, 1887.

Bell, Rob. *Love Wins*. New York: HarperOne, 2011.

Bellis, Alice Ogden. *Helpmates, Harlots, and Heroes: Women's Stories in the Hebrew Bible*. Louisville, KY: Westminster John Knox Press, 2007.

Bernice, Carol. "How Queer Is Celibacy?" In *Queer Christianities: Lived Religion in Transgressive Forms*, ed. Kathleen Talvachia, Michael Pettinger, and Mark Larrimore, 48–52. New York: New York University Press, 2015.

Biale, Rachel. "Sexuality and Marital Relations." In *Sexuality: A Reader*, ed. Karen Lebacqz and David Sinacore Guinn, 46–59. Cleveland, OH: Pilgrim Press, 2000.

Blaedel, Anna. "An Open Letter to the UMC." May 1, 2018. https://www.facebook.com/anna.blaedel.

Bonda, Jan. *The One Purpose of God: An Answer to the Doctrine of Eternal Punishment*. Grand Rapids, MI: Eerdmans, 1998.

Brown, Peter. *The Body and Society: Men, Women, and Sexual Renunciation in Early Christianity (Twentieth Anniversary Edition)*. New York: Columbia University Press, 2008.

Brown, Samuel Morris. *In Heaven as It Is on Earth: Joseph Smith and the Early Mormon Conquest of Death*. Oxford: Oxford University Press, 2012.

Butler, Rex. *The New Prophecy and "New Visions."* Washington, DC: Catholic University of America Press, 2006.

Cahill, Lisa Sowle. *Sex, Gender, and Christian Ethics*. Cambridge: Cambridge University Press, 1996.

Calvin, John. *Institutes of the Christian Religion*, 2:VIII.49. Trans. and ed. John T. McNeill. Philadelphia, PA: Westminster Press, 1960.

Camping, Harold. *Time Has an End: A Biblical History of the World 11,013 B.C.–2011 A.D.* Alameda, CA: Family Stations, 2005.

Cates, Diana. *Aquinas on the Emotions*. Washington, DC: Georgetown University Press, 2009.

Cheng, Patrick S. *Radical Love: An Introduction to Queer Theology*. New York: Seabury Books, 2011.

Colarossi, Anthony. "Man Gets 90 Years in Arson, Murder Attempts on Family." *Orlando Sentinel*. April 25, 2006. http://articles.orlandosentinel.com/2006-04-25/news/GASATTACK25_1_gasoline-kest-hans.

Coogan, Michael. *The Old Testament: A Historical and Literary Introduction to the Hebrew Scriptures*. New York: Oxford University Press, 2006.

Corbett, Julia Mitchell. *Religion in America*. 4th ed. Upper Saddle River, NJ: Prentice Hall, 2000.

Countryman, William. *Dirt, Greed, and Sex*. Rev. ed. Minneapolis, MN: Fortress Press, 2007.

Cruz, Eliel. "Study: 1 in 3 American Young Adults Identify on Bisexual Spectrum." *Advocate*. August 20, 2015. https://www.advocate.com/bisexuality/2015/08/20/study-1-3-american-young-adults-identify-bisexual-spectrum.

"Davey Wavey Wants You to Get Off—And Get In—With Himeros.tv." *Boy Culture*. February 12, 2018. http://www.boyculture.com/boy_culture/2018/02/davey-wavey.html.

Eben, Alexander. *Proof of Heaven: A Neurosurgeon's Journey into the Afterlife*. New York: Simon and Schuster, 2012.

Evangelical Lutheran Church in America (ELCA). "A Social Statement on Human Sexuality: Gift and Trust." Minneapolis, MN, August 19, 2009.

Farley, Margaret. "Sexual Ethics." In *Sexuality and the Sacred*, ed. James Nelson and Sandra Longfellow, 65–66. Louisville, KY: Westminster John Knox Press, 1994.

Fischel, Joseph. *Sex and Harm in the Age of Consent*. Minneapolis: University of Minnesota Press, 2016.

"5 Ex Male Porn Performers Share Their Real Experiences Doing Porn." *Fight the New Drug*, September 29, 2017. https://fightthenewdrug.org/3-male-porn-stars-share-their-most-disturbing-experiences-doing-porn/.

Foster, Lawrence. "The Psychology of Free Love in the Oneida Community." *Australasian Journal of American Studies* 5, no. 2 (December 1986): 14–26.

Goss, Robert E. *Queering Christ: Beyond JESUS ACTED UP*. Cleveland, OH: Pilgrim Press, 2002.

Government of Australia. Royal Commission into Institutional Responses to Child Sexual Abuse. "Final Report." December 2017. https://www.childabuseroyalcommission.gov.au/final-report.

Grenz, Stanley. *Sexual Ethics: An Evangelical Perspective*. Louisville, KY: Westminster John Knox Press, 1997.

Hahn, Heather. "Gay Clergywoman's Case Heads to Top Court." *United Methodist News*, July 7, 2017. http://www.umc.org/news-and-media/gay-clergywomans-case-heads-to-top-court#.WV-3rucQkSA.facebook.

Harding, Sarah. *Paul's Eschatological Anthropology: The Dynamics of Human Transformation*. Minneapolis, MN: Augsburg Fortress Press, 2015.

Harrell, Charles R. "The Development of the Doctrine of Preexistence, 1830–1844." *Brigham Young University Studies* 28, no. 2 (1988): 75–96.

Humphrey, Caroline. "Sex in the City—The New Polygamy." *Cambridge Journal of Anthropology* 29, no. 2 (2009): 21–25.

Hunt, Mary. "Love Your Friends." In *Queer Christianities: Lived Religion in Transgressive Forms*, ed. Kathleen T. Talvacchia, Michael F. Pettinger, and Mark Larrimore, 137–147. New York: New York University Press, 2015.

Jacobson, Malia. "Would You *Bleep* Someone with an STD?" *Women's Health*, June 13, 2012. https://www.womenshealthmag.com/relationships/a19923537/std-sex/.

Jensen, David. *God, Desire, and a Theology of Human Sexuality*. Louisville, KY: Westminster John Knox Press, 2013.

Jersild, Paul. *Spirit Ethics: Scripture and the Moral Life*. Minneapolis, MN: Fortress Press, 2000.

Jung, Patricia Beattie. *Sex on Earth as It Is in Heaven: A Christian Eschatology of Desire*. Albany: State University of New York Press, 2017.

Kafka, M. P. "Hypersexual Disorder: A Proposed Diagnosis for DSM-V." *Archives of Sexual Behavior* 39, no. 2 (2010): 377–400.

Kahn, Yoel. "Making Love as Making Justice." In *Sexuality: A Reader*, ed. Karen Lebacqz and David Sinacore-Guinn, 581–589. Cleveland, OH: Pilgrim Press, 2000.

Kamitsuka, Margaret D.. "Sex in Heaven?" In *The Embrace of Eros: Bodies, Desires, and Sexuality in Christianity*, ed. Margaret D. Kamitsuka, 261–276. Minneapolis, MN: Fortress Press, 2010.

Kephart, William. "Experimental Family Organization: An Historico-Cultural Report on the Oneida Community." *Marriage and Family Living* 25, no. 3 (August 1963): 261-271.

Keufler, Mathew. "Desire and the Body in the Patristic Period." In *The Oxford Handbook of Theology, Sexuality, and Gender*, ed. Adrian Thatcher, 241–254. Oxford: Oxford University Press, 2014.

Kilde, Jeanne Halgren, "A Historical Look at Millenarian Thought." In *Rapture, Revelation, and the End Times: Exploring the Left Behind Series*, ed. Bruce Forbes and Jeanne Halgren Kilde, 33–70. New York: Palgrave Macmillan, 2004.

Kohlberg, Lawrence. *The Philosophy of Moral Development*. New York: Harper and Row, 1981.

Kuyvenhoven, Andrew. *The Day of Christ's Return*. Grand Rapids, MI: CRC Publications, 1999.

Lawrence, Raymond. *Sexual Liberation*. Westport, CT: Praeger, 2007.

LeHaye, Tim, and Jenkins, Jerry. *Left Behind*. Carol Stream, IL: Tyndale House, 1995.

Lewis, Justin Jaron. *Imaging Holiness: Classic Hasidic Tales in Modern Times*. Montreal: McGill-Queen's University Press, 2009.

Ley, David J. "Overcoming Religious Sexual Shame." *Psychology Today*, August 23, 2017. https://www.psychologytoday.com/us/blog/women-who-stray/201708/overcoming-religious-sexual-shame.

Loerger, M., Lehmiller, J. J., and VanderDrift, L. E. "Can Friends Who Have Sex Stay Friends?: A Longitudinal Study of 'Friends with Benefits.'" Paper presented at the Society for the Scientific Study of Sexual Conference, Omaha, NE, November 2014. https://www.lehmiller.com/blog/2014/11/24/can-friends-with-benefits-stay-friends.

Longino, Helen. "Pornography, Oppression, and Freedom: A Closer Look." In *Representing Women*, ed. Linda Nochlin, 155–156. New York: Thames and Hudson, 1999.

May, Catalina. "Porn Made for Women, by Women." *Guardian*, March 22, 2011. https://www.theguardian.com/lifeandstyle/2011/mar/22/porn-women.

McCarty, Richard W. "Objects of the Inquisition, or the Trials of Religion Scholars at Catholic Institutions Who Engage with Sexuality Studies." *Academe*, January–February 2014.

Miles, Margaret. "Sex and the City (of God): Is Sex Forfeited or Fulfilled in Augustine's Resurrection of the Body?" *Journal of the American Academy of Religion* 73, no. 2 (June 2005): 307–327.

Mitra, Indrani. "'There Is No Sin in Our Love': Homoerotic Desire in the Stories of Two Muslim Women Writers." *Tulsa Studies in Women's Literature* 29, no. 2 (2010): 311–329.

Moorhead, James. "The Erosion of Postmillennialism in American Religious Thought, 1865–1925." *Church History* 53, no. 1 (2009): 61–77.

Mouton, Elna. "The Reorienting Potential of Biblical Narrative." In *Character Ethics and the New Testament: Moral Dimensions of Scripture*, ed. Robert L. Brawley, 36–96. Louisville, KY: Westminster John Knox Press, 2007.

Murray, Stephen, and Roscoe, Will. *Islamic Homosexualities*. New York: New York University Press, 1997.

Nelson, James. *Embodiment*. Minneapolis, MN: Augsburg Publishing, 1978.

Nussbuam, Martha. *Sex and Social Justice*. Oxford: Oxford University Press, 1995.

Pagels, Elaine. *The Origin of Satan*. New York: Vintage Books, 1996.

Pelikan, Jarslov. *The Christian Tradition: The Emergence of the Catholic Tradition (100–600)*. Chicago: University of Chicago Press, 1971.

Perez, Chris. "These Christians Swingers Like Sharing Bible Verses, Sex Partners." *New Post*, September 25, 2014. Living. http://nypost.com/2014/09/25/these-christian-swingers-like-sharing-bible-verses-sex-partners/.

Petro, Anthony. *After the Wrath of God*. New York: Oxford University Press, 2015.

Phillips, Richard D. *The Masculine Mandate*. Sanford, FL: Reformation Trust, 2016.

Plante, Thomas. "Six Myths about Clergy Sexual Abuse in the Catholic Church." *Psychology Today*, March 24, 2010. https://www.psychologytoday.com/us/blog/do-the-right-thing/201003/six-myths-about-clergy-sexual-abuse-in-the-catholic-church.

Pope John Paul II. "The Resurrection and Theological Anthropology." *Theology of the Body*, 66. Accessed September 15, 2017. http://www.catholicnewsagency.com/document/66-the-resurrection-and-theological-anthropology-877/.

Pope John Paul. *Catechism of the Catholic Church*. 1992. Paragraphs 2032, 2331–2440; 1008; 997.

Portmann, John. *The Ethics of Sex and Alzheimer's*. New York: Routledge Press, 2014.

———. *Sexual Virtue: A Contemporary Approach to Christian Ethics*. Albany: State University of New York Press, 2015.

"Pseudo-Dionysus." In *Light from Light: An Anthology of Christian Mysticism*, ed. Louis Dupre and James Wiseman, 79–94. New York: Paulist Press, 1988.

Ramelli, Ilaria L. E. "Origen, Bardaisan, and the Origin of Universal Salvation," *Harvard Theological Review* 102, no. 2 (2009): 135–168.
Ramirez, Anthony. "Minister Faces Church Trial for Performing Gay Wedding." *New York Times*, June 17, 2005. New York Region. http://www.nytimes.com/2005/06/17/nyregion/minister-faces-church-trial-for-performing-gay-wedding.html.
———. "Seminary Votes Out Leader over Daughter's Gay Wedding," *New York Times*, February 12, 2005. New York Region. http://www.nytimes.com/2005/02/12/nyregion/seminary-votes-out-leader-over-daughters-gay-wedding.html.
Ranke-Heineman, Uta. *Eunuchs for the Kingdom of Heaven: Women, Sexuality, and the Catholic Church*. Trans. Peter Heinegg. New York: Doubleday, 1990.
Reese, Thomas. "Abandoning Celibacy Won't Stop Sexual Abuse by Priests," *Religion News*, December 19, 2017. https://religionnews.com/2017/12/19/abandoning-celibacy-wont-stop-sexual-abuse-by-priests/.
Reid, R. C., Carpenter, B. N., Hook, J. N., Garos, S., Manning, J. C., Gilliland, R., and Fong, T. "Report of Findings in a DSM-5 Field Trial for Hypersexual Disorder." *Journal of Sexual Medicine* 9, no. 11 (2012): 2868–2877.
Robinson, George. *Essential Judaism*. New York: Pocket Books, 2000.
Ruether, Rosemary Radford. *Christianity and the Making of the Modern Family*. Boston: Beacon Press, 2000.
Ryan, Christopher, and Jetha, Cacilda. *Sex at Dawn: The Prehistoric Origins of Modern Sexuality*. New York: HarperCollins, 2010.
Sandeen, Ernest R. "John Humphrey Noyes as the New Adam." *Church History* 40 (1971): 83.
Saner, Emine. "Can Sex Films Empower Women?" *Guardian*, March 5, 2011. https://www.theguardian.com/commentisfree/2011/mar/05/conversation-gail-dines-anna-arrowsmith?INTCMP=SRCH.
Schaff, Philip. *Creeds of Christendom*. Rev. ed. Ada, MI: Baker Books, 1984.
Schneider, Laurel C. "Promiscuous Incarnation." In *The Embrace of Eros: Bodies, Desires, and Sexuality in Christianity*, ed. Margaret Kamitsuka, 231–246. Minneapolis, MN: Fortress Press, 2010.
Schreiber, Lynne Meredith. "I'm an Orthodox Jew—Here's Why We Have Smokin' Hot Sex Lives." *Yourtango.com*, June 6, 2017. Self, Sex. http://www.yourtango.com/200623/forbidden-desires.
Schwarz, Hans. *Eschatology*. Grand Rapids, MI: Eerdmans, 2000.
Sonsino, Rifat. *Did Moses Really Have Horns? and Other Myths about Jews and Judaism*. New York: URJ Press, 2009.
Spencer, Robert. "72 Virgins Are Waiting for Me in Heaven—So Why I Should Prefer Only One Here?" *Jihad Watch*, August 3, 2015. https://www.jihadwatch.org/2015/08/72-virgins-are-waiting-for-me-in-heaven-so-why-i-should-prefer-only-one-here.

Sporger, John. "In Interview, Mother Details Delusions That Spurred Her to Kill Sons." *CNN.com*, Law Center, April 1, 2004. http://www.cnn.com/2004/LAW/04/01/laney/.

Stevens, Sharifa. "Harold Camping STOLE My Parents." *Manna Express*. Accessed June 19, 2017. http://www.mannaexpressonline.com/harold-camping-stole-my-parents/.

Surnow, Rose. "I Gave a Handjob at Jew Camp." *Vice.com*, May 9, 2012. Travel. https://www.vice.com/sv/article/i-gave-a-handy-at-jew-camp.

Swedenborg, Emanuel. *Love in Marriage: A Translation of Emanuel Swedenborg's The Sensible Joy in Married Love and the Foolish Pleasures of Illicit Love*. Trans. David F. Gladish. West Chester, PA: Swedenborg Foundation, 2015.

"10 Popular Ex-Porn Performers Reveal the Brutal Truth behind Their Most Famous Scenes." *Fight the New Drug*, October 26, 2017. https://fightthenewdrug.org/10-porn-stars-speak-openly-about-their-most-popular-scenes/.

Wallis, Jim. *God's Politics: Why the Right Gets It Wrong and the Left Doesn't Get It*. New York: HarperCollins, 2006.

Watanabe, Teresa. "The Year of Believing in Prophecies." *Los Angeles Times*, March 31, 1999. http://articles.latimes.com/1999/mar/31/news/mn-22793.

Wheat, Ed, and Wheat, Gaye. *Intended for Pleasure: Sex Technique and Sexual Fulfillment in Christian Marriage*. 4th ed. Grand Rapids, MI: Revell, 2010.

Whitbourne, Susan Krauss. "Why Sexual Narcissists Make Unfaithful Partners: New Research into Why Some Partners Are Prone to Stray." *Psychology Today*, December 27, 2014. https://www.psychologytoday.com/us/blog/fulfillment-any-age/201412/why-sexual-narcissists-make-unfaithful-partners.

White, David. "John Humphrey Noyes: Philosopher of Bible Communism." *Philosophy Now* 70. (November–December 2008). John Humphrey Noyes: Philosopher of Bible Communism | Issue 70 | Philosophy Now.

Whittaker, David J. "Early Mormon Polygamy Defenses." *Journal of Mormon History* 11 (1984): 43–63.

BIBLICAL CITATIONS

Genesis 20:3; 22:2; 38:1–11; 44:29;
Exodus 21:2–11
Leviticus 15:19–33; 18:6–18; 21, 20:13
Deuteronomy 7:1–6; 22:20–28; 23:12–14
1 Samuel 2:6; 28:3–19
2 Samuel 22:6
Job 11:8
Psalm 6:5; 19
Ecclesiastes 3:19–22; 8:15
Song of Solomon 4:1–8, 16; 5:4–5, 10–16; 7:1–9

Matthew 19:3–9, 10, 12; 22:23–30; 24:36–44; 25:31–46
Mark 3:32–35; 12:18–27
Luke 19:40; 20:27–40; 23:43; 24:13–35, 42–43, 50–53; 50–51
John 11:25–26; 20:11–18, 19–20, 24–29; 21
Acts 1:6–11; 2:44–45
Romans 5:18; 6:5
1 Corinthians 3:11–15; 7:25–35; 13:12, 15:22
2 Corinthians 5:8
Ephesians 6:5
Colossians 3:22
Hebrews 12:2
1 Thessalonians 4:16
1 Timothy 3:2
2 Timothy 4:3
2 Peter 2:4–5, 9–10; 3:8–10
Revelation 4:1; 19:6–9; 20:1–8, 10; 21:9–10

QUR'ANIC CITATIONS

2:187; 2:223
4:15–16; 124
23:99–100
44:51–44
52:17–20
56:17–18; 34–36
75:1–12

INDEX

abortion, 169, 170
Abraham, 16–18, 20–21
Acts, Book of, 46, 180–81
adultery, 3, 44, 124, 155, 217n9
  See also infidelity
agape, 106, 108
Aida (opera), 155
Akiba, 203n18
Al-Ash'ari, 42, 43
Alexander, Eben, 31
Ambrose of Milan, 66
anal sex, 3, 34, 40, 73
androgyny, 83
angels, 46, 61, 77, 99, 103, 118–19, 127, 204n43
Anselm, 169
anthropology, 152
anti-Christ, 27, 58
Anwar, Ghazala, 40
apocalypse, 8, 29, 57–59, 65
apophatic theologies, 114–16
apotheosis, 49–52
Aquinas, Thomas
  Aristotle and, 200n1
  desires and, 72, 167
  personhood and, 169
  procreation and, 3
  reason and, 3, 21, 214n89
  resurrection and, 5, 91
Aristotle, 200n1

Armageddon, 58
Arrowsmith, Anna, 188–89
asceticism
  overview of, 67–69
  angels and, 118
  eschatology and, 29, 68–69
  eunuchs and, 101
  pleasure and, 111–12
  procreation and, 103, 121
asexuality, 99, 117, 126
atheists, 67, 186
attraction, 147–48, 166, 174
Augustine
  celibacy and, 73–74, 83, 97
  gender and, 83, 92–94, 102
  hedonism and, 213n77
  lust and, 73, 103, 121
  personhood and, 169
  procreation and, 5, 73, 74, 78
  resurrection, 5, 74–75, 78, 83, 102–3
  sin and, 65, 73, 75, 83

baptism, 85–86, 93
Belmond, Vanessa, 184
Bernice, Carol, 131–33
bestiality, 3, 73, 181
Birthright program, 32–33
bisexuals, 44, 85, 93, 107, 175, 177, 199n8
Blaedel, Anna, 22–23
Bonda, Jan, 61

Brokeback Mountain, 151
Brown, Samuel Morris, 50, 51, 200n24
Butler, Rex, 202n24

Calvin, John, 70, 77–78
Camelot (musical), 155
Camping, Harold, 29 30
Cassian, John, 66
castration, 66–67, 69
cataphatic theologies, 116
Cates, Diana, 167, 214n89
Catholicism
    Aquinas and, 21, 200n1
    authority structure of, 24–25
    celibacy and, 20, 76, 97, 192–93
    contraception and, 169–70
    doctrinal codification and, 64
    procreation and, 3, 76
    resurrection and, 75–76, 78
    sexless heaven and, 32
    sexual abuse and, 192–93, 221n65
    sin and, 69–70, 197n4
celestial marriage, 32, 49, 51–52, 54
celibacy
    Augustine and, 73–74, 83, 97
    Catholicism and, 20, 76, 97
    communion and, 105
    eroticism and, 131–33
    eternal, 75, 76, 83, 97, 126
    goodness and, 67–68, 73, 75, 161
    Islam and, 39
    Jesus and, 99–101
    love and, 105, 133, 190–94
    Protestantism and, 97
    sexual abuse and, 192–93, 221n65
    trauma and, 117
censorship, 188
chastity, 1, 76, 108, 109
Cheng, Patrick, 86, 115
child sexual abuse, 192–93, 221n65
Christ. *See* Jesus of Nazareth
Chrysostom, John, 66, 102
Church of Jesus Christ of Latter Day
    Saints (LDS), 48–54
cisgender, 84, 211n14
Clement of Alexandria, 74, 102

coitus reservatus, 46–47
concupiscence, 146
confession, 3
contraception, 3–4, 73, 87, 107, 168–70,
    198n8
Corinthians (epistle), 60, 64
conversion therapy, 84, 107
Council of Nicaea, 66
creation, 2, 36, 40, 73, 83, 197–98
Creel, Richard F., 91
critical realism, 14, 136
crusades, 26
cunnilingus, 35, 101
Cupid, 106

damnation. *See* hell
dating sites (online), 165–66
David (king), 123–24, 216n20
demisexuality, 177
Dines, Gail, 188
divine tests, 18
divorce, 100
domestic heaven
    overview of, 6, 82
    goodness and, 112
    identity and, 116
    Mormons and, 50–52
    promiscuity and, 176
    questions about, 114

Ecclesiastes, Book of, 37, 112
Ellis, Havelock, 47
eros, 106–8
erotica, 36, 182–83
erotophobia, 67
eschatology
    definition of, 6, 11
    construction of, 27
    deconstruction and, 8
    moral reform and, 30
    mystery and, 114–15
    predictions and, 58, 65, 109, 113
    See also specific topics
ethics
    overview of, 6
    dialogue and, 8

interpretation and, 23
resources of, 12
social location and, 26
study of, 18–19
See also morality; *specific topics*
eunuchs, 66–67, 69, 100–101, 124
evangelicals, 3–4
exhibitionism, 172
Exodus, Book of, 18, 21, 169

fall from grace, 70, 72, 73, 83, 121, 146, 198n8
fantasy, 148
fasting, 20
feminism, 92, 109, 182, 183, 188
Fewell, Danna, 36, 203n17
Fischel, Joseph, 182
Fort, Charles, 11
Foster, Lawrence, 46–47
frottage, 73
functional mothering, 95

gay males
    confession and, 3
    creation and, 84–85, 93
    heterosexual marriage and, 150
    pornography and, 184, 187
    reparative therapy and, 107
    social apps and, 166, 184
gender
    overview of, 83–86
    constructionism and, 92–94, 96
    conversion therapy and, 84, 107
    diversity and, 4, 36, 40, 84–85, 118, 151, 177–78
    essentialism and, 92–93
    polygamy and, 179
    resurrection and, 87, 102, 104, 105, 128, 198n8
    See also androgyny; cisgender; eunuchs; LGBTQ; transgender
Genesis, Book of, 17, 34, 84, 119, 198n5
Gnostics, 68
golden calf, 18
Gomorrah, 17
Goss, Robert E., 172

grace
    eroticism and, 36, 105, 108
    fall from, 72
    healing and, 75, 146, 159
    identity and, 85, 87
    love and, 106, 108, 142, 155
    monogamy and, 127, 139, 143, 160
    narcissism and, 150
    promiscuity and, 124–25, 146
    redemption and, 6, 12, 77, 159, 197n4, 208n27
    resurrection and, 74–75
Gregory of Nyssa, 74, 83, 102, 121, 198n8
Grenz, Stanley, 77, 88–89

heaven
    overview of, 4–6, 11–13
    asceticism and, 111–12
    celibacy and, 75, 76, 83, 97, 126, 133, 190
    eroticism and, 86, 88–89, 95, 105
    experiences of, 31
    feasting and, 53, 114, 119
    healing and, 94–96, 117, 167
    monogamy and, 126–27, 131
    promiscuity and, 119–22, 124–25, 161, 165, 173, 178, 187
    sexless, 32, 58–59, 73–78, 162
    See also specific topics
hedonism, 194, 213n77
hell
    fear of, 61–62
    Islam and, 41
    Judaism and, 37
    Mormons and, 50
    proselytization and, 208n27
    sin and, 12, 66, 69, 73, 75–77, 197n4
Henry, Mathew, 207n20
heteroflexibility, 175, 177
heterosexism, 42, 130, 153
heterosexuality, 3, 40, 76, 84, 175, 177
Himeros.tv, 187–88
Himes, Norman, 47
homosexuality, 84, 175
    See also gay males; lesbians; LGBTQ
humility, 8, 24, 113

Hunt, Mary, 174
hypersexual disorder, 155–56, 168

iconography, 181, 187–90
idolatry, 18
immorality, 76, 181
  See also sin
incarnation, 12, 125, 172, 179, 195
Ind, Jo, 83
infidelity, 44, 124, 143–51, 153–59, 217n9
inquisitions, 15, 26
Isaac, 16–18
Isaiah, 32
Islam, 5, 39, 41–43, 53, 54, 204n43
Israel, 32–33, 58, 130, 207n14

Jacobs, Louis, 37
jealousy, 142
Jensen, David, 77–78, 82–89, 92, 109, 118
Jerome (theologian), 74, 102
Jerusalem, 44, 127–28
Jesus of Nazareth
  authority and, 25
  brides of, 87, 128–30
  celibacy and, 99–101
  community and, 180, 207n14
  disease and, 173
  incarnation and, 195
  love and, 87, 128, 148, 163–64, 171–72, 195
  marriage and, 46, 49, 77, 86–87, 98–101, 118–19, 127–30, 139, 181
  prodigality and, 120, 163, 191, 195
  promiscuity and, 120, 124, 163–64
  radical morality and, 194–95
  resurrection of, 5, 90
  second coming of, 29–30, 44–45, 57, 58, 65, 159, 201–2, 206n5
John (apostle), 164
John of Patmos, 32, 82, 127
John, Gospel of, 21, 161, 217n9
Judaism
  apocalypse and, 59
  eschatology and, 5, 37–39, 53, 54
  marriage and, 98, 118, 137

personhood and, 169
pleasure and, 1, 35–36, 38
resurrection and, 37–38, 99, 204n33
ritual purity and, 34–35, 54
Torah and, 1, 33, 34, 100
Jude (epistle), 61
judgment day, 12, 59–61, 64–65, 208n27
Jung, Patricia Beattie, 81, 97–109, 126, 136–37, 185, 214n89

Kahn, Yoel, 36
Kamitsuka, Margaret, 90–96, 109
Kansfield, Norm, 22
Kephart, William, 45
Kethuvi'im, 35
Keufler, Mathew, 66
King David, 123–24, 216n20
kissing, 35, 124, 152, 161
Kristeva, Julia, 94–95
Kuyvenhoven, Andrew, 207n14

Lacey, Marilyn, 191
Laney, Deanna, 15–18, 20–21
Lawrence, Raymon, 119
Lee, Ang, 151
lesbians, 85, 93, 107, 133, 150, 199n8
Ley, David J., 122–23, 186
LGBTQ
  churches and, 23, 199
  conversion therapy and, 84, 107
  heavenly sex and, 125
  heterosexual marriage and, 150–51
  love and, 85, 151
  resurrection and, 93
  See also bisexuals; gay males; heteroflexibility; lesbians; transgender
Long, Ronald, 93
Longino, Helen, 182–83
love
  celibacy and, 105, 133, 190–94
  commandment to, 21, 148–49
  domestic heaven and, 6
  friendship and, 174, 176

healing and, 82, 95, 117, 124, 149, 167, 175
infidelity and, 141, 149, 151, 154–55
Jesus and, 87, 128, 148, 163–64, 171–72, 195
monogamy and, 126–28, 138, 140, 141, 154
promiscuity and, 119–21, 124–25, 164, 167, 175, 187
radical, 115
STDs and, 171–72
types of, 106
See also polyamory
Luke, Gospel of, 49, 98, 118–19, 125, 139
lust
overview of, 147–49
desire and, 103, 107, 108, 121, 147
infidelity and, 149
judgment day and, 61
marriage and, 72–73
objectification and, 148
Lust, Erika, 189

Maimonides, 204n33
Manichaeism, 213n77
Mark, Gospel of, 21, 77, 98–99, 180
marriage
celestial, 32, 49, 51–52, 54
Jesus and, 46, 49, 77, 86, 98–101, 118–19, 127–30, 139, 181
Judaism and, 98, 118, 137
LGBTQ and, 22, 150
lovemaking and, 127
lust and, 72–73
parenthood and, 76
Paul and, 27–28
possessiveness and, 140–42
procreation and, 67–69, 72, 75, 102
promiscuity and, 44–47
resurrection and, 46, 49, 77, 98–99, 118
virgins and, 27, 33
masturbation, 3, 4, 73, 107, 122, 125, 172
Matthew, Gospel of
community and, 180

eunuchs and, 67, 100, 101
judgment day and, 60, 65
marriage and, 46, 49, 98, 100, 101, 139
Mechthild of Magdeburg, 86–87
menstruation, 34–35, 40
Mercer, Joyce Ann, 185
mercy, 3, 27, 144, 163, 217n9
Mishnah, 38
Missal, Hans, 16–18, 20–21
monogamy
overview of, 126–31
goodness and, 138–39, 143–44, 152
infidelity and, 146–51, 154–59
love and, 126–28, 138, 140–41, 143, 154, 159–60
Mormons and, 48–49
New Testament and, 124
polygamy and, 123, 128, 153
theocentric heaven and, 130
as vocation, 131, 140, 143, 160, 194
morality
definitions of, 14
objectivity and, 14–15
philosophical theories of, 19
See also ethics; *specific topics*
Morreall, John, 91
mortal sins, 3, 73, 197n4
Moses, 18, 46, 98
Muhammad, 32, 39
Murray, Stephen, 42
Muslims, 5, 39, 41–43, 53, 54, 204n43

Nachmanides, 36
narcissism, 150
Nelson, James, 117
Neoplatonism, 213n77
New Prophecy movement, 29, 30, 202n24
New Testament, 59–63
See also specific books and topics
Nicene Creed, 64
Novak, David, 37–38
Noyes, John Humphrey, 44–47
Nussbaum, Martha, 167

Obama, Barack, 58
Onan, 34
Oneida Perfectionists, 44–49, 53, 54, 180
open relationships. *See* polyamory; promiscuity
oral sex, 3, 4, 35, 40, 73, 101, 107, 125
Origen of Alexandria, 63, 102
original sin, 72

pagans, 67
Pagels, Elaine, 208n27
Parave, Cristy, 43–44
Parave, Dave, 43–44
parenthood, 73, 76
patriarchy
 Islam and, 42, 43
 Judaism and, 33, 36
 polygamy and, 123, 179
 redemption and, 87, 130
 sin and, 169
Paul (apostle)
 community and, 28, 30
 death and, 71
 heaven and, 136
 identity and, 85
 judgment day and, 28, 60–61, 64, 201n22
 marriage and, 27–28
 predictions and, 113, 136, 201–2
pedophilia, 221n65
 See also child sexual abuse
Pelikan, Jaroslav, 65
Peter (apostle), 25
Peter (epistle), 61, 64
philia, 106–8
polyamory, 47, 119, 139, 146, 153, 179–81, 187
polygamy, 33, 40, 43, 44, 48–49, 123, 128, 179, 220n33
polygyny, 179, 220n33
Pope Benedict XVI, 170
Pope Francis, 3
Pope John XXII, 169
Pope John Paul II, 31, 76

Pope Paul VI, 169, 170
pornography
 overview of 181–190
 addiction and, 185–86
 desire and, 108
 gay, 187–88
 as iconography, 181, 187–90
 immorality and, 181–82
 moral education and, 2
 performers and, 183–84
 Song of Solomon and, 116–17, 203n18
 for women, 188–89
Portmann, John, 42, 154
pregnancy, 168–69
premillennial dispensationalists, 206n5
promiscuity
 overview of, 119–25, 162–64
 boundaries and, 165–66, 180
 demonization of, 138
 friendship and, 174–78
 healing and, 194
 health and, 167–68, 173
 heaven and, 119–22, 124–25, 161, 165, 173, 178, 187
 marriage and, 44–47
 polyamory and, 179–80
 pornography and, 181, 186–87, 189
 prejudice and, 166
 sin and, 146
prophylactics, 123, 171–73
prostitutes, 100, 124, 179, 189
Protestantism
 abortion and, 170
 biblical authority and, 21, 24, 77
 celibacy and, 97
 contraception and, 3–4, 87, 169, 170, 198n8
 diversity and, 4, 23
 grace and, 77, 197n4
 sexless heaven and, 32, 77–78
 sin and, 70, 76
 tribulation and, 27
Pseudo-Dionysus, 115
purgatory, 66

qualitative reflection, 19
queer theory, 85–86, 92
  See also specific theorists
Qur'an, 39–43, 204n43

Ramelli, Ilaria, 63
Ranke-Heinemann, Uta, 67–68
rape, 3, 33, 181, 182, 186
rapture, 27, 29
recreational sex, 166, 174, 177
redemption, 2, 13, 45, 62, 63, 181, 198
  See also salvation
Reese, Thomas, 192
Reform Judaism, 36
reparative therapy, 84, 107
repentance, 77
resurrection
  overview of, 89–92
  Augustine and, 5, 74–75, 78, 83, 102–3
  communion and, 105
  gender and, 76, 102, 104, 105, 128, 198n8
  healing and 95–96
  Islam and, 41, 54, 204n43
  Judaism and, 37–38, 54, 99, 204n33
  LGBT and, 93
  love making and, 104
  marriage and, 46, 49, 77, 98–99, 118
  promiscuity and, 5, 13, 119
  sexual play and, 87–88
  spirits and, 62, 91
Revelation, Book of, 61, 82, 86, 127
ritual purity, 34, 54
Robinson, George, 36–38
Roman Empire, 63
Romans (epistle), 60, 71
Roscoe, Will, 42
Rowland, Christopher, 201–2

Sabbath, 36, 38
Sadducees, 37, 46, 49, 98–99, 118
salvation, 12, 25, 60–63, 69, 72, 163, 208n27
  See also redemption

same-sex experimentation, 175
Samuel (prophet), 37
Schneider, Laurel, 120, 124, 163–64
Schreiber, Lynne Meredith, 34–35
Schwab, Klaus, 81
Schwarz, Hans, 70–72, 111, 135
seduction, 3
Serenus, 66
sex addiction, 155–56, 168, 186
Sex and the City, 157
sex education, 2
sexism, 183, 188, 189
sexual assault, 3, 33, 169, 181, 182, 186
sexual dysfunctions, 122, 185, 192
sexual health, 167–73
sexual theology, 117
sexually transmitted infections, 170–73
shame, 1, 36, 117, 122–23, 156, 186
sheol, 37
sin
  Augustine and, 65, 73, 75, 83, 121
  communion and, 78
  death and, 69–73
  desire and, 67, 72–74, 121, 146
  heaven and, 30, 75
  hell and, 1, 73, 75, 76, 197n4
  infidelity and, 145–46, 159
  LGBT and, 84
  love and, 106, 159
  morality and, 136
  origin of, 198n6
  patriarchy and, 169
  prejudice and, 166–67
  procreation and, 3, 198n8
  promiscuity and, 122, 146, 154, 162
  purgatory and, 66
  redemption and, 2, 12, 45
  terrorism and, 39, 58, 206n5
slavery, 26, 33
Smith, Joseph, 32, 48–51
Snow, Lorenzo, 51
social media, 165–66
Sodom, 17
sodomy, 1, 73, 121, 129

sola scriptura, 24
Song of Solomon, 35–36, 86, 116, 130, 203
Sonsino, Rifat, 38
Stoics, 68
Stuart, Elizabeth, 93
suicide bombers, 39
Surnow, Rose, 32–33
Swedenborg, Emanuel, 126
swinging, 43–44
Synoptic Gospels, 98
    See also Luke; Mark; Matthew

Talbott, Thomas, 208–9
Talmud, 36, 118
Ten Commandments, 21
terrorism, 39, 58, 206n5
Tertullian, 102
theocentric heaven
  overview of, 6, 82
  communion and, 6, 112
  gender and, 93
  metaphors and, 119
  monogamy and, 130
  Mormons and, 50
  questions about, 114
theology
  definitions of, 15, 20
  apophatic, 114–16
  cataphatic, 116
  creation and, 197–98
  interpretation and, 13, 22, 62, 72
  morality and, 6, 13, 15, 18–21, 69
  sexual, 117
  See also specific topics

Thomas (apostle), 90, 164
Torah, 1, 33–35, 100, 217n9
touching, 90, 124, 152, 171, 177, 191
transgender, 85, 93, 107, 150, 199n8, 211n14
trauma, 94–95, 117
Trible, Phyllis, 36
tribulation, 27
trust, 141–42, 149, 152–53

United Methodist Church, 22
universal salvation, 60–63, 66, 82

Vacek, Edward, 106
vaginal sex, 40
virgins/virginity
  Augustine and, 73–75
  Catholicism and, 76
  eunuchs and, 66, 101
  goodness and, 69, 73, 75, 161
  heaven and, 39, 42
  marriage and, 27, 33
violence, 89, 117, 169, 170
voyeurism, 35, 172

Wheat, Ed, 4
Wheat, Gaye, 4
White, David, 46
wrath, 69, 70 140, 142

Y2K, 57–58

Zarathustra, 32
Zeus, 163
Zimmerman, Mary, 135

www.ingramcontent.com/pod-product-compliance
Lightning Source LLC
Chambersburg PA
CBHW030540230426
43665CB00010B/964